Courtship, Love, and Marriage in Nineteenth-Century English Canada

Courtship, Love, and Marriage in Nineteenth-Century English Canada

PETER WARD

McGill-Queen's University Press
Montreal & Kingston • London • Buffalo

© McGill-Queen's University Press 1990
ISBN 0-7735-0749-3

Legal deposit first quarter 1990
Bibliothèque nationale du Québec

Printed in Canada on acid-free paper

This book has been published with the help of a grant
from the Social Science Federation of Canada, using
funds provided by the Social Sciences and Humanities
Research Council of Canada.

Canadian Cataloguing in Publication Data

Ward, W. Peter (William Peter), 1943-
Courtship, love and marriage in nineteenth-century
English Canada
Includes bibliographical references.
ISBN 0-7735-0749-3
1. Courtship—Canada—History—19th century.
2. Marriage—Canada—History—19th century.
3. Canada—Social life and customs—19th century.
I. Title.
GT2713.W37 1990   306.8'0971   C89-090468-5

For Pat

Contents

Tables, Figure, and Illustrations

Acknowledgments

During the course of writing this book I have accumulated an unusually large number of happy obligations. First among them is the debt I owe to my good friend and colleague, James Winter. He has been exceedingly generous with his time, his great knowledge of nineteenth-century Britain, and his prodigal enthusiasm for social history. He has been the best of critics, demanding and encouraging by turns. Our conversations have been one of the great pleasures of writing this book. Susan Houston and Donald Paterson read the completed manuscript and offered many suggestions for its improvement, most of which I had the good sense to take.

Many other friends and colleagues have informed, advised, and encouraged me as well, reading and responding to drafts of work in progress. In one way or another Ivan Avakumovic, Jean Barman, Roderick Barman, George Egerton, Paulette Falcon, DeLloyd Guth, Catherine LeGrand, Tina Loo, Robert McDonald, Richard Mackie, Eric Nellis, Margaret Prang, George Rawlyk, Peter Seixas, Allan Smith, and Alan Tully have all had a hand in this study and I am thankful for their help. Whatever merits this book may have owes much to their well-considered comments. Just as my final revisions were in progress Judith Allen wafted into my office from Australia. Her lively, good-humoured feminism encouraged me to think again about some of what I had written and made me wish that we had met earlier on in my task.

Peter Moogk kindly loaned me some helpful documents from his own personal collection, and Fritz Lehmann generously kept his eyes open for material of interest to me as he laboured through the nineteenth-century colonial press. Constance Backhouse gave me a pre-publication copy of one of her valuable articles, which helped to shore up my modest knowledge of Canadian legal history. Virginia Green assisted with the statistical work in chapter 3. She has worked with me for several years on this and related projects and I am deeply in her debt. Diane Mew, my editor, was an author's delight; this book is much better for her judicious advice.

I also wish to acknowledge Dorothy Hall, Ann Logan, Carolyn Moulton, and Alfred Ward of Toronto, as well as Pat Greenwell of Ponoka, Alberta, who shared their family letters with me. I have attempted to contact those who may hold copyright to the quotations published here and would appreciate being notified of any omissions so that they may be put right in future editions. As for the typist, I have myself to thank. An earlier version of chapter 4 appeared in the March 1987 issue of the *Canadian Historical Review*. This is also a chance to lament the passing of the Leave Fellowship program funded by the Social Sciences and Humanities Research Council of Canada. I was one of its grateful beneficiaries during the course of this study and I still harbour a secret, if naive, hope that someday it may return.

But more than anyone else I am indebted to Patricia Ward. She has been involved with this study since day one and has brought her own special insights to every stage of the project. Over the years she has read, considered, and commented on everything but these acknowledgments and her advice has been invaluable. Most important of all, she has taught me the deeper meaning of married love, the goal which the lovers discussed in this book so earnestly sought for themselves. I doubt whether any of them could have been as favoured as I am.

Courtship, Love, and Marriage
in Nineteenth-Century English Canada

Introduction

We tend to think of courtship and marriage as intensely private matters, which indeed they are. But they also have a public side that is often overlooked. Matrimony and sexual intimacy matter a great deal not only to a couple directly involved in a close relationship but to their families, friends, and neighbours – and more generally to society as well. Because of this communal interest, the relations of men and women are set in an elaborate web of regulations which guide private conduct and sanction approved behaviour. Some of these codes are formal, written, and enforced by institutions, others are informal, unwritten, and ruled by custom; some are widely articulated and openly acknowledged, others remain buried deep in our super-egos. But whatever their form, they act as powerful guides to what we should and should not do in our relations with the other sex.

Much of the recent writing on the history of sexuality and marriage in western societies overlooks this fact. For Edward Shorter the rise of modern marriage in northern Europe is simply a story of growing personal freedom from social and familial constraints.[1] Love, so it seems, conquered all. Lawrence Stone has advanced a more complex interpretation of changes in marriage in early modern England; he identifies several marriage types, each with its own pattern of male-female relationships and distinctive of a particular social class.[2] But despite the great variations in these practices and patterns, the onward march of youthful autonomy in marriage-making was common to them all. Peter Gay's monumental study of erotic and sentimental love among the transatlantic Victorian bourgeoisie pays little attention to the social context of male-female relations.[3] His use of Freudian theory (a model of human behaviour centred upon the personality) to explore the history of intimacy in mens' and womens' lives almost precludes assessing the social milieu and its effects upon private conduct. Similarly, Ellen

Rothman's history of courtship in America treats the progress of love largely as a matter concerning couples themselves, quite apart from their social circumstances.[4]

This book rests on the contrary view that courtship and marriage in earlier times can only be understood in their social setting. Marriage is as much a public as a private event, and the processes leading up to it are as much of social as of personal concern. In uniting a couple, marriage creates the nucleus of a new family, a basic unit of society. Because communities are deeply concerned about the health of their primary elements, they have a great deal at stake in that creative moment when a new family is taking form. For this reason they intrude into the private world of romance, guiding and prodding, teaching and punishing, as the unwed seek one another out and commit themselves to marriage. As a result, the approach to marriage is marked by tensions embedded in opposing aspirations: society's expectations about right conduct in courtship and marriage as against the couple's wish to defend their privacy from the inquisitiveness of others. As we will see, from the late eighteenth century onward these contending forces enveloped those who wooed and wed in British North America.

For more than a decade the history of the family has been one of the great preoccupations of social historians. A generation of scholars has redrawn the map of social relations in earlier times by exploring the contours of family and gender in Europe and America. With a few notable exceptions, however, historians have contributed very little to our knowledge of the family in Canada's past. In particular, the nature and quality of human relationships, what Michael Anderson has called the "sentiments" school of family history, has been almost completely neglected.[5] This book thus enters some unexplored terrain. Broadly speaking, it probes the basis of family formation in a British colonial setting and a maturing capitalist economy at a time of high population growth and rapid economic development. Two great themes lie at the heart of the inquiry. One is the community's ongoing interest in the reproduction and defence of the family as a social institution. The other is the couple's search for privacy and intimacy in the face of public intrusiveness.

When they courted and wed, nineteenth-century Canadian men and women stood at the centre of an interlocking network of regulations. Each of the first six chapters in this book discusses a part of this network. Chapters 1 and 2 examine church and state, whose institutions defined and enforced the formal rules of courtship and married life. Chapter 3 explores the demographic context of marriage, those structural features of a population which directed the choice of a mate in powerful, yet largely invisible, ways. The next three chapters deal with the everyday influence of social custom on those who sought a spouse. Chapter 4 describes the territorial features of courting life, which had such important strategic implications for both genders. In chapter 5 the complex rituals of courtship, betrothal, and marriage are examined to reveal the mark they left on those in quest of a marriage partner. The considerable influence of family and friends on courting behaviour and mate selection is explored in chapter 6. Within this elaborate network of rules and the agents of their enforcement stood the loving couples themselves, enmeshed in the complex ties which bound them to the community at large. Chapter 7 is devoted to them, to their thoughts about courtship and marriage, and to their experiences as they sought and took a partner for life. The book is principally concerned with young love and first marriage; remarriage raises a host of quite distinct considerations.

This study deals with the "long century" from the 1780s to the eve of the First World War. I chose the initial date out of necessity: the sources on which this study is largely based are virtually non-existent for earlier years, when the first tiny settlements of English-speaking people were established in present-day Quebec and Nova Scotia. Thus we must skip over the founding generation of British and American settlers in these colonies, though not those in other parts of British America which developed somewhat later. The terminal date was chosen for much the same reason and also because courting practices shifted dramatically after the First World War, partly in response to the advent of the automobile. From that time onward courtship became an ever more private experience and, in consequence, one ever more difficult for the historian to explore.

Source problems also dictated the cultural and geographic limits of the study: English-speaking central and maritime Canada. Because of insufficient sources, Prince Edward Island and Newfoundland receive short shrift here. Nor do I deal with the nineteenth-century West. The unique marriage customs of the fur-trade community have been discussed elsewhere,[6] while the small settler societies founded late in the century have not left documentary legacies rich enough to support this sort of inquiry. In Quebec, where two cultures co-existed, I have confined myself to the anglophone community and to examples of cross-cultural unions in which British-Canadian influences prevailed.

A further comment is necessary about the literary sources used for this study. Because my primary concern has been to examine the interplay between public and private elements in courtship and marriage, I have drawn heavily on family papers: the diaries and letters written and read by ordinary men and women. These are the only possible sources of direct evidence on how our ancestors experienced the transition to marriage. The major archives of Canada hold a rich lode of private papers, much of it bearing directly on the subject at hand. Yet for all their abundance, the family records left us by the past reflect the lives of but a tiny fraction of all English Canadians. The pure hearts in my profession will object that these sources form a hopelessly biased sample, that they reveal the experiences of an unrepresentative minority, that they tell us nothing about the submerged and silent majority. These objections cannot be dismissed out of hand. For one thing, written records come from the literate population and their use inevitably creates a bias toward the higher social strata. For another, even among the literate, the papers of the noteworthy are more likely to survive than those of ordinary folk. So I confess: the sources are biased.

But not hopelessly so. In wrestling with this problem, three things should be kept in mind. First, literacy was widespread in English Canada, at least by the mid-nineteenth century and probably somewhat earlier. As a result, for much if not most of the period under review, the ability to read and write did not divide the elites from the masses. Silent the majority may have been, but it was not inarticulate. Most of the private papers on which this study rests came from the pens of quite ordinary folk. Secondly, time has winnowed the historical record in predictable ways. The papers of the rich and famous have survived in disproportionate numbers. But most of those whose letters and diaries were consulted for this study won fame and fortune long after they courted and wed. More often than not they came from conventional family backgrounds. Humble? Sometimes. Comfortable? Often. Privileged? Seldom. George Jones, the young Quebec City clerk whose courtship diary provides the central example of this book, is a prime illustration. Thirdly, despite these caveats, there is no doubt that the lower ranks are underrepresented here. The great limitation of these family records is that they reveal little about the lives of the very poor, and about those of the first generation or two of urban industrial workers. Like it or not, this is an obstacle which cannot be overcome and we will simply have to work around it as best we can.

And now a word or two about the knottiest problem of all, the vexing issue of class. Historians wish to understand at least two related characteristics of a community when exploring the question of class, its social structure and its culture. The first set of characteristics concerns the boundaries of social groups, the relationships among these groups, and the access each group has to wealth, power, status, well-being, and so on. The second concerns the distinctive behavioural, institutional, and ideological characteristics of a social group, the "cement" which gives it a sense of common identity and purpose. Class is a particularly slippery problem in any discussion of nineteenth-century Canadian society and the existing historical literature offers us little guidance on the question. The most comprehensive model of nineteenth-century Canadian class relations comes to us from the neomarxist historians, who have appropriated it from industrializing Britain and western Europe.[7] Not surprisingly, it defines a Canadian working class much more carefully than it does any other social group.

But a definition of the working class based upon the British and European model – one consisting principally of skilled and semi-skilled craftsmen and factory labourers – embraces only a small fraction of Canadian labouring people at any time in the nineteenth century. The fact is that, even by the end of the century, no more than 20 per cent of the labour force were employed in secondary manufacturing, and these activities were heavily concentrated in Montreal and Toronto, where only one Canadian in ten lived in 1901.[8] While factory production in these cities grew rapidly after mid-century, few factories were large by international standards of the time. In 1871, the only year for which statistics are available, 3 per cent of Toronto's 572 factories employed 100 or more hands while 87 per cent employed fewer than thirty.[9] Generally speaking, late nineteenth-century Canadian workshops were small, averaging five employees per establishment into the 1890s.[10] On the whole, these circumstances differed sharply from the conditions which moulded the great industrial proletariats in nineteenth-century Manchester, Lyons, Vienna, and Berlin. The forces which defined the British and European working-class communities and which shaped their distinctive cultures were only found in faint outline in Victorian Canada, and then only in a few of its most advanced industrial centres. In fact, Canada remained largely rural until after the turn of the century. In 1901 almost two-thirds of Canadians still were rural dwellers and 40 per cent of the labour force worked in agriculture, by far the largest proportion employed in any economic sector. Another large segment of the work force laboured seasonally in frontier resource industries, migrating from one task to another, and in and out of farming, in patterns which we still do not understand very clearly.

Thus the language of class structure, class culture, and class relations which comes to us from across the Atlantic does not fit the circumstances of nineteenth-century Canada very well; nor can such terms as "working class" and "middle class" be used with much precision when discussing social structure and cultural patterns. Therefore I have avoided them. No doubt they have a place, carefully defined, in historical writing about Canadian society, but I leave it to others to find one. The language of status and rank is more flexible and comprehensive, and therefore more useful for describing social differences. It, too, suffers from serious limitations, for it is a good deal less than precise. But it has the virtue of not implying sharply defined social categories where social boundaries were unclear. And it does not mislead us into confusing small social groups for large ones when we think about the past.

Prologue

"[Today I made an] acquaintance with that most amiable young Lady
Miss Tanswell. I must say that I never met with so amiable & lovely a
young Lady. She belongs to the Catholic religion and I am a Protestant.
My Mother is a Catholic too, and – but I am foolish, and always thinking
of Miss Tanswell. My sisters say her Christian name is 'Honorine'." So
begins one of the most remarkable diaries kept in nineteenth-century
Canada. Its author, George Stephen Jones, was a young Quebec City
clerk. Between 22 October 1845 and 5 April 1846 he kept a daily
record of his courtship of Honorine[1] Tanswell. Each night before retiring
he noted the day's events – the words they spoke, the activities they
shared, the relations and friends they saw, the letters and gifts they
exchanged. A touching record of flowering youthful love, the diary is
an earnest and often painful account of emotions deeply felt. It is also
the most intimate record of courtship in Canada we ever are likely to
have.

George began to keep the diary when he was eighteen. The son of
an Irish father and a French-Canadian mother, his father was a grocer
in the faubourg St Jean. Late the previous June, not long before he
began to keep the diary, the family had lost everything in a disastrous
fire which burned over much of the city, destroying thirteen hundred
buildings. In reduced circumstances and confronted by a serious housing shortage – the fire and another a month earlier had left eighteen
thousand (half of the city's populace) homeless – George, his parents,
and his two sisters lived in a single room behind their small shop on
St Louis Street. An older brother, Edwin, who was in business with
their father, no longer lived at home. George worked as a clerk for
Abraham Joseph, a Jewish wholesale provisioner in the city.

The Tanswells were a well-established Anglo-Canadian family with
roots in early post-conquest Quebec. Since the late eighteenth century

they had married into the French Catholic community and adopted its faith. Honorine's father, paternal grandfather, and paternal great-grand-father had all taken French-Canadian wives and her sister had recently married a French Canadian. The Tanswells were people of some standing in Quebec City. Grandfather Thomas had been master of the Académie de Québec, and father Stephen was a gentleman of independent means. Fate had spared their home on rue Dauphine from the terrible fires of spring, and during the period of the diary Honorine lived there comfortably with her parents and two younger brothers. She was twenty when she met George, the only daughter remaining at home, her younger sister having recently died of consumption.

As a suitor, George proceeded cautiously. The day after their first meeting he confided to his journal:

Every person that knows Miss Tanswell speak of her as being clever, amiable and lovely, and by what I have seen and heard of her, I think she is all that. I have not heard whether she is loved by anyone but I suppose she is, for a young Lady of her accomplishments cannot be without a Lover. But enough of this for I am always thinking of her and every time I do so I ask myself these questions. "Why am I thinking of her, why am I so anxious to see her to speak to her," and my answer is "I do not know." I must take care lest I should be deceived. It is true I like to be in company with Ladies, particularly when they are pleasing, but so far, I have felt no real love for any.

On the verge of manhood, George felt the first stirrings of romance but was uncertain of his new-found emotions. He was very young for serious courtship, rather unsure of himself with the opposite sex, and unfamiliar with the bachelor role now opening before him.

George's thoughts were filled with Honorine for ten days after they met. They encountered one other twice on family visits to each other's home, but mostly George was alone with his reflections. On 31 October he wrote, "I don't know why, but I am always anxious to see Miss Honorine. I never felt so about any other young Lady." Next day he identified the reason. Having passed the evening at the Tanswells, where Honorine played the piano and sang for several guests, he returned home to inform his diary:

Every time I am in Miss Tanswell's company I feel a pleasant sensation, which I never felt before. I sometimes become melancholy & speak very little. They then perhaps say I have no sense. It is true I have not much sense. Still when I am in company with Ladies, I generally talk & amuse them pretty much, but when in Miss Tanswell's company I am thoughtful. I speak very little but think a great deal. All this has made me come to the resolution of examining myself to see from whense the sensation I feel when in Miss Tanswell's lovely company and why I am so anxious to see her to converse with her. And when I am with her, why I am afraid as it were to speak to her. I have this evening examined myself, and find that love is the cause of it all, yes I am really in love for the first time in my life and it is Miss Honorine Tanswell I love. Yes I am in love with her and she knows it not, nor will I tell her for I am afraid she does not love me, she cannot love me, therefore I will love her in secrete. Love has taken possession of my heart, and that heart I have given to Miss Honorine. O if she could love me, how happy I would be.

On her part Honorine surely noticed George's attentions, however silent, for she returned them in kind. The day after love's dawning, when he passed by her home with one of his sisters, Honorine invited them in and gave him a song which she had written.[2] The following week she offered him more encouragement, calling on his family and inviting them to call on hers. One evening after playing whist she told his fortune and predicted that he would have trouble in love.[3] A few days later she "teased me about Adele Paquet, a young girl with whom I used to play when a child."[4] Then at her mother's encouragement she gave him a Philippina, a nut with two kernels which, according to custom, should be shared with one of the opposite sex. At their next meeting the one who first said "Philippina" was entitled to a present from the other. By now the diffident George was grateful for any sign of reciprocal feeling. "I dont know if I am mistaken & am afraid to think so, but I think Miss Honorine loves me a little. O happy thought, I hope it is the case." As for the Philippina, it gave him a welcome opportunity. "I will lose it & then I will give her a present," he planned. And lose it he promptly did, when he came home to dinner at noon the next day and found Honorine waiting for him there.

George could scarcely contain his overflowing ardour. A day after he lost this little contest, he wrote, "I have not yet declared my love to Miss Honorine but I must tell her soon for I cannot live this way." He must have confessed soon after but, unfortunately, twenty-four crucial pages are missing from the diary at this point, including those on which he presumably recorded the scene of love's tender avowal. Honorine must have replied in kind because, when the diary resumes some two weeks later, the pair were on much more intimate terms. They had begun exchanging love letters in French.

But George soon learned the truth of the fortune Honorine had told him, for he soon began to grow troubled. At the end of November he was cast into despair. "Honorine told me that her parents wants her to marry Gingras, but she says she will not. If she dose I will be the most mesirable man on earth and I will never marry. No never."[5] On top of this, her father discovered one of George's love notes and told Honorine he would speak to George about it. The dreaded admonition never occurred, George attended the Tanswells more faithfully than ever, and Honorine consigned his letters to the purifying flame (though she did save their ashes). But from this point onward interfering parents blighted the lovers' affection.

Deeply disturbed by thoughts of losing his loved one to a rival, George redoubled his attentions toward Honorine and her family. He called on her almost daily. He accompanied her on evening walks. He brought her a selection of rings and asked her to choose the one she liked best. But this raised the awkward question of her parents' approval. George recorded that she said "she could not find words enough to express her thanks to me. She also said 'I will wear the ring but if my Parents will not allow me to wear it, you will take it back.' I said 'no Honorine, I will never take it back. If your Parents will not allow you to wear it keep it in secrete, and perhaps one day you will be allowed to wear it.' We talked of love, of that love we have for one another, and we were happy."[6] Next day she wore the ring, with her parents' consent. Honorine reciprocated with gifts for George, a seal for his watch chain and a handsome pencil case. They professed their love for one another at every meeting and even talked of marriage.

Meanwhile Gingras, Mr Tanswell's candidate for Honorine's hand, lurked in the background. He too called regularly at the Tanswells and from time to time took Honorine for drives in his cariole. Evidently he pressed his suit forcefully. According to Honorine, "Gingras was getting ready to get married, and … she feared he would ask her. But she says she will refuse for the third time."[7] The situation had divided the Tanswell family. Honorine told George that "her Father had a conversation with Mrs. Lemieux [Honorine's recently married older sister] about me. The former says I am too young for Honorine & the latter said there was not much difference between us since I was only one year younger than Honorine, and that if she was in Honorine's place she would prefer me to Gingras."[8]

In January Honorine's parents made their position clear: they would never permit her to marry George.[9] They also forbade her to wear the ring he had given her (although she evidently defied them). Over the next two months the lovers continued to meet, usually in the company of members of their families, and whenever they had a few moments alone they reassured one another of their undying devotion. But George remained very unsettled. He tried to ingratiate himself with Mrs Tanswell who, according to Honorine, liked him very much. He bought small gifts for his love and sent her a valentine on 14 February. He took her and her mother to the theatre. On a more practical note, he asked his

father and older brother to take him into the family business so that
he might have enough income to support a wife. They refused. At the
Tanswells the family discussions continued. Honorine's father was the
voice of prudence, her mother the voice of young love. "Her father said
I was too young," George noted, "& her mother said that if Honorine
& I loved one another, there was no use trying to prevent our doing
so."[10] And Gingras continued to call.

Pressed on all sides, Honorine finally began to rebuff George's attentions. On 7 March he wrote,

I went to see Honorine after tea. Mr. Drome was there. He left soon after with
Theophilus. I gave Honorine an engraving to put in her Album & to Mr. Tanswell
I gave ½ doz Principes. Honorine played several tunes on her Piano. She did
not look pleased. I asked her what was the matter. She said, "nothing". I said,
"yes Honorine, there must be something. O tell me lovely Honorine." She said,
"You will know it soon enough." I told her I would try and get some fine engravings
for her Album. She said "do not get any for I will not take them. You have given
me too many things already." I left her at ½ past 9. Honorine came into the
passage with me. I took her hand & pressed it. I said, "Honorine what is the
matter? Does your parents say anything because I come to see you every
evening." She said "I will tell you another time"...I said, "O Honorine do you
still love me." She said "Yes", and I left. I would give anything to know what is
the matter with lovely Honorine. Something strange is coming to pass. All the
family receive [me] coldly. Even Honorine does not seem to love me so much
now as usual. But can I doubt her love – no, no. She told me again this evening
that she loved me. O that she may always love me. She told me to go & see
her tomorrow afternoon.

Caught between her parents' demands and her own inclinations, Honorine began to lean in the only sensible direction. George had not yet
come to man's estate and could offer her little but love. The path of
prudence lay where her father indicated: marriage with an older man
who had established himself in life.

George was distraught. "Last night I threw myself on my bed and
cried until 1 o'clock. I cried like a child. And now I have a great headach.
O Honorine, if you knew how unhappy I am you would perhaps try to
console me. I did not see her today nor any of the family. I hope she
is well. That she may be happy is my prayer. The more I think of my
unhappiness the more I feel the weight of it. My eyes are sore from
crying. 11 o'clock. I will go to bed & try to think of happier times."[11]

For a week he mostly kept to his room to nurse his dejection. Then
all was explained. At a painful meeting Honorine told him that her
parents said she must marry Gingras if he asked her. She reaffirmed

her love for George but bowed to her parents' will. Over the next few weeks the unhappy pair saw little of one another. Whatever passed through Honorine's mind, George was in deepest despair. With circumstances combining against them their remaining encounters were troubled and inconclusive. A melancholy pall hangs over George's last entry in the diary:

Sunday 5 April, 1846

Rose at ½ past 7. Fine warm weather. I stopped in my room all day. I passed a very lonesome day thinking of my unhappiness.

I think Honorine dose not love me so much now as she did some time ago. As she already forgotten the letters she wrote to me. If so I have not, for I have read them all over today, and when I think how she loved me, I cannot believe that she loves me so little at present. O if she knew how my love has not changed, perhaps she would not be so indifferent, but she dose not seem to care whether I love her or not. If I had never loved her I would not be so unhappy, but now that I know the power she has over me I can never think of loving another. No never! I have sworn & swear again that I will never marry another.

I went out at 6 o'clock and met Honorine walking with my sisters & Edwin. Honorine went home soon after. She told me she would not go out this evening. After tea I went out and walked about trying to forget my unhappiness, but I might as well try to forget that I am in existence. I came home at 9 o'clock, and was no little surprised to find Honorine & her brother here, particularly after telling me that she would not go out this evening. Had I known that she would come here this evening I would not have gone out. But at all events I was back in time to accompany her home, which I did at 10 o'clock. She did not speak much to me.

O Honorine, Honorine, have you forgotten your love for me. The only Consolation (if it is one) I have at present is her letters & her hair, which I kiss often.

11 o'clock going to bed.

End of Journal A or no. 1

CHAPTER ONE

The Christian Setting of Courtship and Marriage

When George and Honorine courted they took part in a series of rituals whose roots lay deeply embedded in the religious culture of the western world. For most of the past two thousand years the primary institutional influence in the West on human sexuality has come from the Christian church. Church law on marriage and religious ideals about sexual conduct have disciplined sexuality in the interests of the social system. For the most part this has meant that the church has subordinated personal desires to the needs of social institutions. In particular, by constructing a framework of rules and ideals within which courtship and marriage took place, it has played a vital role in creating and defending the family. Thus the origins of matrimony in Canada, as in all of the western world, lie deep in the Christian past. For this reason, before we can learn much about courtship and marriage in nineteenth-century Canada, we need to explore the place of Christianity in the history of family formation.

From the dawn of the Christian era the Roman church upheld the superiority of virginity.[1] Pauline doctrine advised that, since the unmarried cared for things of the Lord and not things of the world, theirs was the higher calling. But Paul also declared marriage to be an honourable estate, for "every man had his proper gift of God, one after this manner, and the other after that."[2] The church built its teachings about sexuality and marriage on the tenets of St Paul. According to the medieval historian Michael Sheehan,

the first thousand years of the Church's life can be seen as a period during which Christian doctrine, confronted by a bewildering profusion of marriage customs, concentrated its efforts on defending and enhancing the moral value of matrimony. Steady insistence on the permanence and sanctity of the relationship of husband and wife, and on the limitation of erotic sexuality to that relationship, gained significant acceptance by society, even though individual practice and the different civil customs and laws lagged well behind. The Church's position was often locally stated, was not always consistent, nor was it organized and complete.[3]

The French medievalist, Georges Duby, has sketched a fascinating portrait of the development of Christian marriage in northern France during the eleventh and twelfth centuries. The product of a complex interplay among ecclesiastical, political, economic, dynastic, ideological, and sexual aspirations, Christian matrimony gradually supplanted a host of older, secular marriage practices in which the church was scarcely involved.[4] For churchmen and laymen alike, Duby argues, "marriage was an instrument of control. The leaders of the Church used it as a means of holding their own against the laity, and in the hope even of subjugating it. The heads of families used it as a means of keeping their power intact."[5] For the better part of two centuries the two groups struggled over the issue, secular lords in pursuit of their dynastic goals, spiritual lords seeking to extend their religious and temporal power. But by the end of the twelfth century the contest was resolved, a consensus was established and the central tenets of Christian marriage were being taught throughout north-western Europe.

Foremost among them was the doctrine of consent: free agreement of the two to be married was the only necessary element in the marriage bond. While certainly desirable, witnesses, special forms, priestly intervention, and the assent of others were not required to establish a binding tie. Consent alone made marriage. The union which it created was permanent and exclusive. Husband and wife bound themselves to one another alone so long as they both lived. Catholic doctrine also held marriage to be sacred and the marriage rite a sacrament – one of seven defined by the teachings of the church. "The symbolism of matrimony," a Catholic authority has observed, "is gathered from Scripture. The union between man and wife is representative of the union between Christ and the Church ... It is a union in virtue of which Christ is bound to the soul by ties of love so close that conjugal affection alone affords a term of comparison."[6] As the priest had no effective role in forming the nuptial tie, the couple administered the sacrament of marriage to one another at the moment they exchanged their consent.[7]

The Roman church also extended control over matrimony by defining and enforcing stringent rules against incestuous marriage. Medieval Christianity forbade unions between men and women related in some measure by ties of blood, marriage, or godparenthood. The prohibited degrees varied over time, the general tendency being toward extension and elaboration. The process reached the point at which, in 1059,

Pope Nicholas II forbade marriage up to the seventh degree of affinity, a measure so comprehensive it would have precluded virtually all licit marriage in most communities throughout Europe. The Lateran Council of 1215 reduced these prohibitions to the fourth degree (marriage with a third cousin), the point at which calculations of kinship in medieval Europe usually ceased.[8] For the next seven hundred years marriage to someone within these bounds was forbidden by church law, though bishops could provide dispensations from impediments in the third and fourth degrees on payment of a fee.[9]

The development of the medieval ideal of Christian matrimony has been interpreted in several ways. George H. Joyce, the Catholic historian of marriage, considered it a momentous achievement, "a great formative factor of civilization."[10] Sheehan has described it as the expression of a humane ideal, the church placing the good of the couple before all other interests.[11] The anthropologist and historian Jack Goody, however, has taken a more sceptical view. Private consent and prohibitions on kin marriages, he notes, weakened the influence of families over the marriages of their young. By enforcing strict codes of forbidden alliances the church set itself against systems of collateral kinship in favour of the nuclear family. In doing so it frustrated strategies aimed at accumulating and preserving wealth through marriage within kin groups. The doctrines of spousal consent and the sacramental character of marriage similarly opposed the authority of parents over their childrens' choice of mates.[12] Far from acting in the interests of the couple to be married, Goody has argued, the church had its own distinctive ends to serve in seeking control over marriage. It hoped to increase its power over common men and women, and to aggrandize its wealth by encouraging those with property to bestow some or all of it on the church rather than their kinsmen. Goody is equivocal about the extent to which the church pursued these ends consciously as they formulated the rules of Christian marriage. But he leaves no doubt that, whatever its overt intent, these were the consequences of its growing role in marriage.[13]

Not surprisingly, Catholic marriage teachings aroused strong objection in many quarters. Dissenters repeatedly challenged priestly influence on matrimony – for example, the Cathars of early fourteenth-century Montaillou who denied church authority over marriage.[14] Kinsmen with disappointed expectations of inheritance also resisted Catholic marital regulations and forced their modification; in particular they demanded dispensations from the rules forbidding close marriage.[15] Refusing to yield up their power over matrimony, parents, too, claimed that their consent was necessary to marriage.[16] More generally, popular marriage customs, which often varied widely from those officially approved, persisted everywhere in pre-Reformation Europe.[17] Secret marriages – between those who simply exchanged vows in private – caused serious concern. Although in accord with Catholic doctrine that consent by itself made a binding union, clandestine marriage flew in the face of church teachings about the duties that children owed their parents. It also created problems for religious authorities by opening the door to widespread abuse. According to one sixteenth-century church rubric, "Clandestine marriages are forbidden for two reasons: first, lest the expectation of marriage lead to fornication; and secondly, lest those who are really married be unjustly separated. For in secret marriages it often happens that one of the parties alters his mind, and sends the other away destitute of all evidence and powerless to obtain remedy for the wrong."[18] In other words, secret marriages followed the letter, though not the spirit, of Christian marriage law.

The Reformation divines, like earlier religious dissenters, took issue with some central principles of Catholic marriage doctrine. Luther, Calvin, and others denied the sacramental nature of marriage, considering it instead a civil contract, though Protestants continued to regard matrimony as sacred and therefore a matter for religious oversight.[19] The long-run consequence of this radical shift in understanding was the progressive secularization of western beliefs about marriage. The reformers also disagreed with Catholic views about the validity of clandestine matrimony, which they took to mean marriage without parental consent. The principal Reformation theologians considered unions void if they lacked the approval of each spouse's parents. Luther – whose teachings on matrimony varied over time – once held that a father could annul the marriage of a child who wedded without his permission.[20] Reform thought also disputed Catholic regulations about the prohibited degrees, though on this point the reformers differed among themselves. Luther considered the Levitical prohibitions a complete list, while Calvin regarded them as illustrative and extended them in strict parallel to all relationships as close as those mentioned in Leviticus.[21] The Anglican reformers followed Calvin and drew up a table of prohibited unions for publication in the Book of Common Prayer and display in every church. Whatever the forbidden alliances, Protestant doctrine, unlike Catholic, considered them part of God's law from which there was no dispensation. Some reforming theologians also admitted the possibility of divorce and remarriage, though on such narrow grounds that this was extremely difficult, more difficult in their eyes than annulment of marriage in the Catholic communion.[22]

Confronted by dissent, the Roman church considered the issue of marriage at the Council of Trent, called in the mid 1540s to consider church reforms and to address the Protestant challenge. As a first step,the council affirmed the doctrine that marriage was a sacrament, "an outward symbol to which Christ has attached a gift of inward grace."[23] Then it amended the rule that consent was sufficient for marriage, from which the problem of clandestine unions had flowed, to require public nuptials. Thereafter no marriage would be valid without three witnesses, one of them a parish priest or priestly delegate. Secret marriages remained sacramental unions, but simple consent was no longer enough to create a valid marriage.[24] By instituting obligatory forms the council recognized matrimony as a social as well as a private and sacramental act, though it continued to deny parents any formal control over their children's marriages. Finally, Trent reaffirmed the church's position on consanguinity and affinity, and the possibilities of dispensation from some impediments to marriage.[25] As a result the Catholic church continued to impose more stringent, but also more flexible, restrictions on matrimony than did the Protestant communions.

The three centuries following the Reformation era saw relatively little change in the tenets of Christian marriage among Catholics and Protestants alike. The act of marriage itself was thought sacred, if not a sacrament, the wedded state a condition blessed by supernatural sanction. Matrimony remained a lifelong, exclusive relationship (though some churches countenanced divorce and remarriage in highly exceptional circumstances). Marriage was founded on mutual consent freely exchanged before witnesses, although some denominations emphasized the supplementary need for parental agreement. Close kin, related either by blood or affinity, were forbidden to marry one another, the extent of these prohibitions varying somewhat from one faith to the next. Erotic sexuality was confined to married life, and each church devised its own means to detect and punish offenders, goals which they pursued with shifting zeal over time. Together these rules formed the common core of Christian marriage doctrine in the modern western world.

The European missionaries who settled in Canada brought with them Christian ideals on sexuality and marriage, all the major religious denominations in the colonies playing an active part in this process.[26] But only the Catholic church taught its marriage doctrines systematically in the course of everyday religious life. Following the precepts of the Council of Trent, bishops periodically reminded their priests of the sacramental character of matrimony, of their obligation to explain this truth to their flocks, and of the need to uphold Catholic marriage law on all occasions.[27] In Upper Canada from 1840 onward, church ordinances required that Catholic doctrine on the sacrament of marriage be preached annually from every pulpit. The catechisms so widely used for instructing youths and children also emphasized the central principles of Catholic matrimony. *Butler's Catechism*, one of the most popular in nineteenth-century North America, had this to say about marriage:

Q. What is Matrimony?

A. A sacrament which gives grace to the husband and wife to live happily together; and to bring up their children in the fear and love of God.

Q. Do they receive the grace of the sacrament of Matrimony, who contract marriage in the state of mortal sin?

A. No, they are guilty of a very great sacrilege, by profaning so great a sacrament, and instead of a blessing they receive their condemnation. Ephes. v 32

Q. What should persons do to receive worthily the sacrament of marriage?

A. They should make a good confession, and earnestly beseech God to grant them a pure intention; and to direct them in the choice they are to make.

Q. Should children consult their parents on their intended marriages?

A. Yes; and be advised by them according to reason and religion; they should also give timely notice to their pastor.

Q. Can the bond or the tie of marriage be ever broken?

A. It never can, but by the death of the husband or wife. St. Matt. xix; Rom. vii and 1 Cor. vii

Q. What is the reason that so many marriages are unhappy?

A. Because many enter into that holy state from unworthy motives, and with guilty consciences: therefore their marriages are not blessed by God. 1 Cor. vii 28.[28]

J.B. de la Salle's popular *New Treatise of the Duties of a Christian Towards God*, which circulated throughout Canada in both languages during the last third of the nineteenth century, also discussed Catholic marriage doctrine. Like all such texts, it placed heavy emphasis on the sacramental nature of marriage and the need to enter it in a state of spiritual grace. Before deciding to marry, de la Salle counselled, a person should pray fervently to know God's will on the question. Like Butler he also emphasized the advisory role of parents. "Parents have at heart the interests of their children, and know better than they do the means by which they can be promoted. Children should, therefore, follow their advice, rather than blind inclination, in an affair so important, and on which their happiness for time and eternity is so dependent."[29] De la Salle's insistence on the role of parents in matrimony was no retreat from the traditional Catholic view that a valid marriage could be made without parental consent. But popular tracts on Church doctrine, this one included, commonly upheld the authority of fathers and mothers by insisting that their advice be taken in matrimonial decisions.

The Catholic church enforced its ethical standards on marriage and sexuality through a hierarchy of tribunals. Priests dealt with common lapses of conduct in the confessional. They referred more serious questions to their bishops, who had much broader authority over these matters. In some instances bishops, in turn, would place a case before the papacy, the ultimate authority within the Roman faith. When enforcing its moral law the church generally strove to attain three primary ends: it defended its principles; it tried to reconcile offenders with the church and submit them to its authority; and it demanded penitential gestures from transgressors – outward signs and inward gestures – for these blotted out the stain of sin and aligned the erring one's thoughts and actions more closely with Christian principles.

Unfortunately for us the confessional is closed to the historian's eyes. Spoken confessions on matters of private conscience leave no written traces behind. From time to time renegade priests have dropped the veil of secrecy (for instance, the good Father Chiniquy, whose reports of scandalous tales heard at the confessor's grill in mid-nineteenth century Quebec are far more titillating than informative), but these sources can scarcely be believed.[30] Thus we will never know much about the Catholic treatment of common marital and sexual misdeeds in nineteenth-century Canada.

But on serious questions church records are more informative, for when priests encountered problems beyond their competence, they had to consult their bishops, and enough of their correspondence survives to provide revealing glimpses of at least some major misdemeanours. Priests occasionally encountered cohabitation outside marriage, a grave offence that required a bishop's advice. The extent of cohabitation in nineteenth-century Canada can never be known, but it likely was fairly widespread. Catholic archives certainly reveal signs of a popular sub-culture of illicit, consensual unions largely hidden from public view. Usually at least one partner in such liaisons had been married and deserted, a common predicament in societies with high rates of immigration and population mobility. Certainly Mary O'Brien, that astute observer of Upper Canadian social customs, considered desertion common in the 1830s.[31] The Catholic doctrine of lifelong matrimony encouraged illicit liaisons by refusing remarriage to those with a living, estranged spouse. Cohabitation also was easy to conceal, given the high population mobility of nineteenth-century Canada. On arriving in a new locale a couple only need call themselves married to be accepted as such, for no one else would likely know of their antecedents. Nor was there any reason why unchurched unions would ever come to light unless conscience goaded men and women to disclose the state of their affairs, a prospect perhaps more likely in Catholic circles because of its confessional rituals.

The church dealt with these problems according to the circumstances of each case. If at all possible, it quickly and quietly married the offending couple. In 1838 Edward Gordon, a priest at Niagara, wrote Bishop Gaulin about one such case. A woman gravely ill with consumption confessed that she had never married the Protestant whose wife she was reputed to be and by whom she had had several children. She begged Gordon to marry them before her imminent death. He demurred and sought Gaulin's advice, however, for a priest had no authority to perform mixed marriages. But before the bishop's reply arrived she failed so quickly that Gordon married them privately without his superior's consent (which subsequently arrived); she died soon after with her conscience at rest.[32] In 1870 a priest in Napanee petitioned his bishop for authority to marry a cohabiting pair without banns and thus avoid a local scandal. The two had lived together for several years and had always been considered husband and wife. They had five children, were very poor, and lived in part on local charity because the man was a cripple. In this instance, too, the bishop permitted a private marriage.[33] But when cohabitation persisted in the face of Catholic authority, the church used its full disciplinary power to chasten the offenders. In 1850, when an unmarried couple near Belleville continued to live together despite church condemnation, Bishop Phelan commanded that a letter admonishing them to separate be read before their congregation on three successive Sundays. If they still failed to comply they faced public excommunication.[34]

When one of the couple seeking marriage had been wedded before, the church proceeded cautiously. Another marriage would be bigamous in Catholic eyes unless the absent spouse were dead, and this the Catholic hierarchy scrupulously tried to prevent. Such cases were not uncommon. In 1833 James Farling, a Protestant from Penetanguishine who wished to become a Catholic, asked Bishop Macdonell's permission to marry his housekeeper. He had married in 1815 and his wife had left him and their four children in 1826. Farling now questioned the legality of his first marriage because it had been performed in the United States by a British official, and he hoped these grounds might permit Catholic nuptials.[35] Two years later Jean Baptiste Morin, a priest who ministered to the French-Canadian population of south-western Upper Canada, told Bishop Gaulin of a similar case involving a woman whose husband had abandoned her with four children and who now wished to marry the man with whom she lived.[36]

James O'Flynn, the priest in St Thomas, placed still another case before Gaulin in 1840. In this instance an Irishman had separated from his wife of four months when she bore another man's child. He had then come to America and later wed a second time according to Catholic rite, without divulging the fact of his first marriage to either his priest or his new wife.[37] Unfortunately the bishop's response is unknown in each case.

The Catholic position on remarriage was clear and rigid. "The rule I have followed," Bishop Macdonell told one of his priests in 1832, "is never to marry a person separated from a wife or husband let the period never be so long till there be a satisfactory evidence, or at least a strong presumptive proof of the decease of the absentee & from this rule I could not allow the least deviation."[38] On this basis priests refused to marry those who had been married before and who could not prove that their spouse was dead. But some Canadian bishops used latitude in dealing with these cases. In one instance Bishop Power excommunicated a couple who lived together in the face of church censure. They could only be readmitted to the sacraments after separation, repentance, atonement, and a lengthy waiting period.[39] But Power took a more lenient view of other less flagrant circumstances. A woman who unwittingly wed a married man who had no proof of his wife's decease was advised that it would be best if she lived with him chastely, though Power did not forbid their cohabitation unless the first wife was discovered alive. The bishop denied her husband absolution and the sacraments unless he lived with his second wife as a brother would a sister.[40] In a third, similar case Bishop Horan simply instructed a priest that he should follow whatever course would produce the most good.[41]

Mixed marriages created another ongoing problem for the church. The Holy See considered them dangerous to the faith and instructed bishops to discourage them.[42] But because Catholics were a minority in English Canada – and not an especially powerful one at that – the prospect of marriage outside the faith was an ever-present threat. The Catholic church responded by raising barriers to it. It required the dispensation of a bishop, who insisted that the petitioners explain their motives, assure the faith of the Catholic party, and promise to raise their offspring in the Catholic faith.[43] The Protestant partner in such unions commonly signed a promise not to interfere in the religion of his or her spouse and their children.[44] As to the priesthood, some bishops were stern disciplinarians in matrimonial affairs. Bishop Power threatened to suspend any priest who performed mixed marriages without his consent.[45] But at best these strictures may have curbed the practice somewhat, for it remained a chronic problem.

Still, while Catholic marriage law was stern and unyielding, the religious diversity of nineteenth-century Canada limited its effects. The Roman communion competed in a religious market-place with several Protestant churches, all of them with less restrictive and less energetically enforced marriage laws than its own. Not surprisingly, when Catholic marriage regulations seemed too confining, some couples approached Protestant clergymen instead. The correspondence of Catholic bishops in nineteenth-century Ontario is sprinkled with cases of their members who were married by Protestant ministers. In many instances these couples were lost to the faith. In others, one or both parties later sought reunion with the church and the priesthood used these occasions to assert their rights over marriage. In 1842, when two Catholics in St Catharines were married by a Protestant minister to evade the publication of banns, their priest preached against scandalous marriages and refused them entry into the parish church.[46] Some twenty years later a Catholic couple from Cornwall, married by a Protestant clergyman in the United States, were required to atone for their sins before their former congregation as part of the reconciliation process.[47] But these incidents were rare. While the church would not compromise its doctrines, it could not require too harsh punishments for fear of driving some of its adherents into irreligion or the waiting arms of less exacting faiths.

As these various examples indicate, the authoritarian, hierarchical features of Catholicism shaped the system of discipline which the church employed in nineteenth-century Canada. Its control lay in the hands of bishops and priests who used graduated penalties to enforce the ethical codes of Catholicism. Regular confession, imperative for the faithful Catholic, drew misdemeanours to priestly notice, thus bringing offenders before those who dispensed the moral law of the church. This body of law and the forms of its enforcement had evolved over more than a millennium of Christian history. They were part of the colonial religious inheritance and drew nothing from the Canadian environment. For this reason Catholic church discipline in nineteenth-century English Canada differed little from that practised throughout the western world.

For the most part the church exerted its discipline behind closed doors, relying on the spiritual, moral, and social authority of the priesthood to alter behaviour and attitudes. Penitents performed their acts of contrition in private. Church leaders only appealed to congregational opinion in support of Catholic law in exceptional cases, when offences were public and flagrant. They did so in two ways. Occasionally they required public confession and repentance before an offender could be reconciled to the church. In other instances they excommunicated the stubborn, placing them outside the fellowship of believers. In both circumstances the church used public humiliation to direct community opinion against deviant behaviour. The process might succeed in coercing a delinquent and reforming his or her conduct. It might also fail and lead to ostracization. In either event the lesson would be salutary for the faithful.

The religious context of marriage evidently concerned Canadian Protestants much less deeply than it did Catholics. Protestants, unlike Catholics, had no tradition of pastoral teaching on marriage, for the spiritual nature of matrimony lay outside the field of their active interest. Where Catholicism persistently reminded the faithful of the goals of Christian marriage, Protestantism quietly accepted these as common truths. The Anglican church paid little heed to matrimonial questions until the later nineteenth century, when the issues of divorce and marriage with a deceased wife's sister absorbed Catholic and Protestant alike. Similarly, marriage was peripheral to the Methodist preoccupation with conversion and the achievement of saving faith. Perhaps it had greater weight with some Presbyterians, who took right conduct in this world as a sign of election in the next, but even their interest in marriage doctrine was slight. All of the major Protestant churches stated their marriage canons simply and without qualification, in forms dating back to the post-Reformation century. The central principles of Protestant marriage applied without qualification, unlike those of the Roman church which, while rather more stringent, could be bent somewhat on occasion.

The weight of Protestant concern lay instead on pre-marital sexual offences, and thus on the process of courtship. Here, too, the basic problem was one of enforcement. Once again the written record tells us less about these matters than we would like to know. Each church had its own means of dealing with those who misbehaved, and most tried to do so as circumspectly as possible. Methodists simply refused delinquents admission to class meetings, an informal process invoked by class leaders which left no trace behind. Anglicans seem to have denied the sacraments to flagrant offenders. Bishop Strachan proposed this course in one of the few such instances which has come to light. He told a minister who had complained of a parishioner living in adultery that the offender should be denied communion until he repented and separated from the woman with whom he was living. Whether the minister should do this openly was quite another matter, given what Strachan described as "the present lax state of church discipline." He advised public exclusion if the legal evidence was sufficient, if the congregation would support it, and if its effects would be beneficial.

Otherwise he counselled discretion.[48]

The Presbyterian communion, in contrast, had a long-standing tradition of formal rebuke for those who offended church law. Calvin had held that the reformed church should enforce strict social discipline, and from the mid sixteenth century onward his Scottish followers did so energetically. The kirk session, a body of elders elected by each congregation, joined the minister in supervising the faithful. They employed a graduated scale of corrections, ranging from private admonition to public confession and repentance. Although sessions dealt with many offences, sexual misdemeanours were their paramount concern. Any reading of Scottish church records before the nineteenth century reveals that elders' courts dealt incessantly with these questions, pre-marital intercourse in particular. Disciplinary practices varied widely from one congregation to the next, but kirk sessions normally imposed shaming punishments and if the accused would not submit, they expelled him or her from church membership.[49]

The Scots began migrating to British America in the second half of the eighteenth century, when moral policing in Scotland was less energetic than it once had been. The corrective zeal of the eldership was in decline, and population growth and the spread of religious dissent had made church censure easier to avoid. But after the turn of the century, when the tide of emigration swelled, an evangelical Presbyterian movement refurbished the church's ancient concern with sin.[50] The tens of thousands of Scots and Scots-Irish who arrived in the British colonies after the Napoleonic wars thus came from communities with strong traditions of religious discipline and with a revived concern about social misconduct. After founding new Presbyterian congregations in Canada they lost little time in choosing elders – leading lay members of the church – to oversee popular morality in their new world setting. Here we see a clear example of cultural conservatism at work. The Presbyterian churches in early nineteenth-century British colonial society were ethnic institutions; their members were almost entirely Scots and Ulster Scots who clung tightly to their religious and cultural roots. If the Canadian wilderness promised them freedom from old world constraints, they turned their backs on the offer. Instead they resurrected one of the most traditional of Scottish institutions, kirk session governance, and this at a time when its influence in Scotland was clearly on the wane, despite the puritanism of the evangelical revival.[51]

We catch some instructive glimpses of kirk session discipline at work in eastern Upper Canada in a recent study of the Presbyterian eldership in rural and small town congregations. It reveals the Scots' common preoccupation with sexual transgressions, especially pre-marital intercourse.[52] Some sessions hunted offenders more energetically than did others. The Presbyterian church in Franktown, a small, predominantly Scottish community between Ottawa and Perth, showed remarkable zeal in this pursuit. Between 1837 and 1879 the Franktown elders dealt with forty-four sexual offences, all but three of them premarital intercourse.[53] They did so as part of a deliberate plan to revive traditional Scottish discipline, for the elders declared in 1839: "Altho the Law obliging those guilty of scandalous offenses to profess publicly penitence for the same, has in many Parishes become obsolete in Scotland, & has not, so far as is known to Session, been fully acted upon in any Scotch Congregation in this Province, still the Session being unanimously of opinion, that the observance of this Law would be beneficial, it was resolved that it should be enforced."[54]

Enforcement commenced with a summons to appear before the kirk session. When confronted with a charge, the offender usually admitted guilt and professed penitence. The elders then formally admonished and absolved the delinquent, and after some time admitted him or her to church membership. Any children illicitly conceived were then accepted for baptism. In the far less common instances of graver sin – adultery or multiple fornication – the elders insisted on public rebuke and penance before the entire congregation on one or more Sundays. The Franktown elders also excommunicated the obdurate, as well as those who broke church law by marrying within the forbidden degrees.

In Presbyterian Ontario kirk session discipline lasted until late in the nineteenth century. Session minutes speak of occasional cases well into the 1880s, though by this time formal church discipline had been in decline for more than a generation. In fact it had always been somewhat inappropriate in its new world setting. Elders' courts were one of the many forms of social discipline in pre-modern Europe which used shaming punishments to regulate personal conduct by directing community opinion against unacceptable behaviour. The Scottish kirk session combined elements of popular and elite control, for the elders ruled by general consent. In Canada kirk sessions formed part of a transplanted ethnic and cultural institution. But the use of public humiliation to regulate behaviour – very much on the wane in western Europe by the early nineteenth century – had shallow roots in British America. The criminal law abandoned shaming punishments during the reforms of the 1830s, following the examples offered by British and American penology.[55] Though some have argued otherwise, the charivari was never a powerful instrument of social discipline in English Canada, and what little influence it had dwindled as the century progressed.[56] By the 1850s most secular practices directed at shaping private behaviour through appeals to community opinion had been abandoned in English Canada. Always an alien form of correction, kirk session courts grew increasingly anachronistic and incongruous with passing time. As a new generation of Canadian-born Presbyterians replaced the immigrant generation of Scots, they gradually abandoned the old world punishments, introduced by their forbears, for less overt forms of influence over matrimony.

Evangelicals faced special problems overseeing courtship and marriage, among them the exclusivist tendencies of evangelical organizations which limited the range of acceptable mates. Methodists, like Roman Catholics, opposed marriage outside the faith. The first *Form of Discipline* widely used in Upper Canada interpreted Paul's caution "be ye not unequally yoked together with unbelievers" to forbid marriage with the unawakened, and called for the expulsion of those who disobeyed.[57] Later versions of the *Discipline* relaxed these requirements somewhat, advising members to consult their most serious brethren before taking steps toward matrimony and admitting the possibility of marriage outside the faith, as long as the intended spouse possessed the form and sought the power of godliness.[58] Punishments for the disobedient were also rather less harsh. Those who wed an unbeliever were merely exhorted to godly conduct and placed on trial for six months, after which they were readmitted to church fellowship if their conduct had been satisfactory.

The emotionalism of evangelical preaching and worship placed a special pitfall before those who walked the narrow paths of right conduct: the possibility of confusing spiritual with secular passions. The fervent emotions of revivalism ostensibly expressed an aroused love of God and no doubt they normally did. But revivals also encouraged the creation of a loving fellowship, the expression of deep feelings and desires, and the normally forbidden exchange of caresses among those who were not kin; all of this could blur distinctions between love for God and love for man or woman. The evidence on this point is maddeningly slight for we still know very little about evangelical religion in early Canada. The youthful Egerton Ryerson provides us with one stray clue. In 1825, newly embarked on a career as a Methodist circuit rider at the age of twenty-two, he told his mother that "I have many temptations to contend with and many trials to weigh me down at times. These I will not attempt to describe but would only remark that sometimes they proceed from unbecoming forwardness in young females to which I oppose retirement."[59]

An episode in 1793 involving rumours about the improper conduct of Harris Harding, a Nova Scotia New Light preacher and follower of Henry Alline, is also instructive. According to one of Harding's supporters in Annapolis, Harding had been the subject of "many cruel and false reports that he has not deserv'd." In her opinion, Harding

was not overcome with any indecent behaviour but I think the Young Woman had a great natural fondness for him and thought all his tender expressions for hers and other Souls was the effect of natural passion which she wish'd to be the case to her, and when she found she was mistaken she was fill'd with confusion and shame, Expressing herself in such words as would best Answer to clear herself, and tho she has told many stories which do not all agree with each other, Yet some have feasted themselves on reporting them, and Mr. ____ has been foremost in it.[60]

To view the matter most favourably, Harding and the young woman were victims of an emotional ambiguity inherent in evangelicalism.

But perhaps Harding did not deserve the benefit of our doubt. Three years later he impregnated a woman outside marriage and wed her a few weeks before she bore his child.[61] Given the long-standing reputation of evangelicalism for moral austerity, Harding's role in these two incidents might seem to place it in a surprisingly wanton light (even more so because these events did little to impair his standing as a leading evangelical in Nova Scotia). But there seem to have been other signs of licentiousness among New Lights in Nova Scotia during the early 1790s.[62] George Rawlyk argues that Maritime New Lights and Baptists practised sexual openness during the Second Great Awakening (c. 1790–1810) until their increasingly conservative preachers, anxious to establish more respectable institutions, insisted on orthodox discipline. Possibly these incidents were confined to the Maritimes; until we know more about revivalism in British America we cannot be certain. Still, they do suggest the presence of sexual tensions deeply embedded in evangelical Christianity, tensions which created special disciplinary problems for revivalism in colonial society.

Ministers were sources of special concern. Like Ryerson and Harding, evangelical preachers tended to be young and unmarried. They usually travelled alone, often amongst relative strangers. In these circumstances, some of the behavioural constraints which bound most men did not tie them so tightly, even though they were men of God. They often had close contact with young, single women, for intense religious experiences were common amongst girls in late adolescence.[63] Recognizing the special perils inherent in these circumstances, Canadian Methodists insisted that ministers consult a superior in the church before taking a wife.[64] They also watched carefully over the conduct of their preachers. Intermittently throughout the nineteenth century, church courts sat in judgment over ministers accused of improprieties, ranging from excessively frequent visiting at the home of a married woman to indecent behaviour and illicit intercourse.[65] Churches were particularly vulnerable to pastoral misconduct for two reasons. First, ministers probably had more opportunity for indiscretions than most other men in nineteenth-century Canada because their profession brought men and women together much more often than did most other callings. Secondly, the Christian churches were leading defenders of orthodox opinion on marriage and sexuality, and they as much as their public expected ministers and priests to behave in a manner beyond reproach. No lapses could possibly be tolerated among the clergy, though those of more frail mortals might be accepted with regret.

From our perspective, church discipline in the past is extremely illuminating for it helps us identify the bounds of acceptable behaviour and the penalties incurred for crossing them. Although it was far from the only influence on private conduct in nineteenth-century English Canada, the authority of religious beliefs and institutions, and the face-to-face character of most towns and rural communities, must have made religious discipline an effective check on personal behaviour. The church thus influenced the matrimonial process in fundamental ways. Doctrine established the primary rules of Christian sexuality and marriage, and defined the boundaries of normal family life. Discipline enforced the basic constraints on sexual relations between men and women. By means of both the church supervised courtship and marriage, and in doing so oversaw the process by which the institution of the family perpetuated itself in Anglo-Canadian society.

Church regulation of sexuality and marriage in nineteenth-century Canada served three further ends. First, it promoted church interests. By the time the first settlers laid the foundations of English-Canadian society, religious institutions in western society had long since lost their monopoly over marriage. What authority they still had now derived from the state. But this influence was far from negligible, for residual control over marriage gave churches an important role in one of life's primary events, and thus an opportunity to tighten their bonds with their adherents. In nineteenth-century English Canada, where religious diversity created a competitive market-place for marriages, denominations jealously guarded their matrimonial authority. They recognized the claim it gave them to influence over their parishioners. This matter lay at the heart of the dispute over the legal right to perform marriages, which pitted Upper Canadian Anglican and Methodist church leaders against one another before 1831.[66]

Through its supervision of marriage and sexuality the church defended traditional ethical standards. Long the chief guardian of Christian matrimonial ideals, it had always emphasized the moral value of continence and fidelity. Christian dogma held marriage to be permanent, exclusive, and sacred, and insisted that eroticism be limited to the married state. In nineteenth-century Canada all Christian denominations occupied this same doctrinal ground, though they differed on some points of teaching. They differed, as well, on the means of enforcing these ethical standards. But in their distinctive ways, the confessional, the kirk session, and other agents of church discipline all sought the same ends: the safekeeping of Christian principles on marriage and sexual life.

Finally, as civilization's chief instrument in regulating sexual life,[67] the church defended the primary institution in western society – the family. This was as true of nineteenth-century Canada as it was of all modern western societies. By insisting on the sanctity of marriage, by confining sexual love to married life, and by enforcing these doctrines amongst their adherents, the Christian churches fortified family stability. Each family member benefited from this influence, but women and children – economically the most vulnerable – profited most. Family life was crucial to their well-being, for outside its bounds life usually was precarious. Historically the church has never entirely succeeded in using matrimony to bridle sexual impulses and, as we have seen, this was true of nineteenth-century Canada. But partial failure should not cloud the fact that, imperfect though it was, this was probably the best defence the family ever had before the age of the welfare state.

CHAPTER TWO

Law and Property in Courtship and Marriage

Though George and Honorine scarcely considered it at the time, their growing commitment to each other had complex legal implications. Like most young lovers, they were oblivious to the fact that the law invaded every phase of the process of courtship and marriage, enveloping even the most private acts in a web of public regulation. Both civil and criminal law framed the lives of courting couples with a latticework of constraints, which grew ever more intricate the nearer the marriage day approached. In one sense the law is an instrument of definition: it determines what is legal, what is illegal and, by omission, what lies outside the realm of law. Thus it was with the laws concerning courtship and marriage in nineteenth-century British America. The laws of the colonies determined what acts were licit, what were illicit, and what lay beyond legal regulation.

The law touched courtship at two important points: it validated a promise to marry, and it dealt with pre-marital sexual intercourse. In the first instance the common law gave men and women a remedy against suitors who promised to marry them but later refused. The aggrieved party could launch a civil suit and, if proof were offered that a promise had been made, he or she was entitled to damages at a jury's discretion. While available to both sexes, breach of promise actions were primarily a woman's defence against deceit in courtship. They rested upon the presumption that her honour, her future marriage prospects, and her sentiments were injured if she were cast off by a suitor who — to use that fine Victorian phrase — trifled with her affections.[1]

A breach of promise case from eastern Ontario in 1874 reveals the close links between this aspect of the law and popular attitudes toward courtship. In October of that year Lucy Jane Vanalstine, of Clarendon Township, Frontenac County, sued John Leason, the manager of a lumber company in the same place, for breach of promise of marriage. Several witnesses testified that John had courted Lucy for more than four years, regularly taking her to parties, prayer meetings, and other social occasions. According to a press report, "it was consequently considered by all the neighbours and friends that the parties were engaged and would soon be wedded. In fact Leason on several occasions spoke of the plaintiff as his wife. They were nearly always in company together and seemed much attached to each other."[2] The court also heard letters from John to Lucy in which he wrote of his intention to marry her soon. The jury found for her and awarded her $1,500. One telling feature of this case is the legal standing of public opinion about a private matrimonial arrangement. In the eyes of the community the fact that the couple had been seen together regularly over a long period of time was proof of their betrothal, and a court of law accepted this as evidence of the fact. Most likely the compelling bits of evidence, seen from the judge's perspective, were Leason's letters of intent. In this instance law and popular sentiment reinforced one another.

A larger body of law related to sexual misdemeanours in courtship, especially pregnancy and childbirth outside marriage. The extent of pre-marital pregnancy and illegitimacy in nineteenth-century English Canada is hard to know. The only estimates of the former we have suggest that a significant proportion of women were pregnant when they married – the known range varied from one in twelve to one in five – but, based on a small sample as they are, these figures are not much more than impressionistic.[3] Illegitimacy was comparatively uncommon. Best estimates suggest that illegitimate births probably ranged between 2 and 4 per cent of all births in English Canada throughout the century.[4] If so, the incidence of illegitimacy in nineteenth-century Canada was as low as it was anywhere in the western world at that time.

When an unmarried woman delivered a child, one possible way of obtaining restitution was a civil action for seduction. Because the concept of seduction in the British common-law tradition implied female consent and therefore responsibility, relief was not available to the woman herself but only to her father or, if he were dead, her mother or some other close relation with whom she lived. In this instance the father would sue for loss of filial services. He had to prove that his daughter resided at home both at the time of her seduction and when her child was born, and that she performed simple domestic chores. Damages were to be based upon the plaintiff's financial losses as well as his distress and dishonour, the loss of his daughter's society, and the cost of rearing an illegitimate child.[5] In Upper Canada, legislation passed in 1837 eliminated the need for plaintiffs to prove loss of services. As Chief Justice Sir John Beverley Robinson observed in 1843, "the wound given to parental feelings, the disgrace and injury inflicted upon the family of the person seduced," became the real injury to be redressed in such actions.[6] But judicial interpretation later returned the basis of action to its former, narrower grounds.

Although theoretically available to all, this remedy was inaccessible to most unmarried mothers and their relations. The legal historian Constance Backhouse conducted an extensive search in Ontario case reports and court records, most of them from the second half of the nineteenth century. She uncovered 152 suits for seduction, representing only a tiny fraction of the thousands of illegitimate births that occurred in the province during these years.[7] The financial and social costs of these lawsuits limited them to the better off and the thick-skinned, for those who took putative fathers to court paid a high price in legal fees and tarnished family reputations. And the outcome of a lawsuit was far from certain. Ultimately three-quarters of the plaintiffs whom Backhouse examined received a verdict in their favour, but defendants appealed a third of all cases, adding to the plaintiffs' costs and uncertainties. Moreover, the size of the award could not be predicted. Average awards generally ranged between $300 and $400 plus costs during the latter part of the century.[8] This was about the annual income of a working man at the time, not a trivial sum, but by no means substantial either. Nor were all seducers good for the money; some were too poor, while others developed a wish to see the world when irate fathers pursued them on their daughters' behalf. More often than not actions for seduction probably never came to trial. A newspaper report of 1888 noted that, of nine seduction cases in North York over the previous two years, all but one had been settled out of court.[9] Perhaps the best protection the law could offer was the possibility of a lawsuit. The threat of legal action must have been enough to force many a defendant to pay the plaintiff for the wrong which he and his daughter had sustained. No doubt it also overcame many a reluctant groom's misgivings about marriage.

In terms of financial support, the legal standing of unmarried mothers and their children differed from one colony to another before Confederation. In the early years of each colony, Nova Scotia and New Brunswick modelled their welfare provisions on the English poor law and gave local authorities the power to order putative fathers to pay for their child's delivery and subsequent maintenance. In these matters the uppermost consideration was not the welfare of mothers but that of ratepayers, anxious to be spared the financial costs of illegitimacy.[10] In Lower Canada and, later, Quebec, the civil code gave bastard children the right to demand maintenance from their parents but took no account of their mothers' welfare.[11] In this instance, of course, someone would have to sue on the infant's behalf. The Upper Canadian government made no provision for poor relief when the colony was founded and therefore unwed mothers initially had to rely on uncertain private arrangements for assistance. From 1837 anyone responsible for raising an illegitimate child could sue the child's father for its support.[12]

The criminal law on birth control, abortion, and infanticide also touched upon courtship, as did laws relating to abduction, rape, and other sexual offences.[13] Although seldom invoked, they nevertheless formed part of the framework surrounding the progress of marriage. This is not to suggest that they exerted much direct influence over the conduct of courting couples. The most powerful rules governing intimacy were social and ethical, not legal. Yet the civil and criminal law exerted a strong subliminal influence over the whole of the courtship process. It defined the basic rules of fair dealing and it provided penalties and redress for those who overstepped the bounds of sexual propriety.

To the extent that it affected courtship, the law simply governed private behaviour. Marriage, however, was a public act to which the community's welfare was intimately linked. As a result, the law shaped the form and content of matrimony. Three facets of this relationship are particularly important. The law defined whom one could or could not marry, it conferred the power to perform marriage ceremonies, and it defended the integrity of married life.

The key to understanding the marriage law of British America lies in England, for colonial laws derived from those of England. Two statutes in particular established the basic framework of the subsequent law of marriage in English Canada. One, enacted during the reign of Henry VIII, forbade marriage within the Levitical degrees of affinity.[14] The other, Lord Hardwicke's Marriage Act of 1753, insisted on parental consent for those who married under the age of twenty-one.[15] It also required public nuptials before a clergyman and denied the legality of clandestine matrimony by insisting that marriages be celebrated only in churches and other approved locations at approved times. The common law also incorporated a complex body of matrimonial regulation, the stipulation that the minimum age for marriage was twelve for females and fourteen for males, to choose one example. In nineteenth-century British North America the law of marriage differed somewhat from one colony to the next. It combined English common and statute law as it existed on the date when Parliament created each colony with colonial laws passed and judicial decisions made after that time.

Once the British North American colonies had inherited their marriage laws they made very few changes.[16] As soon as most colonial legislatures were constituted, they quickly confirmed the legal basis of matrimony within their jurisdictions and validated any marriages performed in the region before each colony came into being. Here the primary concern was to ensure the legitimacy of children and their capacity to inherit.[17] Pioneer legislators also authorized certain clergymen to officiate at weddings.[18] But beyond these requirements they prescribed little else as necessary for marriage, and even relaxed some of the more stringent regulations in Lord Hardwicke's Act because they were inconsistent with the circumstances of frontier communities. Lower Canada was an exception, for its marriage law rested on French colonial foundations, confirmed by the Quebec Act in 1774 and later embodied in the civil code compiled during the 1860s. Though similar in substance, Lower Canadian marriage law differed greatly in detail from that of the other colonies.

The only major alteration in the law of marriage made during the nineteenth century broadened the range of possible spouses by allowing a man to marry his deceased wife's sister (and a woman her deceased husband's brother). In this instance the colony mimicked a contemporary British debate when the issue emerged during the 1870s. Although Leviticus only forbade such unions by inference, some denominations prohibited them outright. But opinion differed amongst the various Christian churches and within some of them as well, and the status of these marriages remained clouded. At one end of the spectrum stood Catholic, Anglican, and Presbyterian convictions strongly opposed to any hint that these were licit unions. At the other end lay the official views of Canadian Methodism as revealed in an extremely telling incident involving the Reverend Morley Punshon. Punshon was a leading English Methodist who came to Canada in 1867 to become president of the Canadian Wesleyan Methodist Conference. He wished to marry his late wife's sister, which was still forbidden by British law. When Punshon put the question to Egerton Ryerson, the leading Canadian Methodist of his time, Ryerson wrote that such unions had never been questioned in Canada and that prominent Wesleyans in Ontario – including his brother, a minister himself – had married in this fashion. He then proposed that Punshon and his bride-to-be come to Toronto by way of New York and Niagara Falls, that he meet them at the border, and that they marry immediately on their arrival. He even offered to obtain the necessary licence and arrange a private wedding for them in a Niagara Falls hotel.[19]

Parliament spent a lot of hot air on the issue during the 1870s and this provoked intermittent skirmishes among religious pamphleteers.[20] Eventually in 1882 it declared that a man might lawfully marry his deceased wife's sister and this put an end to doubt about the question.[21] This little tempest bears an important message about religion, the state, and marriage in Victorian English Canada. At the heart of the controversy lay a challenge to the traditional incest taboos of the Christian church. The unfolding debate revealed deep divisions within the religious community. Roman Catholics and conservative Protestants upheld a strict interpretation of Leviticus, moderates a liberal view. But no matter how vigorous their assertions, the conservatives defended the minority position, one based on the conviction that marriage was a sacred estate. While moderates never denied the religious significance of matrimony, their position was a further step along the path toward a secular view of marriage. In this instance the state accepted the liberal interpretation and reinforced the secularizing trend.

Beyond determining who could marry and who could perform weddings, the law also defended the state of matrimony. Most important of all, it made divorce exceedingly difficult. In this instance colonial circumstances rested firmly on British precedent which, from the early seventeenth to the mid-nineteenth century, made marriage virtually indissoluble. The only possible means of divorce was by act of Parliament, a process so costly that only the wealthy could afford it. Between the late seventeenth century, when the practice began, and 1857, when civil divorce courts were established, only about two hundred divorces were granted in England.[22] Nova Scotia, New Brunswick, Prince Edward Island, and British Columbia entered Confederation with divorce courts and they were the only jurisdictions to possess them until the federal government gradually gave the other provinces similar authority after the First World War. Previously a statutory divorce or an annulment were the only other means of legally dissolving a union in Ontario or Quebec. As in England, this process was costly and thus was only available to the wealthy. Between Confederation and the turn of the century Parliament granted seventy-one divorces. Yet even in provinces where matrimonial courts provided somewhat easier access, divorce was extremely uncommon. The courts granted fewer than two hundred divorce decrees during this same period.[23]

The civil law also offered husbands redress against men who seduced or, in the legal jargon of the day, had criminal conversation with their wives. A celebrated Halifax case in 1820 (the transcript of which an enterprising publisher printed and sold for a shilling) provides an illustration. In this instance William Henry Hall claimed damages of £5,000 from Major George Barrow "for the destruction of his peace and tranquillity, and social happiness as a husband, and for the injury he has sustained in the loss of the society, domestic comfort, and assistance of his wife."[24] After hearing a good deal of testimony – whose juicy details no doubt roused the publisher's entrepreneurial instincts – the jury awarded Hall £400. At this point we do not know how often such lawsuits were pressed or how widely their damages varied, though we know that only men could pursue these actions. But even a casual reading of the colonial press indicates that editors and journalists revelled in scandals like these. Reports of local lawsuits eagerly followed gossipy testimony in all its sinuous detail, and newspapers also gave generous coverage to celebrated British and American suits for matrimonial causes. In this way the law as well as the publicity surrounding its administration reinforced the bonds of marriage.

We could add other examples to this list, the criminal sanctions against bigamy to name one. But by now the point should be clear: through its use of law, government reinforced the stability of marriage. It defined the range of acceptable spouses, it established the terms under which men and women married, it empowered the agents authorized to perform wedding ceremonies, it frustrated the dissolution of marriage, and it punished those who transgressed its bounds. In these ways the state put its weight behind the traditional Christian concept of marriage.

M arriage united possessions as well as bodies and souls. It should come as no surprise, then, that the law on marital property touched on a central issue in the relations of husbands and wives. Although they may not have realized it at the time, when men and women courted they negotiated a property transaction which would affect their economic lives as long as their marriage lasted. The bargain they struck conformed to clearly prescribed rules about the differing property rights possessed by each spouse. Domestic law in Canada during the nineteenth century is a complex subject, not only because of intricacies in the law itself but because two separate legal traditions shaped the law of matrimonial property in nineteenth-century Canada, one English and one French.

The simplest approach is to consider the question of marital property and women's rights. A popular saying aptly summarized the English common law tradition: "In law husband and wife are one person, and the husband is that person."[25] In England a woman's property became her husband's when she married and any which she acquired during her marriage fell to her husband as well. She could not legally hold property apart from him. However, the law did treat women's real or immoveable property somewhat differently from her personal property. The common law provided that a husband could not dispose of his wife's real property without her consent.[26] In fact he was its guardian rather than its owner, for upon his death she regained full control over any real property which she had brought to or acquired during marriage. Through dower rights she also enjoyed a life interest in one-third of her husband's real property, though this ancient practice was eroded after the turn of the nineteenth century.[27] Thus, the common law defended a wife's real property interests in some measure. It was not so with personal property. According to the British historian Lee Holcombe, "the law relating to personal property held that all such property that belonged to a woman at the time of marriage and all that she acquired after the marriage were her husband's absolutely. He could use and dispose of this property in any way he chose during his lifetime without his wife's consent."[28]

Despite its primary importance, the common law was not the sole arbiter of matrimonial property. Equity, a separate body of law administered by its own courts, opposed the injustices of the common law tradition. Holcombe notes that equity was considered "the guardian of the weak and unprotected, such as married women, infants and lunatics."[29] In the matter of marital property it established a set of rules opposed to those of the common law, rules which gave at least some women special property rights "not only equal but in some ways superior to the rights of their husbands and of unmarried women." It did so by allowing separate property for a woman's use to be held by a trustee. Any form of property could be administered in this way, including real and personal, and such a trust could be established either before or during marriage.[30] Normally trusts were established through written documents, marriage settlements for example, but even verbal or tacit agreements could be deemed to constitute separate property for women. The property rights which a woman had in such cases would be restricted only by the terms of the agreement constituting the trust. Equity did not give married women equality with their husbands, rather it offered them a special status with circumscribed rights and diminished responsibilities. In social terms, the high cost of establishing and administering trusts meant that only well-to-do women could use the law of equity in defence of their interests.

Lower Canada apart, women in British North America shared these same legal disabilities. Until the 1850s married women in the Maritime colonies and Upper Canada had no legal right to hold or use property except as provided in equity (though a husband required his wife's consent to sell her real property and, through dower law provisions, she retained an interest in his real assets). In fact, in terms of civil law, a married woman had no independent existence. She could not make a will, sell her property, sign a contract, or engage in business without her husband's consent. The *Upper Canadian Law Journal* put the matter quite bluntly in 1856. "The *natural* rights of man and woman are, it must be admitted, equal; entering the married state, the woman surrenders most of them; in the possession of civil rights before, they merge in her husband; in the eye of the law she may be said to cease to exist."[31] Access to the protection afforded by equity varied widely in British America before the mid-nineteenth century. Colonial governors exercised informal equity jurisdiction in the Maritime colonies during the eighteenth century (in Nova Scotia, at least, from the earliest days of the colony) but an equity court was not established in Upper Canada until 1837.[32]

Reform came gradually to most provinces during the second half of the century. First came a limited measure, enacted in New Brunswick in 1851, which allowed abandoned or deserted wives to control their own property, with a single additional clause entitling married women to own real or personal property.[33] In 1859 the Canadian legislature enacted a more comprehensive statute giving all married women in Canada West ownership of their property independent of their husbands' control. Women who married after the act became law could enjoy their real and personal property without spousal interference. Those already married had the same rights over any property which they acquired later, though not over possessions which they had brought to their marriage.[34] But these powers were subject to telling limitations: for example, women still could not sell their property without their husbands' consent, and husbands retained their claim over their wives' earnings.

The initiative for reform in Canada West came from two quarters: a few influential members of the colonial Legislative Council, and a petitioning movement during the later 1850s. Petitioners and legislators both took inspiration from campaigns in Britain for similar reforms and, even more, from agitation for and change in the legal status of women in the United States – notably a New York State law passed in 1848 which gave married women control of their own property.[35] Between 1855 and 1858 a series of petitions circulated in Canada West. Campaign organizers gathered several thousand signatures from women and men alike on the printed petitions which they circulated and presented to the colonial legislature.[36] The legislature considered bills to give married women separate property rights each year from 1856 to 1858 but all three became mired in the legislative process and failed to become law. The measure passed in 1859 was far from all that the petitioners sought. Still, it was a singularly important step, for it marked an important departure from past Canadian thinking and practice about women, property, and family relations.

In Ontario and the other common law provinces, legislators sporadically broadened married women's property rights throughout the rest of the century, struggling against judges who tended to narrow the scope of statutory reforms through judicial interpretation.[37] A series of laws passed across English Canada gave married women the power to hold and dispose of property in their own right, to retain control of their own earnings, and to conduct business apart from their husbands. By 1900 women in English Canada had attained a degree of control over their own property and earnings which, if not yet equal to that of men, was far greater than anything their mothers or grandmothers had enjoyed.

The nineteenth-century law of marital property in Lower Canada and Quebec – significant to us here because it applied to English and French Canadians alike – had quite different origins. Derived from the Coutume de Paris of seventeenth-century France, matrimonial property law remained essentially unchanged throughout the nineteenth century. The law prescribed that, unless otherwise stipulated, spouses would share a community of goods during their marriage. The only property not shared in this way was that received through inheritance.[38] As in the English tradition, masculine supremacy and feminine incapacity distinguished the legal rights of each gender, but special defences partly offset women's legal disabilities. A husband could unilaterally dispose of the spouses' common property as long as this was for the good of the matrimonial community. He also could enjoy the fruits of his wife's inherited property (though he could not dispose of it without her consent) on condition that he support the family expenses. At the death of one spouse the survivor had a right to the *préciput* (personal property or money of a value stipulated in their marriage contract), after which the matrimonial community usually was divided in half between the survivor and the other heirs of the deceased.[39] A widow, however, had further options. She might renounce her share in the community (if, for example, it were encumbered with debt). She could also remove, in whole or in part, her initial contribution to the community if this were to her advantage. Widows also had a right to the *douaire*, a life pension whose value was fixed either in the marriage contract or by custom. During the life of a marriage a husband had no power to dispose of any property assigned to the *douaire*.[40] Although it reformed other aspects of the law, the civil code adopted in 1866 made few significant changes in domestic law. In this respect, as in many others, Quebec women remained legally disadvantaged until well into the twentieth century, if somewhat better off than most other women in nineteenth-century British America.[41]

Thus marriage involved the pooling of wealth, however great or modest the amounts, and it looked forward to future acquisitions. It also anticipated the redistribution of property when death dissolved the union. For these reasons domestic law had important implications for courting couples long before they took their marriage vows. Marriage settlements usually provide us with the best means of exploring the relationship between property and marriage in the past. In early modern Europe these were common legal devices drawn up in anticipation of marriage. They normally determined how a husband and wife were to enjoy their property during their lifetimes and how it would be divided among their children after their deaths.[42] In nineteenth-century England the landed elite used marriage settlements extensively, but even small property-holders often made settlements before marriage. Unfortunately, outside Quebec, very few marriage contracts from the nineteenth century can now be found in Canada. In addition, despite the great importance of property matters to marriage and family life, the family letters and diaries of nineteenth-century English-Canadians tell us surprisingly little about the role of material assets in matrimonial affairs. Thus we confront another question. Why are English Canadian marriage settlements so scarce? Is it because the records have not survived, or because few settlements were made in the first place?

The second answer seems more likely. If we widen our angle of vision a bit we can see that the custom of bestowing property at marriage was part of the larger process of inheritance, the passing of wealth from one generation to the next.[43] Most of the available evidence on inheritance in nineteenth-century English Canada comes from David Gagan's work on Peel County, Ontario. Gagan discovered that real property normally passed from one generation to the next upon the death of the land-owning father. The heir (normally the eldest son) then assumed responsibility for maintaining his mother and for paying each of his brothers and sisters a stipulated portion of the inheritance. In some instances this payment may have served as a dowry for those who wished to wed, but these arrangements were intended primarily to compensate each child for his or her contributions to the family economy, not to facilitate marriage.[44] In other words, though Gagan suggests otherwise, marriage did not depend on the transmission of wealth from parents to children in the way that it so often did in early modern Europe and New England.[45]

It is worth a moment's speculation to consider why this might be so. European systems of inheritance varied widely but in almost all rural communities both men and women brought property to marriage and this fact made marriage an important instrument in the transmission of wealth.[46] One reason was that resources were relatively scarce in much of pre-modern Europe. In rural communities the land supply often was fixed, so sons and daughters commonly had to be provided for out of the family holdings before they were able to wed. Nineteenth-century English Canadians faced vastly different circumstances. Land remained reasonably abundant in Canada West until at least mid-century. By the time the Canadian land supply began to dwindle even larger amounts could be had in the American mid and far west and, at the end of the century, the Canadian plains as well. Those who sought an urban destiny could also find one in the many growing cities south of the border or their scattered counterparts in the British colonies. The international border was no barrier to migration and those who chose to could move freely in search of opportunity.[47]

A fascinating letter written in 1823 from Simeon and Eunice White, an elderly farm couple in Barnston, Lower Canada, to their son in New York State illustrates these circumstances vividly. The senior Whites were growing old and they wished to retire. They wanted Simeon Jr and his wife Lydia to return and live with them in their old age:

You have wrote that you had about concluded not to come back to live [here]. If you think you cannot be contented as [in the] States after receiving one more letter from you I shall forbare writing on that subject. But Simeon I ever expected if you came back that we should give you our property ... [I]t is our wish for you to come if you and Lydia think that you can come and undertake the task to live with us. It is uncertain that perhaps we may live 5 or ten years and perhaps not one – that is unknown to us. But perhaps your prospects is to good now that you feale loth to leave it. But one thing Simeon I would just state to you – you ought to remember that when your strength is weakened by sickness then your income must stop. I think that the income of a small farm is much better than a macannick.[48]

The letter continues at length, discussing the nature of filial duty and a recent family quarrel. But this brief excerpt is enough to make the point. The senior Whites hoped that their son would return to care for them in their old age. Evidently Simeon Jr and his wife were reluctant to comply, and the only inducement his parents could offer was the promise of the family farm. The prospect must not have been very attractive, either to Simeon Jr and Lydia or to the Whites' other children who were living near their parents, for the discussion pre-dating this letter had caused ill feeling in the family. We do not know what happened to the elder Whites' appeal, but such a letter could scarcely have been written in early modern rural Europe, where a queue of heirs formed beside the dying land-holder's bed. Admittedly a single letter does not make a case (though in this instance the point is reinforced by the high rates of transiency in nineteenth-century North America, as families and family fragments drifted across the continental landscape).[49] Economic opportunity in Canada varied widely from time to time and place to place. But here is a straw in the wind, a sign that what our Victorian ancestors politely called "expectations" bound adult children to their parents much less tightly in English Canada than they did across the Atlantic. The young need not wait for the old folks' money to marry. They could do so whenever they could support themselves. In these circumstances, what use would most men and women make of marriage contracts?

Still, a small handful of British-Canadian marriage settlements are scattered in the nineteenth-century court records and family papers from Ontario, and a somewhat larger number can be culled from the notarial archives of Quebec. These contracts are like fragments of a long-lost jigsaw puzzle retrieved from a summer cottage cupboard on a rainy August afternoon. Some pieces are torn, others are missing, but parts of the puzzle can be assembled with a bit of care. An interesting case in point is a sample of seventy-six nineteenth-century Anglo-Canadian marriage contracts from the Archives nationales du Québec in Montreal.[50]

The most striking feature of these contracts is their number. If the index to Montreal marriage contracts used to create this sample is a reliable guide, very few English Canadians in Quebec drew up marriage contracts before they wed. French-Canadian marriage contracts commonly accepted the civil code's provisions regarding community of matrimonial goods, one of their primary functions being to specify the amount of the *préciput* and the *douaire*. The British-Canadian marriage contracts differed strikingly from this pattern, for the primary clause in all but seven of those sampled here established that there would be no community of goods between spouses. In addition most (four out of five) prospective brides agreed to relinquish their customary dower right in return for some other provision for themselves in the event of their husband's death.

One characteristic of these agreements is the unusual advantage they conferred on many of the women who signed them. As we have seen, with very few exceptions married women in Canada West and the Maritime colonies had no control over their own property until the 1850s at the earliest, and their counterparts in Canada East were in the same situation. But long before it was common, half of the women who agreed to separate matrimonial property also obtained the right to administer any property they brought to their marriage or acquired later in life.[51] The motives behind this departure from Canadian practice are not clear from the contracts themselves. But the documents leave some room for speculation. It is not hard to imagine, for example, that well-to-do parents might wish their wealth to pass to their daughters and not their sons-in-law. The records offer some encouragement for this supposition because, while the occupations of only twenty-two of the brides' fathers are noted, sixteen of them were merchants, professionals, and gentlemen – in other words, men likely of sufficient standing to take some pains about how they passed their wealth on to the next generation. Not surprisingly, seven of the thirteen widows whose contracts appear in the sample also kept control of their property.

If some women had a clear advantage in contracting out of the matrimonial community of goods, what of their prospective husbands? Why would they agree to separate property in marriage when they normally could expect the profit from their wives' assets? Here, too, the occupational profile of the men who signed these contracts provides a clue. Over a third of those for whom occupations are known (twenty-six out of seventy) were merchants, and another quarter (nineteen) were military officers, professionals, and gentlemen. A further eighteen were skilled tradesmen. In other words, most of them probably had business interests or significant economic assets of one kind or another. For men of business, marriage contracts offered a way to limit liability in case of bankruptcy. Without a marriage contract, a businessman's domestic property might be attached to pay his debts. According to one mid-nineteenth-century legal authority, unless a contract of marriage were properly registered it was void in respect of a bankrupt's creditors. A businessman could not be discharged from bankruptcy unless he could prove to the court that his marriage contract assigned or assured his property to his wife or children.[52]

A Montreal lawyer underscored the significance of marriage contracts in 1887 when he advised my great-grandfather, Alfred Ward, about the legal implications of entering a business partnership.[53] As a partner, Alfred was told, he would be responsible for the debts of the firm if its property could not cover them. His wife's real property could not be attached. But because the Wards had no marriage contract, her movable property was at risk because it formed part of their community of goods and thus was liable for his business debts. (Alfred soon moved his family to Hamilton where Ontario law greatly reduced the downside risk.) Thus a marriage contract which placed domestic property in a wife's hands was a type of insurance for men of affairs. It could guarantee that family assets, at least, would survive a business failure. This seems the most likely explanation why the young men who agreed to these contracts so willingly relinquished all claims to their future wife's property. It also suggests a reason for the limited use British Canadians in Lower Canada and Quebec seem to have made of marriage contracts. While beneficial to men of affairs who wished to shelter their personal assets, these agreements did not confer the same advantages on most prospective grooms. For them the community of matrimonial goods, which placed family property securely under male control, offered by far the greater advantage.

Marriage settlements from Upper Canada and Ontario are few and far between. Doubtless more of them survive than the fourteen which I have unearthed, but there seems little profit in searching so many haystacks for so few needles. Four of these contracts come from the records of elite families in the province. In one, John S. Cartwright settled a yearly income after his death on his future wife, Sarah Hayter Macaulay, "in lieu and stead of her estate of dower."[54] Another between the Irish-born doctor William Charles Gwynne and Anne Murray Powell (granddaughter of the early colonial jurist William Dummer Powell) established a trust to hold Anne's investments apart from her husband and gave her a yearly income from him free of his control.[55] A third settlement between yet another member of the Jarvis, tribe, William Dummer Powell Jarvis and Diana Irving set up a trust under her sole direction to administer real estate and investments for them during their marriage.[56] In 1870 Remigius Elmsley, of a prominent Roman Catholic family in Toronto, gave his future bride, Nina Bradshaw, a life income of $2,430 a year.[57]

The remaining ten settlements are noted in the records of cases heard before the Ontario Court of Chancery between 1869 and 1875. In this instance the marriage contracts themselves have not survived but their contents have been described sufficiently to reveal their basic provisions. Most of them seem to have been drawn up between prosperous rather than wealthy individuals, both rural and urban. In one of the ten a widow preserved control of a mortgage which she owned by placing it in a trust when she married again.[58] Another anticipated that all money, property, and personal goods acquired by a woman in marriage would be held for her exclusive use in trust.[59] Three settlements transferred land or money from parents to children to aid in establishing a new family unit.[60] In the largest number, six (including one of those just noted) grooms gave their brides property or sums of money in trust to provide them with a separate matrimonial income.[61]

Considering the fourteen Ontario marriage settlements as a group, all but three of them established a trust to provide a separate income for a wife, and in eight instances some or all of the property placed in trust was a gift from the groom to his bride. But it is difficult to read the broader meaning of these documents. No doubt the practice of drawing up marriage contracts was exceptional in Ontario. Thus, while they tell us something about marriage among the well-to-do, they shed no light whatsoever on that among the plain folk of the province.

To this point we have treated the law as a powerful force in the private lives of nineteenth-century English Canadians. But there are limits to the reach of the law, even in those matters which are normally within its grasp. A celebrated murder in Port Hope on 23 September 1856 graphically illustrates this point. George Brogdin, a Port Hope barrister, shot Thomas Henderson in the back while Henderson stood at the bar on board the steamer *Arabian,* which had just arrived at the town dock. Six weeks earlier Henderson, also a lawyer, had run off with Brogdin's wife and subsequently had further insulted Brogdin. The murder occurred in view of some three hundred people gathered on the wharf to watch the steamer tie up. Brogdin had evidently come down to the dock armed with a revolver and the knowledge that Henderson would be on board.[62] The murder convulsed Port Hope, where sympathy for Brogdin ran high. Within a day of the tragedy, a coroner's jury of eighteen returned the verdict that Henderson had died at the hands of Brogdin, "who fired under great and justifiable provocation," and they expressed "the strongest reprobation of that course of licentiousness on the part of the deceased which proceeded [*sic*] such a fearful retaliation."[63] When Brogdin came to trial in early November public opinion inclined in his favour. But when instructing the jury, Sir John Beverley Robinson, the leading Upper Canadian jurist of his day, declared it impossible in his view that there could be a plainer case of murder. The jury disagreed. After a half-hour's deliberation they declared Brogdin not guilty.

This episode reveals the presence of a competing, popular sense about right and wrong in matrimonial offences. The two juries obviously thought that the injury done to Brogdin's marital happiness (and perhaps his patriarchal authority) justified the murder of his antagonist. In the jurors' eyes, whatever Brogdin's guilt, he was more sinned against than sinning and therefore popular justice should prevail over that of the law. By itself this incident is just an illustration; it touches on only one of society's many regulations about male-female relations. But it points to a more general characteristic about the rule of law. As the anthropologist Sally Falk Moore has observed, "ordinary experience indicates that law and legal institutions can only effect a degree of intentional control of society, greater at some times and less at others, or more with regard to some matters than others."[64] In other words, many areas of human conduct lie beyond the reach of law. Some laws, in fact, oppose or are inconsistent with the rules of social life. Brogdin's case was not a simple matter of law and deviance but one of two conflicting sets of rules, one formal and institutional, one informal and popular. Thus while colonial law established a framework within which courtship and marriage unfolded, a separate body of social rules performed some of the same functions and with far more pervasive influence. These rules centred upon popular notions of fairness and honour in the relations between men and women. They did not always conflict with the law as dramatically as in Brogdin's case, but they derived from the authority of public opinion and they had a vigorous life of their own.

Finally, we should note the obvious point that the legal arrangements examined here all expressed a deeply patriarchal sense of family relations. They speak of a world of masculine authority and feminine deference, of parents' rights and childrens' duties. Their origins lay in the colonies' legal inheritance from eighteenth-century England where, as in all of pre-modern Europe, the family was the basic unit of economic enterprise. The early modern family revolved about the father who, because of his central position in its productive life, held authority over every member of his household. As the Austrian historians Michael Mitterauer and Reinhard Sieder have noted, "from the time he took over the farm until his death or retirement, the farmer was both household head and business manager, and he wielded unrestricted power, as did his wife in the narrower sphere of work allotted to her."[65] What Mitterauer and Sieder observed of farmers' families was equally true of artisans' and merchants' – indeed almost all – families.

This patriarchal spirit suffused the first laws of English Canada which touched on courtship and marriage and, given the conservative outlook of most jurists and legislators, it persisted during the nineteenth century. Throughout most of these years the assumptions and values embedded in these laws reflected the dominant beliefs and practices of a society whose economy rested on small-scale family enterprise. Toward the end of the century, the rise of the city and the factory began to loosen the economic bonds of family life and to challenge a husband and father's authority, just as it had done in other lands.[66] As is often the case, the law lagged behind these changes, although we have seen that, where married women's property was concerned, legislation gradually became aligned with these new circumstances. But by the early twentieth century, the laws which touched on marriage and gender relations still bore clear marks of their patriarchal ancestry, though time had eroded some of their most highly visible features.

On the surface, the patriarchalism embedded in these legal arrangements seems to express the domination of women by men which, we often assume, pervaded social arrangements in the past. The law, so it appears, reflected and reinforced the unequal status of the sexes, augmenting the power of men at the expense of women. This certainly was one of the most visible characteristics of the laws governing courtship and marriage in colonial society. Yet it would be a mistake to conclude that this was their only, or even their primary, purpose. The patriarchal family was not just a group of biologically related individuals each of whom possessed different rights and obligations. It was a small corporation, a social unit in itself, which owned common property, pursued common ends, and enjoyed a common standing in community life. The corporation's legal business was conducted in the name of the patriarch, normally the father, in whom formal authority resided. In law the other family members were subordinate to him. But – and this is a bigger but than we sometimes realize – the patriarch was not inevitably male. A wife succeeded to that office when her husband died, often obtaining control of family assets which had previously been vested in him, normally regaining possession of her own property (which he had held in trust during his lifetime). In fact, widows enjoyed a broad measure of control over family property. They also could exercise patriarchal rights where their children were concerned. To choose an example already discussed, the right of action for seduction belonged to a young woman's mother when her father was dead.

Thus there was much more to patriarchal laws than men's supremacy over women. Patriarchalism embodied a set of relationships among parents and children as well as husbands and wives. It preferred the interests of the family group to those of individual family members, even those of fathers who in theory were to subordinate their personal interests to the good of the entire family. And it is here that we find a clue to the deeper meaning of these laws. By placing the interests of the family group before those of each family member, the law defended the family as a social institution. It reinforced the subordination of wives and children to a male patriarch or, in his absence, of children to a female patriarch. It buttressed the familial basis of the family's economic enterprise. It strengthened the family as the primary unit in community life. The law gave no consideration to equality within the family. Instead it lent its support to the solidarity of family life.

CHAPTER THREE

Marriage Age and the Marriage Market

George Jones's romantic troubles stemmed from his age. At nineteen he was too young to marry. If he had had enough income to support a wife and family perhaps Honorine's father would not have objected to him. But in order to marry in early Victorian Canada, a man required the financial competence which only years might bring, and this is precisely what George so obviously lacked. Honorine, on the other hand, was of an age to marry. At twenty, both she and her parents thought it was time that she should.

George and Honorine's dilemma raises three important questions. How old were nineteenth-century Canadians when they wed? How did their marriage opportunities vary with their age and sex? What proportion of men and women never married at all? These are fundamental issues in the history of society, tied to the cultural, ideological, economic, and social structural characteristics of the community. Through their influence on fertility they are also closely linked to the size of individual families and, more broadly, to a society's basic demographic patterns. Here our interest is centred upon the process of marriage. By itself age is an important factor in matrimony. It also illuminates some dimly lit corners in the history of love, corners we could explore in no other way. In particular it offers us insights into the roles of gender, ethnicity, religion, and social status in mate selection.

Marriage age data were not published in Canada until 1921. As a result they can only be recovered from manuscript sources, the most usually reliable being marriage registers kept by clergymen. In Ontario, bridal age was regularly recorded from 1858 onward, though almost never before that date. Even when not recorded, marriage age can sometimes be recovered from parish records through family reconstitution techniques by matching marriage and birth or baptismal registers. These methods have been fruitfully employed for some western

European communities as far back as the sixteenth century. But prospects are dim for comparable success in nineteenth-century English Canada, especially for the earlier decades. For Upper Canada particularly, the available parish records are too few, too fragmentary, and too imperfect to support sustained analysis of this sort. One alternative source of age data is the decennial census, conducted in Canada since 1851. While marriage age has never been noted, averages can be estimated from census statistics on age and marital status, but these lack the greater precision offered by parish register data.

Nevertheless, several attempts have been made to establish marriage age means from 1840 onward, either for Canada as a whole or for specific communities within it.[1] The community studies have exploited parish registers, the national surveys aggregate census data. Together these inquiries have yielded three facts. First, in the 1850s Canadian men married in their mid-twenties on average, women two or three years earlier. Secondly, over the next half century the marriage age for both sexes gradually rose, somewhat more for brides than for grooms. And thirdly, the proportion of women married – the nuptiality ratio – declined from the mid-nineteenth century onward, in 1891 reaching the lowest point in the known population history of English Canada. These facts reveal that English Canada conformed to the western European marriage pattern: comparatively late marriage, small age differences between spouses, and significant numbers of unmarried.[2] They also leave the unmistakable impression that it became progressively more difficult to marry from the 1850s onward. Unfortunately, however, they tell us little else about the marriage market in nineteenth-century Canada.

Before proceeding further we must take a short detour around celibacy. Marriage was by far the most common experience for nineteenth-century English Canadians. At most only about 10 per cent of adult women never wed.[3] No comparable statistics for men are available but they could not have differed much from those concerning women. Still, the rate of spinsterhood rose during the second half of the century and the cause of this change is unclear. Because we know very little about the historic experience of being single in Canada it is tempting to assume that rising barriers to marriage frustrated the matrimonial hopes of a growing proportion of the population. In the case of bachelors this may or may not have been true. Among women, however, the rise of spinsterhood may well have reflected the growth of other forms of feminine livelihood and a decline in the necessity of marriage. This certainly was the case in late nineteenth century England.[4] The point to keep in mind is that marriage was not the goal of all men and women. Therefore rising rates of celibacy should not be seen simply as a measure of those who failed to obtain a spouse, but also (and perhaps largely) as an index of changing life alternatives and of the willingness of men and women to pursue them.

To return to marriage itself, a closer examination of marriage registers offers us some additional insights into the nature of Canadian matrimony during these years. Twenty-three registers were chosen from scattered communities and major denominations in Upper Canada and, later, Ontario.[5] Only one which lists marriage age has been discovered for the pioneer era, that of Trinity Anglican Church in Cornwall, and it notes age for only a short span of time, from 1817 to 1829. Until more ages are unearthed or parish records suitable for family reconstitution are found, these few marriages must substitute for a larger body of data, and in these circumstances we should keep in mind that they may not be representative. The remaining registers were kept for varying lengths of time between 1858, when the colonial government first required all clergymen to submit annual returns of the marriages they performed, and the end of the century. In all, 6,436 marriages were analysed. These records reveal little enough about past marriage patterns, but whatever their deficiencies they still can tell us much more than we presently know about marriage norms in Victorian English Canada.

The registers confirm the general trend toward rising marriage age throughout the nineteenth century, though the increase for men was slight compared to that for women. The Cornwall figures for 1817 to 1829 suggest that in the pioneer era women married slightly younger than, and men as young as, at any later time in the century. It appears that marriage age rose by a year for men and by three years for women during the century. The increase in male bridal age occurred suddenly at the end of the century, while that of women occurred much more gradually.[6]

These trends differed somewhat for immigrants and the native-born.* Among English Canadians bridal age increased steadily throughout the later Victorian era, by two years for men and three for women. During the Confederation decade immigrants (at least the great majority, who had come from Britain and Ireland) married one to two years later than did Canadians. But after 1880 the marriage ages of the native-born and newcomers gradually converged. In the 1880s and early 1890s British- and Irish-born grooms married as young as or younger than at any previous time, while the mean age of brides fluctuated by a year or two. Among the three groups from the British Isles, Irish brides and

---

* For readers who are interested in further details the data on which this discussion is based are found in the Appendix on pp. 197-82.

Figure 1
Age at First Marriage
Upper Canada/Ontario, 1817–1900

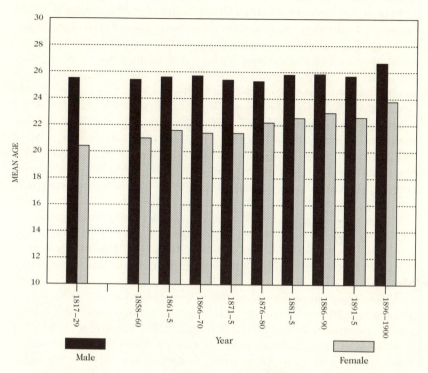

Scottish grooms were the oldest, and English brides and grooms the youngest, though in all instances the differences among them were slight. The evidence thus suggests a relationship between migration and somewhat delayed marriage, at least for men. This might be expected if the migrants were adults seeking to better their economic lot, but it would be more difficult to explain if they had arrived in the new world as children. Since nothing is known of the timing of their migration, the cause for this shifting pattern of the marriage age amongst the migrant population is far from clear. But what is much more important, the differences in marriage age amongst the various immigrant groups and native Canadians were never very great and they diminished over time. This would suggest that, as far as marriage age is concerned, ethnic factors had little to do with the Anglo-Canadian marriage market. In particular, the Irish clearly abandoned their post-famine custom of extremely late marriage when they embarked for the far Atlantic shore.

Among the four major religious denominations in Upper Canada and

Ontario, marriage ages were highest for Roman Catholics and lowest for Methodists, though the gap between the two was but a year for grooms and only slightly more for brides. Denominational variations were most pronounced amongst the Canadian born; in contrast, those of the Irish, divided as they were by a major religious cleavage, were relatively slight. Nor were residential, and therefore economic, patterns associated with significant disparities in marriage age. On average men and women in rural Ontario married at the same point in their lives as did their town and city cousins.[7] Differences were also small amongst the various urban areas examined. Brides and grooms married at about the same age in industrializing Toronto and Brantford as in stagnating Kingston, agricultural Chatham and Perth, and frontier Barrie, despite striking differences in the social and economic structures of these communities. All sub-groups in these parishes shared the trend toward rising marriage age, and disparities among them were relatively slight.

The reasons for the rising trend in the marriage age remain obscure. The demographer Ellen Gee has argued that the prolonged depression of the later nineteenth century encouraged marriage postponement.[8] But she admitted that this could only have aggravated the trend toward higher bridal age already established. Nor does this explanation jibe with the fact that the depression was basically agricultural. In Ontario and Quebec rapid industrialization stimulated economic growth after 1870 and generated sustained increases in real incomes for at least some economic groups.[9] Gee also stated that the trend toward higher female marriage ages derived from sex ratios which were increasingly adverse to women's marriage chances. The disproportionate outmigration of adult males during the last third of the century shrank the pool of eligible mates, thus increasing the mean age of brides.[10] But this suggestion does nothing to explain the rising age of grooms. If demographic factors alone were at work, these sex ratios should have increasingly favoured earlier marriage for men, and this did not occur.

While exploring land availability and inheritance strategies in mid-nineteenth century Peel County, David Gagan also discovered a trend toward higher marriage age.[11] He considered it one of the many adjustments made by a rural community during its transition from a frontier wheat economy to a diversified pattern of commercial agriculture. Declining land availability and growing population pressures combined with pioneer attitudes toward land use and inheritance to prolong youthful dependence and raise the age of marriage in the community. Gagan viewed the rising marriage age as a local response to changing local circumstances. Simultaneously, he suggests, similar changes were occurring throughout much of rural Ontario, as they had in times past and would in the future on other North American agricultural frontiers, presumably with similar implications for marriage age. On the surface this argument seems persuasive. But confined as it is to one rural community at one phase of its development, it does not help much to explain a nation-wide tendency occurring in such a broad range of locations. And when the extent of the trend and the diversity of social and economic environments are recognized, one might quite reasonably wonder whether bridal age in Peel County rose exclusively, or even primarily, as the result of local factors. In fact, age at marriage can be quite insensitive to immediate population and economic trends.[12]

Furthermore, Canadian circumstances were far from unique. The marriage age also seems to have been rising in those countries most closely tied to Canada by migration, in particular England, Scotland, and Ireland.[13] Irish marriage age means rose sharply immediately after the famine, a trend that continued until, by the 1920s, Ireland had among the highest marriage ages and celibacy rates in western population history.[14] The American evidence is poor and somewhat contradictory. But whether it reveals a rising, falling, or more or less constant trend in marriage age, the degree of probable fluctuation was relatively slight.[15]

Thus the causes of the nineteenth-century rise in the marriage age in Canada are something of an enigma. The case for its relationship with social and economic change in rural communities seems tenuous at best, and the argument that depression caused the increase is a good deal less than convincing. Industrialization, sometimes cited as a factor in declining marriage age,[16] seems not to have affected the overall Canadian trend, though some claim to have detected the beginnings of such an influence in Hamilton during the 1850s and 1860s.[17] Nor did the productivity gains of the later nineteenth-century Canadian economy lower marital age as might have been expected. Some students of marriage age in the United States have concluded that "massive immigration, westward population movement, and both urban and industrial growth left surprisingly little trace on the age at marriage of both males and females during this period."[18] The comment could well be applied to Victorian Canada. If marriage age trends had connections with those in countries closely tied to Canada by migration, the links remain obscure. At this point the nineteenth century rise in the Canadian marriage age can be observed but not adequately explained.

We should also note that, even though rising, the average age at marriage in Ontario was low when compared to the rest of the transatlantic world at this time. Among men the differences were relatively small. At most a year and a half divided the age of Ontario grooms from those in England, Scotland, and the United States. For women the gap was rather greater, as much as three years and more below means recorded elsewhere in the English-speaking world.[19] The Ontario marriage ages also were as low as or lower than those in France and lower still than the means found in other European countries, notably Belgium and Germany, where bridal age was then falling from even higher levels.[20] Whatever the origins of these differences in national marriage patterns, the relationships among economic, social, and ideological factors and nuptiality obviously were a great deal more complex than has so far been acknowledged. Still, Victorian Canada was the promised land for those who wished to wed. Chances were very high that both men and women would not only marry but marry younger – women considerably younger – than if they lived almost anywhere else in western Europe or North America.

The opportunity to find a spouse is determined first of all by the availability of potential mates. Thus the ratio of single men to single women in a community is the primary structural feature of its marriage market. In mid and late Victorian Ontario about 90 per cent of women wed for the first time between the ages of eighteen and twenty-eight, 90 per cent of men between twenty-one and thirty-two.[21] The aggregate census only provides marital status information in broader age categories, so sex ratios can only be calculated for single men and women between fifteen and forty. Because the range of normal marriage age for women was three to four years lower than that for men, the number of marriageable women in each age cohort would exceed that of men by roughly 10 per cent if single men and women were present in more or less equal numbers. Thus a ratio of 110 single men to 100 single women at any age in the prime marrying years would give both sexes more or less equal marriage opportunities. Lower ratios would favour the marriage chances of men, higher those of women.

The sex ratios of the unmarried in the communities sampled here fell into three distinct categories. Lowest by far were those in Toronto and Kingston. There single women of marriageable age outnumbered single men in the same age group by 10 to 15 per cent throughout the second half of the century, the female surplus tending to grow over time. This was a common feature of large nineteenth-century urban places throughout the western world, Canadian cities included. Theoretically, at least, these circumstances placed women at a considerable disadvantage in the marriage market. Next were a group of well-established towns such as Chatham and mature agricultural communities such as Scarborough, Markham, and Pickering townships, which provided roughly equal marriage opportunities over time. In Huron and Simcoe counties, outlying districts of more recent settlement where single men outnumbered single women by 40 per cent and more during the 1860s, the disproportionately large presence of young, single males would seem to have offered women a substantial advantage in getting a mate.

By themselves, however, sex ratios seem not to have had much impact on marriage age. Other things being equal, communities where the balance favoured bachelors should have had relatively low nuptial ages for grooms and relatively high ones for brides. In opposite circumstances the contrary should have held. But other things seem not to have been equal. Kingston, where single women most consistently outnumbered single men, had among the highest marriage ages for both sexes. In Colgan, Simcoe County, where very high male to female ratios prevailed during the 1860s and 1870s, bridal age was just as high for both. Caledonia, Markham, Bobcaygeon, and Dunbarton, other rural communities where sex ratios favoured women's marriage chances, recorded among the lowest marriage age means in the sample. Seemingly the availability of mates affected the opportunity for marriage, not the age at which it occurred.

Another point to consider is the age gap between spouses. According to Peter Laslett, "in the West the number of years separating husband and wife has always been relatively few, with a relatively high proportion of wives older than their husbands, and marriage tending toward the companionate." These, he declares, have been among the most important features of the family in western history. In particular the marriage of older women to younger men, which Laslett claims constituted between one-fourth and one-fifth of all unions, was "the most consistent indicator of 'Westernness' in familial matters."[22] Remarriage most likely accounted for a large proportion of brides-older unions because the late age of the western marriage and the relatively small age difference between spouses tended toward fairly high mean ages at widowhood. This, in turn, gave widows considerable opportunity to marry men younger than themselves. No doubt the proportion of first marriages with elder brides was considerably lower than Laslett's figure. In nineteenth-century Ontario the proportion of older brides at first marriage was well below his estimate. In pioneer Cornwall only 6 per cent of brides took younger grooms when they first wed, while in the province more generally the average was 12 per cent during the second half of the century, with an upward trend over time. Four of five marriages during the 1850s and 1860s were between older men and younger women, a proportion which declined to two in three by the end of the century. During the same period, unions between those of like age almost doubled, from 7 to 12 per cent.

The average age discrepancy between husbands and wives was far

greater when the husband was the more mature spouse. In early Cornwall, grooms were nearly six years older than their brides, and in
Ontario during the second half of the century the difference ranged
between four and five and a half years, though the gap narrowed a little
with passing time. On the other hand, when brides wed younger men
they took spouses closer to them in age. On average the difference was
slightly less than three years. Nor was there significant deviation from
these general patterns on ethnic, religious, or other social grounds.
Immigrant and native-born, Protestant and Catholic, urban and rural,
the age differentials in grooms-older and brides-older marriages both
fell within these general ranges.[23]

The size of the age gap between spouses, however, was a function of
the age at which people married. Brides in their teens almost invariably
married men considerably older than themselves, on average six years
their senior in the parishes sampled here. But by their later twenties
women were more likely to marry someone their own age or younger
than someone older, and the older they became the more likely they
were to marry youth. Moreover, the age difference between women and
their more mature husbands diminished as the age scale was ascended
while that between women and their younger mates grew proportion-
ately. The oldest quarter of brides with older husbands were three and
a half years younger than their spouses; the oldest quarter of brides
with younger mates were almost five years their senior.

The converse was largely true for grooms. The older men grew, the
more likely they were to take a younger wife, and the greater the spread
in their ages. One-quarter of grooms in their late teens and early
twenties married an older woman, their brides on average three years
older than they. Grooms of the same age who took younger brides were
on average just as much older. On the other hand, men in their late
twenties and early thirties wed younger women nine times out of ten,
and the average age gap between them was eight years. In general, age
spreads were lowest when brides and grooms were in their mid-twenties.
Those who married when either younger or older normally took a spouse
further removed from them in age.

Both Peter Laslett and Edward Shorter have argued that great age
disparities were the hallmark of pragmatic marriage while small ones
signified marriage for love.[24] Shorter has also claimed that the shrinking
age gap between spouses during the last two centuries signified the
rise of the romantic marriage. But what are we to make of the great
variation in age differentials of spouses in nineteenth-century Ontario?
Three marriages in ten during the last four decades of the century
linked partners more than five years apart in age. Were these unions
founded any less firmly on affection than those of spouses closer in

years? Were marriages less companionable when a nineteen-year-old bride took a husband six years her senior than when her twenty-four-year-old sister wed a man who was twenty-six, or when her thirty-year-old brother took a wife of twenty-two? For want of evidence we cannot find an answer, though it seems improbable that it could be yes. In truth, statistics have little to tell us about the world of the emotions. Any age is the age for love, and companionship exists where one can find it. As we shall see, love was the usual basis for marriage in nineteenth-century English Canada, companionship one of its primary goals. For us the importance of marriage age lies elsewhere: in the demographic structure of the marriage market itself.

The fact of the matter is that by investigating patterns of age difference at marriage we can learn a great deal about how the marriage market functioned. In Victorian English Canada, most women took husbands somewhat older than themselves and most men wed somewhat younger brides. The leading consequence of this was that the marriage market for women was the mirror image of that for men. Because most women married up the age scale, the pool of available mates was largest when they were youngest. As they aged it continually shrank, for each marriage reduced the stock of potential husbands by one. Immigration might replenish the bachelor supply somewhat, but death and emigration would also deplete it in greater or lesser measure. Thus the older a spinster grew, the more her chances of marrying someone still older diminished. To offset this disadvantage and broaden the range of selection, with every passing year more women adopted the dominant male marriage strategy and took younger mates. At thirty, more than twice as many women chose a younger spouse as one older, despite the fact that, at that age, the pool of available bachelors was still five times the size of that of the remaining spinsters.[25] If by that time they still cherished matrimonial hopes, this offered the best chance to stem the ebb tide of choice.

For men, the market in brides worked in converse fashion. The conventional male preference for a younger spouse and the financial prerequisites for matrimony, borne largely by men, postponed marriage somewhat longer for grooms than for brides. In addition, the range of possible spouses accessible to a man in his early marriageable years was relatively limited, confined as it was to women near his own age. These were also the years of most frequent female marriage, and therefore competition for brides was especially intense. But with advancing age the scope of a man's choice of mates continually expanded, at least until his mid or late thirties, when most bachelors stopped actively searching for a mate. While marriage, migration, and mortality depleted the pool of single women, larger numbers of entrants to the market

Table 1
Sex Ratios of the Single at Marriageable Age, Canada West/Ontario, 1851–1891

Year	Ages	Males/100 Females
1851	15–39	145.0
1861	15–39	130.4
1871	16–40	123.3
1881	16–40	114.8
1891	15–44	113.7

Source: Canada, Census, 1851–1891.

continually restocked it. Thus, by marrying down in age, men gained access to an ever-growing supply of possible mates. The older men were within the normal range of marriage ages, the broader the selection from which they could choose. As they matured, prospective grooms had to seek brides further from them in age. Because the proportion of women married at any age was always higher than that of men, the supply of unmarried women of near age was increasingly depleted as men grew older. But continued access to young women newly arrived on the marriage market more than offset this disadvantage and gave men greater choice of marriage partners with every passing year.

The marriage market thus had a crystalline inner structure. But unlike most crystals, it was not especially rigid. The dominant patterns of preferred bridal age were flexible enough to absorb significant changes in supply and demand without frustrating the goal of marriage. Unless especially sudden, these changes could be accommodated by adjustments to the age gap between the spouses and to the prevailing pattern of grooms-older and brides-older marriages. The higher the ratio of women to men, the more the age spread would narrow, and the higher would be the proportion of older brides. The converse would hold as the ratio declined. In other words, when sex ratios created an advantageous marriage market for one sex at the expense of the other, the latter could adjust its behaviour to counter its disadvantage and broaden the range of possible mates.

This is probably why the marriage age of Ontario women rose more rapidly than that of men during the later nineteenth century. Single men of marriageable age always outnumbered single women in the province at this time. The sex ratio varied considerably from one locale to the next, and urban centres typically had a surplus of spinsters. In general, circumstances favoured women's marriage chances; even in the cities, where they did not, internal migration seems to have overcome their disadvantage. But provincial sex ratios favoured women much more at mid-century than at its end.

As this table indicates, in 1851 there were three marriageable bachelors for every two eligible single women in Canada West; by 1891 there were only eleven for ten. Where once women had held a clear advantage, now their chances of finding spouses were little better than those of men. The emerging equilibrium of supply and demand gradually eroded women's demographic advantages in the marketplace for mates and prolonged their wait before marriage.

Age apart, what influence had other factors – geography, religion, and ethnicity in particular – on marriage patterns in the past? Here, too, parish registers offer some useful insights. They reveal that, for anyone seeking a spouse in nineteenth-century Ontario, the marriage market had clear geographic limits. Two out of three men and women married someone from their own community.[26] Country girls usually wed boys from the next concession, while their city cousins normally found husbands in their home town. Even today most North Americans tend to marry someone who lives nearby, and it should scarcely be surprising that they did so in former times, when mobility was much more limited. Since the emotional intimacy leading to marriage usually develops over repeated encounters, distance itself was a major factor in nineteenth-century courtship. Residential patterns involve more than travel time, however. People who live near one another usually share important social and economic characteristics, both in rural and urban areas. Those who courted their neighbours likely did so for more complex reasons than simple propinquity. We might reasonably suppose that farmers' sons wedded farmers' daughters, and that urban working men took wives from their own social ranks, but the only hint we have on this point comes from a small sample of marriages in Hamilton during the early 1860s, which found almost no marriage outside class boundaries.[27]

Religion and ethnicity also had some bearing on the choice of a spouse, though perhaps not as much as might be suspected. While in this case the evidence is slender, it suggests that two out of three brides and grooms married someone of their own faith.[28] Intermarriage between Protestants from different denominations accounted for a further quarter and more of all unions, and Protestant-Catholic marriages the remaining 5 per cent. Religious endogamy was relatively high, though it declined somewhat with passing time.

Seen from the perspective of national origins, Ontario marriage patterns were rather more diverse. In the late 1850s and early 1860s, the close of the first great period of British migration to North America, the English-, Irish-, and Scottish-born wed their own countrymen almost as often as not. But by the 1890s ethnic preference had dwindled to one marriage in four or five. Unlike the British immigrant groups, the American-born (who, like Canadians, shared no common cultural inheritance) married one another much less often. The contrast between their patterns of mate choice and those of newcomers from the British Isles reveals that common ethnic origin remained significant when selecting a spouse, particularly amongst the Irish. It was not an especially powerful factor, however, and its importance diminished as the century progressed. Most likely this occurred because ethnic cultural differences gradually declined as an Anglo-Canadian nationality took form toward the close of the century.

The Canadian-born, in no sense an ethnic group, had much higher rates of intramarriage, and these increased with passing time. In the decade before Confederation half to three quarters of Canadians married their own countrymen, but from the mid-1870s onward nine in ten did so. No obvious cultural ties were at work in making these matches, although a second-generation ethnic preference may well be hidden in the data. But the relative weakness of ethnicity in these Ontario marriage patterns is easily explained. First, cultural differences amongst British immigrants and their Canadian descendants were comparatively slight and therefore presented no great impediment to overcome. Secondly, and more important, the foreign-born constituted a small and declining proportion of the population during the later nineteenth century. Thus the pool of single men and women was increasingly heavily peopled by the Canadian-born. In the normal course of events, anyone seeking a spouse would encounter far more unmarried Canadians than immigrants. Not surprisingly, the native-born shopped for partners where the selection was greatest. Meanwhile, faced with a limited and diminishing supply of mates with origins like their own, the English, Irish, and Scots enlarged their marital options by taking more and more spouses from outside the bounds of their own national groups.

The opportunity to marry was always high in nineteenth-century English Canada. If at least nine out of ten men and women married at some point in their lives, few who earnestly sought a spouse could have failed to find one in the end. But the search for a mate was not always easy. The rising bridal age and the falling female nuptiality ratio indicate that the goal of marriage receded as the century progressed, rather further for women than for men. Why this occurred is not entirely clear, though some of the answer lies in the declining demographic advantage which women had in the marriage market. Yet the picture was far from bleak for, even at its nineteenth-century peak, the English-Canadian marriage age was low when compared with that in other western societies, then as in the more remote past. In addition, the parish registers seem to suggest that marriage was more or less equally accessible to all social groups. Ethnicity, religion, place of residence, and migration status had little influence on the age at which people wed, and the slight differences which existed at mid-century diminished over time.

The marriage market also had characteristics which imposed limits on marriage opportunities. The contrary functioning of the markets for brides and for grooms was the most basic of these features. Women married in a contracting market, men in an expanding one. This meant that marriage chances varied obversely for the two sexes at any age. Geography, too, imposed limits on the range of marriage opportunities. At all times and in all places chances were high that people would marry within their own community. Social rank presumably limited the range of mate choice as well, but deficiencies in the evidence provided by parish registers obscure this fact from view. Finally, while religion and ethnicity had little effect on marriage timing, they had greater influence over the choice of a spouse. Brides and grooms showed a strong preference for marriage partners of like religion and, among British immigrants at least, perhaps a slight one for someone of the same ethnic background. As the century drew to a close, however, these predilections began to diminish. The range of potential mates, if not the chance to wed, broadened accordingly.

CHAPTER FOUR

The Territories of Courtship

Nineteenth-century English Canada gave each sex separate territory. Men moved in one world of work, power, and associations, women moved in another. The economic, familial, and civic roles of the sexes were bound up with these social territories. Man's domain encompassed the field, the workshop, the tavern, and civic affairs; woman's included the house, the garden, the family, and the church. For the most part mutually exclusive, sometimes these spaces overlapped. The home was shared space even though women presided. In the urban workplace each sex had its own special terrain. Men and women also possessed the church jointly, though they had distinctive parts to play in its ongoing life. Despite the strength of the Victorian patriarchy, space was not always ordered hierarchically. A woman's sphere might well have been narrower than a man's, but it was not necessarily subordinate. In the world of work the family welfare relied as heavily on women's labour as on men's. The family was an economic partnership in which each adult performed separate but complementary duties. While the great instruments of political, legal, and economic authority lay almost entirely in male hands, this should not obscure the fact that women, too, had inviolable realms, spaces under their own governance largely apart from male authority.

Perhaps the most striking feature of the system was its complexity. This was far from the world of contemporary Provence, with its strict segregation of the sexes, which Lucienne Roubin has described.[1] Sharp sexual boundaries existed in some areas of Canadian society, blurred ones in others. Circumstances varied according to status, age, marital state, and place of residence. In frontier communities the pioneer economy tended to break down the walls of the separate spheres. Yet here we also see widespread variation. Those genteel British women who left us such rich memoirs of life in the backwoods clung to the traditional domestic space of their sex. But we should not conclude that theirs was the common lot of rural females. Women shared the rough work of pioneer agricultural development, as the Langtons, the Traills, the Moodies, and the O'Briens often unreflectively noted when observing the many servants who paraded through their homes. During the second half of the century, at least, the territory of the sexes varied considerably in an urban context as well. Women of some wealth and social pretension led lives more rigidly bounded by family, friends, and church than did those in the urban labour force. Even though we still know little about the circumstances of both women and men in nineteenth-century English Canadian society, the available evidence suggests a community with gender boundaries much more sharply defined than our own, yet rather less rigid than those of most contemporary western European nations.

The sociologist Erving Goffman has pointed to the fact that we commonly control the boundaries of our social worlds by admitting some individuals to our company while denying admission to others.[2] As a general rule we make ourselves open to social encounters. But not all encounters are welcome or suitable, and therefore we admit or bar others according to our beliefs about what relationships are desirable. The boundaries of social engagements are particularly important in courtship, for they determine the size and content of the pool of potential mates. From the time the young gained the initiative in making their own marriage choices, no later than the late eighteenth century in most of the English-speaking world, they courted and married within the bounds of their acquaintanceship. This circle of friendship was as much a spatial as a social reality. By examining the physical setting of courtship we can learn much about the social constraints on romantic love and the extent of feminine autonomy in the making of marriage arrangements. Both issues had great significance for men and women in the past as they took one of life's great decisions.

The principles of sexual segregation were aimed at keeping unrelated men and women apart, the young and unmarried in particular. As a result, courtship required neutral spaces where youths and young adults could pass time together, places to meet and grow acquainted, settings defined and governed by clear and well-understood rules. Nineteenth-century Anglo-Canadians found this space in various locations. The family was the pre-eminent setting for courtship, love blooming under the watchful eyes of friends and relations. Social institutions also brought youths together. Churches played a prominent role in matrimony long before the wedding day. In drawing community members together, religious observance allowed intimate social, as well as spiritual, contacts. Popular amusements and recreations – balls, house parties, skating, sleighing, picnics, concerts, plays, and summer excursions – all provided courtship opportunities as well. The range and extent of possibilities enlarged with the rise of the city and the growing diversity of urban pastimes. But whatever the context of courtship, the important thing to note is that the unmarried met in supervised settings. The forms of supervision varied from one setting to the next but, wherever it occurred, the search for a spouse inevitably fell under the discipline of the community. George Jones and Honorine Tanswell tried to shield their emotional lives from the scrutiny of outsiders, but in their case, as in most others, the community enforced customary rules which governed their intimate affairs. And like all courting couples, they yielded to social dictates about the process of taking a spouse.

The locations of courtship's prescribed spaces varied with the phase of the courting process. In the normal course of events courtship followed a predictable sequence of stages. The nature of the relations between men and women varied considerably from one stage to the next, as did the settings of their encounters and the rules of conduct appropriate to them. Before active courtship people in their late teens and early twenties normally passed some time in mixed company with no open intent to look for a mate. George was at this point in his life when he met Honorine. During the next phase, prospective brides and grooms tested the marriage market by surveying some of its candidates. Then they singled out one individual for more intense courtship and a deepening relationship. When successful this led to the following stage, betrothal, a period of private (and usually public) commitment to matrimony centred on the couple's emotional and material preparation for married life. The process culminated in the final step, marriage itself. Of course, not all courtships developed precisely in this manner. Some couples skipped entire stages. George seems to have settled on Honorine without any market research at all, though she had considered at least one other suitor. The length of each stage also varied from couple to couple. Some spent years in the earliest stages of the process while others moved with great haste. But despite the diversity of experience, the successful nineteenth-century courtship usually conformed to this pattern.

Balls and assemblies were among the most popular amusements in nineteenth-century English Canada. These events brought together men and women – young and old, married and unmarried – for evenings of music, dancing, and dining. They were some of the earliest social occasions in frontier communities. Mather Byles III, the loyalist Anglican clergyman, recorded an elegant assembly in St John in 1786.[3] In 1792 Elizabeth Simcoe, wife of the colonial governor, noted in her diary that residents in the town of Niagara planned fortnightly

subscription balls during the winter months. According to her inform-
ant, at the most recent one "there were fourteen couples, a great display
of gauze, feathers and velvet, the room lighted by wax candles, and
there was a supper as well as tea."[4] Hannah Peters Jarvis, wife of office-
holder William Jarvis, described a lively ball in Newark (Niagara-on-
the-Lake) in 1793. She opened it with a minuet but, to her dis-
pleasure, country dances took up the rest of the evening. After the
customary eleven o'clock supper "the company returned to the Ball
Room when two Dances finished the Nights entertainment with the
Sober Part of the Company – the rest stayd until Day light & wd have
stay longer if their Servants had not drank less than their Masters."[5]
Although often socially exclusive, assemblies were not the preserve of
elites. Together with some of his friends, Ely Playter, the York publican
and farmer, organized a private ball in 1802, though he abandoned
the attempt when several of the invited guests could not attend.[6]

Some pioneer communities held assemblies infrequently, but as colonial towns and cities matured, they soon became regular pastimes. The
acerbic Joseph Willcocks complained in 1801 that York offered no
public amusements but an annual subscription ball.[7] By 1815,
however, Harriette Eunice Peters, a member of the extensive Jarvis
family connection, spoke of numerous assemblies in town during the
winter.[8] In the same year fortnightly balls attracted the socially pre-
occupied young women of leading Halifax families, some of whom held
informal dances in their homes as well.[9] The many British garrisons
in colonial society, each one constituting a large pool of bachelors, took
leading roles in organizing these festivities. Montreal long offered its
Anglo-Canadian community a busy annual round of balls and assemblies, as might be expected of the largest city in the colonies.[10] But
even small towns held similar public gatherings on a regular basis.
Caroline Wallbridge, daughter of a Belleville merchant and farmer,
informed her sister in May 1838 that there had been several parties
and balls in town during the spring.[11] A quarter-century later James
Reynolds, a young Prescott lawyer, told his fiancée "there's a dancing
assembly every week in P___ now & we hope to have a dining party
& a military ball ere the winter is over."[12] During the early industrial
era the factory ball also made its appearance in some communities.[13]

Driving or sleighing clubs provided another variant of the assembly.
In January 1868 Samuel Jarvis Jr, still another member of the
Upper Canadian Jarvis clan, told his mother from Kingston that "We
have a driving club here this winter which increases the sources of
amusement for the young ladies of the place. The Club gave a dance
at a Country Tavern about 5 miles from Kingston on Friday last. There
were nearly 50 people at it. And we had the Rifle Band and their

Messmen. It was very well done and we got home about ½ past 12. We drive twice a week and there are also small carpet dances for the young people every Tuesday evening at ½ a dozen different houses each taking their turn. The lady of the house doing Chaparone for all."[14] Whatever their form, these gatherings remained common features of English-Canadian social life throughout most of the nineteenth century.

Parties like these, whether public or private, reflected the sharp social divisions in colonial society. James Robb, a young lecturer in chemistry and natural science at King's College, Fredericton, remarked on this feature of colonial life soon after arriving from Scotland. "There could be no place where sets are so decided," he told his mother in 1839. "The upper set know not the common set (storekeepers, etc.) but when on business."[15] He elaborated in a later note to his sister.

A Fredericton party would however astonish you, because official people, be their office ever so small, always make a great show. Many of them only give one party a year and that one is a good one – others give them once a fortnight and they are meagre enough. I go everywhere and anywhere when I am at leisure, or rather I go to all of the people of the set. There are two sets in Fredericton. 1st, the Government officers, Clergy and professional men – that is my set. 2d, shop and store keepers and businessmen. There I am found by exception only and on rare intervals. It is death without benefit of clergy if you are caught out of your set.[16]

Assemblies and balls were central institutions in the colonial marriage market. Few other formal occasions created neutral ground where the sexes could meet for convivial ends. In these settings the young could seek out one another for friendship and perhaps romance. To choose only one example, the youthful W.H. Merritt met his wife-to-be, Catherine Prendergast, at an assembly in St Catharines just before the War of 1812.[17] These events allowed the young to mingle beneath the gaze of responsible adults in the community. Older married men and women invariably acted as patrons and young women normally attended with an older relation. The rules of respectable social conduct required chaperons for unmarried girls and young women in particular, to vouch for their decorous and honourable behaviour.

At this point we should note an important implication of the sexual division of space. Men and women rivalled one other for control of courtship territory and, thus, influence over the marriage market. Normally the bachelors of a community organized balls. They sold subscriptions to meet the evening's expenses and issued all the invitations, to unmarried young women as well as single men and married couples.[18] These parties gave their organizers the chance to shape marriage markets to their own particular ends. Since they drew up the guest lists they could invite and exclude as they wished, and like as not they selected with their own matrimonial prospects in mind. Certainly Ely Playter did when he and his bachelor friends attempted to organize their dance. From his point of view the primary reason for the ball was the chance to be with Sophia Beman, a neighbour's daughter, whom he was then courting. Her father strongly opposed Playter, however, and refused her permission to attend.[19]

The genteel English emigrant John Langton, a lonely bachelor in the backwoods near Peterborough, relished these occasions in his prolonged quest for a wife. In 1834 he told his father, "I certainly never expected on coming to Canada that I should be one of the Bachelors who gave a ball to between 80 and 90 & meet with two of the best waltzers I ever figured with. A tremendous thunderstorm luckily coming on we kept it up with unabated vigour till daylight, as there are no covered carriages in Canada."[20] Balls gave him the opportunity to meet large numbers of young women whom he otherwise seldom encountered. A year later he reported, "Balls in Canada are no joke; when one comes forty miles to dance one does not like to make such a journey for a trifle & one takes a spell of dancing sufficient for an average winter at home. We commence at 7 or 8, and, as the roads are hardly safe for the Ladies to drive home by in the dark we contrived, on the 27th at least, to keep them employed till daylight. We had about 40 dancing ladies present & when I came to reckon up in the morning I had danced with all but 2 & with some of them two & even three times."[21]

Women controlled other social spaces and thus had their own means of shaping the marriage market. While men normally organized public assemblies, women usually sponsored private parties. Given their informal, familial nature we know rather less about such events, but the guiding role of women in domestic hospitality is clear, as is the part played by house parties in female matrimonial strategies. Private dances gave the power of invitation to women. Propriety forbade men from inviting others to social occasions in their homes unless they were widowers with young, marriageable daughters or they shared the duties of host with a mature female relative. With guest lists at their discretion, young women and their mothers could invite or exclude local bachelors at will, and thus manipulate opportunities for courtship in their own interest.

The most revealing of these events, the coming-out party, formally placed young women on the marriage market. The Canadian coming-out ritual, though but a pale colonial imitation of the royal court debut in London, served the same purpose for young colonial women as it did for society debutantes in Great Britain.[22] In nineteenth-century

English Canada, socially prominent and ambitious families often "presented" their daughters at private gatherings to which they invited friends and eligible young men from other acceptable families. In 1831 Mary O'Brien, that perceptive observer of Upper Canadian social customs, noted the arrival in York of a Miss Stewart, daughter of a prominent Peterborough area couple, who had come to town for her debut.[23] Six years later, in Belleville, a rather gossipy Lewis Wallbridge told an older sister that "Louisa Ridley and Elizabeth Brenkenridge made their debut at Mrs. Murney's lately afterwards at Mrs. Samsons again at Mrs. Dougall at the first two of which places I had the pleasure of being invited danced and waltzed with the two dear little creatures and came home."[24] Toward the end of the century the practice had changed little. In 1892 nineteen-year-old Fanny Marion Chadwick, daughter of a leading Toronto lawyer, came out at the home of a friend. The event failed to impress her. "They all say I should have said I had 'a glorious time'," she told her diary. "But I never had a glorious time at an old dance in my life & never expect to. Met nearly all new men."[25] Her diary at this time repeatedly notes the debuts of other young women friends.

As we can see, custom divided opportunities to organize marriage markets between men and women. Yet the division was far from equal, and the balance shifted over time. Until mid-century, at least, the leading role young men took in organizing public dances probably gave them more influence over social life than that exercised by women. But thereafter the bachelor's ball faded away and single men discarded their collective influence in matrimonial affairs. More generally, parties organized by plain people gradually lost their formality and their public character while those of elites grew more exclusive if not more formal; increasingly they centred on the parlour, the garrison, and government house. Meanwhile women clung tightly to their sphere of social authority and the influence which it gave them in making marriage alliances. By the end of the century they possessed far greater collective influence over marriage markets than did men.

Why this shift occurred is not entirely clear. Perhaps some part of the explanation lies in the profound structural changes taking place in Canadian society during these years, as urban influences increasingly pervaded rural English Canada during the second half of the century. It may also be that the growing rigidity of sex roles in Victorian Canada narrowed the scope of women's social activities while enlarging those of men. The evidence also suggests that, in Ontario at least, women's marriage chances may have diminished during the second half of the century. Thus, as competition for husbands grew, concerted efforts to win a spouse may well have assumed ever greater importance. Whatever the reasons, the facts themselves seem clear. By the end of the century men seeking a spouse found that free agency served their interests well, but most women still clung to their traditional means of shaping the marriage market.

Communities had many other places for courtship, spaces between male and female territory where the sexes could mingle quite freely. To choose a few obvious examples, the unmarried often gathered at camp meetings and work bees in backwoods communities, church services and social clubs in towns and cities. Here and elsewhere the paths of men and women intersected. Seen from the courtship perspective, these spaces differed from those of assemblies in one important respect: because men and women met voluntarily rather than by invitation, public gatherings could not easily be manipulated by either sex to shape marriage opportunities. Here social contacts occurred in a classical free-market setting. There were no barriers to entry; all who hoped to find a spouse could attend if they wished.

The next step in our inquiry is to examine the courting world of men and of women in turn. By doing so we can see how the courtship system worked, how men and women sought one another out in a world of separate spheres, how each used their own territory, as well as the neutral ground in between, to their own advantage. We should also be alert to the changing social context of courtship. Economic development, rapid population increase, territorial expansion, industrialization, and urban growth gradually altered the contours of English-Canadian society during the nineteenth century. In 1800 British North America was a series of small, isolated colonies with a few tiny urban centres and fairly simple economies. By 1900 it had become an incipient nation with a substantial population, a diversified agricultural and industrial economy, and a broad urban base. These developments and attendant ones in social structure had important implications for courtship and marriage. The changing character of social groups and social relationships, as well as the growing differentiation of urban and rural society, worked their transforming power on the shape of social territory. Most important of all, the line between private and public space grew more sharply etched over time and this, in turn, meant new freedoms and new restraints for all of those who courted.

The bachelor letters of James Walton Nutting offer some penetrating glimpses into the world of unmarried young men during the early nineteenth century. In later life a lawyer, editor, and leading Baptist layman, Nutting was nineteen, an Anglican and a student at King's

College in Windsor, Nova Scotia, in 1806. Over the next six years he wrote a series of chatty and sometimes ribald notes to his close friend and contemporary, Edward James Jarvis, a student at law in St John, New Brunswick. These letters reveal the great preoccupations of a relatively privileged youth on the brink of adulthood: courtship and getting established in life. His amorous adventures and those of his friend absorbed much of his attention. In August 1806 he wrote, "Fraser had engaged me to drink tea at Campbells, but we stop'd to eat cherries with Eliza & Ann and while Ben was walking with Ann in the garden I took Eliza in the chaise and drove up to the bridge. poor Fraser was quite astonish'd especially as I did not drive very fast, so he went and [illegible], for which I can assure you I was very angry at him. Damn it, Ned, its almost too much for flesh & blood to bear. But thank God I am not such an amrous [sic] Sot as you are. Armstrong is most desperately in love with Kitty, & A. Campbell both."[26]

In March of 1808 he boasted:

You dont know how I got acquainted at Thomson's. dont trouble yourself it is not the first time I was brought to an anchor under Betsy's Flanks & a devlish commodious harbour it is I assure you[.] As for the Loveliness or satyre you speak of as for the first it must require a sharper fellow at those affairs than I am to perceive it. There is oddity enough if that will answer & for the second I mean Satyr. I see nothing like it in her unless it is that she is built like one. Fraser is eternally there. As for Master Cupid I have lately kicked his A ____ & sent him packing, unless when he has made his appearance in quite a different manner from his former "Lack-a-daisical" one. The little Son of a whore shall be my [illegible], but "Devil burn me" if he shall be my master again, if I can help it ... I did not know what to make of your letter I think Mr. Lawyer about to be that your invention of the Terms Shaggor & Shaggee &c will one day raise your name to celebrity in yr Profession. But let me ask you if in your engagement with Miss Poor she Did not become Poxor (if I may put her in ye Mascul. G) and you poxee or rather pocky[,] or what made you and Clarke so great when I told him to write to you. What says he, has he got it. O, young man I am perfectly ashamed of thee. As for your commission with repect to Greasy Belly. You must certainly excuse me. Her eyes have been continual fountains of corruption since she came down.[27]

Within a year or so, however, Nutting had turned misogynist. Smarting from a disappointment in love, he told Jarvis from Halifax,

Well Ned I have been at Mrs. Thomsons when I met The ____[Ann Monk] and in spite of myself spent an evening of careless pleasure[.] God knows it was far from a happy one. I did not once speak to her. you may judge of my sensations. with A. I had a long conversation on general subjects of chat. Lady W. [Wentworth?, wife of the colonial governor] the old Whore has been the "primum mobile" much good may it do her as it shall me hereafter for Damn me if I ever get my tackling entangled again with any frigate. Oh this damned reflection if I would let it, it would kill me.[28]

What do these letters tell us about the territory of privileged young men in the colonies during the earliest stage of courtship? Most obvious is the strong hint of the predatory male. Nutting and friends were on the prowl and they ranged quite freely in pursuit of young women. It is difficult to know quite what to make of the innuendo in the letter of March 1808. Was this youthful braggadocio or was seduction really the primary object of the quest? We cannot answer the question. But two features of the courtship system seem clear from Nutting's accounts. First, from at least the beginnings of the nineteenth century young men had a great deal of autonomy when seeking out female company. They took the initiative in arranging encounters and they circulated with few restrictions on their movements. Secondly, despite the ambiguity of Nutting's lewd remarks, affection seems to have lain at the heart of the quest.

Ely Playter's diary leaves much the same impression.[29] Though far less aggressive than the youths in Nutting's circle, and not at all ribald, Playter moved through similar space in his search for a wife. He was older than Nutting, twenty-seven at the time he began to record his courting career, and perhaps this partly explains the more restrained tone of his account. But much more important than differences in tone are the similarities he describes in a male's courting territory. Playter passed time with a number of unmarried women, calling at their homes, dining with them, walking and riding in their company. He even joined a three-week pleasure boat excursion on Lake Ontario with several young friends, including some unmarried young women (among them Sophia Beman, whom he later married).

Living as they often did far from eligible young women, backwoods bachelors such as John Langton had to seize opportunities for courtship as they presented themselves. In 1835 he spent a week at the home of a friend, a Major Hamilton, whose family had taken him in. The ostensible purpose of the visit was to attend the major, who lay seriously ill and whose mill, brewery, and distillery had recently burned to the ground. But Langton also found the major's three marriageable daughters a compelling attraction. "What I did each day is hard to say," he told his father.

Immediately after breakfast I generally spent an hour by the Major's bedside, after which I as regularly found my way among the young ladies where two or three more hours used to pass away in conversation, my hands being kept employed in the ignoble occupations of unpicking, marking, darning, &c.; another visit to the Major concluded the morning. After an hour or two for dinner a chat or a walk with the ladies occupied the afternoon; the Major generally appeared at tea, & after he had retired, chat, music, &c. concluded the day. All very agreeable but exceedingly unprofitable, and you may perhaps say that the Major's daughters had as much to do with my stay as the Major himself – Maybe.[30]

When Langton left, another man replaced him at the major's side, perhaps with the same ambiguous motives in mind. In this case, so it seems, illness provided the occasion for courting.

The following year Langton described another courtship opportunity distinctive to the frontier. In September he joined a boating party of a dozen or so friends on a five-day outing in the Peterborough area. The party consisted of at least one married couple and several unmarried young men and women. In his words,

I went home at night but returned before daylight for a hunt in which I was to have the honour of taking Miss Fisher in my canoe. Our hunt was unsuccessful, but after losing the deer we all continued up to Balsam Lake, Miss Fisher being under the guidance of myself & Griffin and in celebration of such an honour my canoe by especial permission was christened the Jeanet Fisher. This young lady you must know occupies so conspicuous a place here not only because she is the first who had ever been so far back, but also because she is in herself a remarkably agreeable person & the best suited to the backwoods of any young lady I have seen in Canada. She is however too high game for such as me I am afraid having a very nice fortune of her own; but I am of opinion that this expedition was decidedly a fishing expedition, Wallis being the prey which it was sought to ensnare – the fish however did not seem inclined to take the bait.[31]

This event offers us two instructive insights. First, in Langton's view the outing was organized for courtship purposes; someone – perhaps Jeanet Fisher herself with the connivance of her chaperons – had created special territory for matchmaking. If this was so, Langton proved extremely perceptive. The prey ultimately took the bait and Wallis married Miss Fisher in 1840.[32] Here also is a clear example of the strong concern for wealth, status, and hierarchy in matrimonial arrangements which genteel Victorian British migrants brought with them to the new world. Langton obviously found Miss Fisher attractive but, though he was on the lookout for a mate, she could not possibly be a candidate because of her higher social position.

By the Confederation era a rural bachelor's courtship space had changed very little, as we can see from the diary of J.H. Wooley.[33] A nineteen-year-old farm boy from Simcoe County, Ontario, Wooley kept a record of his social life in the early 1860s. Unusual in one respect (he still attended school at an age when most of his contemporaries did not) in others he was a remarkably ordinary rural lad. While still some years from marriage, he found young women attractive and sought their company at every opportunity. At this point he was just entering the marriage market and had no immediate matrimonial object. His social life revolved around private parties, church meetings, community events and drives through the community – by cutter in winter, buggy in summer – with male and female friends. He took various girls with him at different times on these excursions, sometimes alone, sometimes accompanied by a male friend and his female escort. When he had no formal engagements he often called on a girl to pass the time, either at her home or riding with her about the neighbourhood. Yet, while he had no exclusive partner, the prospect of marriage was very much in his mind. On returning home from a four-day trip to Brantford for the May 24th celebrations, where he had met a number of friends, he wrote, "the whole trip was as good a time as I ever took. Burkley stopped here to tea & I went a piece with him crost the fields (and we had quite a private conversation) about the matrimonial state of things."[34]

Maurice Harlow, a small-town merchant in Queens County, Nova Scotia, noted similar experiences in his bachelor diary later in the century. During the 1880s, while in his early and mid-twenties, he moved freely in the society of women. His social life centred on the Baptist church and a small circle of friends. Older than Wooley, Harlow perhaps was anxious to find a wife, and he moved about more purposefully and rather less widely than Wooley did. But like most other nineteenth-century rural and small-town men, he called on his female friends, escorted them to and from church, met them at picnics and parties, and in the process came to know Dora Waterman whom he later married.[35]

In his mid-Victorian diary Thomas Dick, a young Ottawa Valley farmer, described social customs reminiscent of those youth-controlled courtship institutions in early modern Europe recounted by Edward Shorter.[36] On New Year's Day, 1867, Dick noted,

I called into Mrs. Brocks and George and I had a new years kiss from Jennie. Mrs. Brock would not kiss us and then we had a glass of wine and a cake chatted a while and started. I drove George home and then I come home got dinner and then got reddy and Bob Walker and me walked up to a surprise party at Roberts Rennick. George took his horses and took all the young people on the street up to it. We had a great time. Had hard work to get a fiddler. It was late when we got one but when we did get him we put him through till five in the morning. Then we broke up and every one went to his or her home. George brought us all home in the morning each to there place. Bob Hall & Bob Walker & I walked down from Brock's gate. George brought us that far & then he took Jennie in.[37]

Dick's diary outlines the general pattern of youthful visiting in the Valley. Unmarried young men and women, singly and in small groups, called frequently at one another's homes in the evenings or on weekends, the men usually taking the lead. Like the New Year's Eve surprise party, these were spontaneous gatherings, initiated and governed by the youths themselves. Though nominally overseen by parents, youths in their late teens and early twenties regulated these informal meetings with no adult supervision. In this way they created free space where friendships between the sexes could flower.

The urban bachelor courted in different terrain, but like his rural counterpart he could roam more or less at will. Among town and city young men of higher social standing, calling was a common bachelor social pastime, just as it was in genteel British society. Invitations for dinner or tea and visits on designated days when women were formally at home to friends, as well as more casual calls, often introduced men into the company of unmarried young women. A fragment of a letter from Charles Askin to his cousin in 1810 offers a brief glimpse of calling in Montreal during the early nineteenth century. Having taken tea at a Mr Airds the previous evening, where he had met the young woman to whom one of his friends was attached, he remarked, "she is not so handsome as I thought her but I like her manners very much. I was so much pleased with her conversation and that of her sisters and the old Lady, that I staid till half after nine, much later than I ought to."[38] Arthur Henry Freeling provides a later example. Posted to Canada as a young junior officer in the Royal Engineers, Freeling kept a record of his social life in Toronto from 1839 to 1844. He visited in a circle which included his superior officers and their families, and many of the city's leading civilian families: the Robinsons, the Boultons, the Hagermans, and others. These were the only settings in which he met young women of his own social standing.[39]

Larratt Smith, an articling student in Toronto at the same time, followed a similar course in much the same social milieu. Smith fell under the patronage of Mrs W.H. Draper, wife of the lawyer to whom he was articled and a leading politician of the day. "A fortnight ago, Mrs. Draper, after choir practice talked a good deal about calls, she wished me to call at Government House. I therefore called there, put my name down & left my card & just a week later got invitation to Govt. House Ball for 3rd December."[40] Dutifully, though not energetically, Smith followed the young bachelor's customary round of social calls in the years before he wed.

Kept more than a generation later, the diary of Laura Ridout (a member of one of Toronto's oldest leading families) reveals that the young men of the urban elite still continued the practice of calling. In 1873–74, when Laura recorded her diary, the Ridout household consisted of Laura herself, her widowed mother, two unmarried sisters, and two or three unmarried brothers. During the year and a half spanned by the diary both she and an older sister were courted and engaged; her older sister married, as did Laura, early in 1875. Callers virtually besieged the Ridouts throughout these months. Invited and uninvited, visitors dropped by their home almost daily, many of them young bachelors attracted by a household of marriageable young women. There the guests dined, took tea, escorted the Ridout girls to and from church and on walks about town and, with chaperons, accompanied them to parties and public amusements.[41]

J.J. Kelso kept a diary between 1885 and 1891 when he was in his early and mid-twenties. It is one of the most revealing accounts of bachelor life we have from late Victorian English Canada. Although he later became a prominent public figure, Kelso's family provided him few social advantages. He was the eighth of ten children in an impecunious Irish Protestant family. His father George had owned a starch factory in Dundalk, County Louth, but had come to Toronto to recoup his fortunes when a fire destroyed his business. Success eluded him, however; increasingly dependent on alcohol, he failed to provide enough for the large Kelso family. Stung by a deep sense of disgrace at her husband's alcoholism and the family's reduced circumstances, Kelso's mother strove as best she could to advance her children's interests, but the task was beyond her limited means. As a boy Kelso took menial jobs to provide added family income. When he started his diary he was struggling to secure better-paid work, and throughout this period he strove to shore up his family's modest social and economic standing. To say the very least, his position in Toronto society was well below that of the young men who pirouetted about the Ridout girls.[42]

Kelso was powerfully attracted to young women, and his diary overflows with tales of his romantic encounters. Well aware of his ardent character, he fancied himself the idealized lover of the Victorian novel. In a highly self-conscious apostrophe in April 1888 he wrote, "Ah why is it that my heart is so disturbed by every pretty face, by the pressure of a little hand, the glance of a pair of eyes, the utterance of a few words? Every day my heart is torn and lacerated afresh with a pleasure that is almost pain in its deliciousness."[43] But more important than his amorous nature, at least from our point of view, is the field of his courting activity. Kelso's domain was much larger than those of the other urban bachelors we have encountered to this point. Calling remained one of his principal means of seeing young women, but he also met them in a wide range of more impersonal, public settings: parties, dances, toboggan slides, church services, libraries, trains and streetcars, to name only some. The young women he met in these circumstances seldom were chaperoned. Some were at work, others were on errands, while still others were attending parties or public events with family or friends. By no means forward or familiar, Kelso normally sought introductions to those who attracted him. When no mutual acquaintance was present to offer such services, he sometimes introduced himself but usually did so with reluctance. In other words, while deeply interested in these chance meetings, Kelso was far from predatory. Nor did his object seem to extend much beyond the pleasures of conversation.

The larger meaning of Kelso's behaviour is much more apparent when we contrast it with that prescribed by the rigid code of social conduct of the Victorian British elite. In *The Best Circles* Leonore Davidoff analysed the mechanisms of social placement used by society leaders in England to establish status relationships in a community where traditional forms were being undermined by new wealth, urban growth, and greater geographical mobility. According to Davidoff, "the rules of Society and the confining of social life to private homes made possible the minute regulation of personal daily life. It also made possible the evaluation and placing of newcomers in the social landscape."[44] An elaborate, formal system of etiquette regulated access to and conduct within polite society. A large part of etiquette concerned the terms of entry into social relationships or, in Davidoff's words, "the introduction of new individuals and families into group membership and activities." As she observes, "in a system where the aim was to keep those below you at bay while gaining access to the next higher group, introductions were vitally important."[45] Since the oversight of male-female relations in general, and the regulation of the marriage market in particular, were primary functions of this system, the etiquette of introduction was especially significant in courtship. Introductions invariably were formal and required the agency of a third party known to both introducees.

Kelso's behaviour often bore little resemblance to these rigid rules. He saw nothing wrong with introducing himself to unaccompanied young women if the usual formalities of introductions could not be observed. Nor were his attentions rebuffed. These facts are noteworthy in themselves, for they reveal that the mechanisms of social exclusion were far more relaxed in late Victorian Toronto than in the upper ranks of contemporary English society. It might be objected that Kelso was an aggressive social climber and therefore not a representative figure. But when he put himself forward he normally received encouragement, whereas in England he would have been cut, and this fact also speaks of a more open new world social climate. The other mid and late nineteenth-century diaries and letters noted here support this conclusion. None of them, even that of the Toronto blue blood Laura Ridout, indicates that the rules of polite conduct were as stringent as those governing the English social elite. Lacking an indigenous Canadian body of nineteenth-century etiquette literature, we will probably never know the details of English-Canadian behavioural codes. But the evidence indicates clearly that, well before the end of the nineteenth century, youths like Kelso and his young female friends had far more opportunities to meet and be met than existed in Britain.

The examples we have examined reveal four features of a male's courtship territory. First, the space allotted young men was broad and extensive, and they enjoyed virtually unrestricted movement within it. As a result they had many opportunities to meet unmarried women in a wide variety of socially approved settings. Youths such as Nutting and Kelso, Playter and Smith, could come and go at will. This gave them the initiative in making contact with eligible women, though the encounters usually occurred, not in man's domain, but in neutral space where the community permitted the unmarried to mingle or in the home, woman's realm.

Secondly, two crucial features of male territory changed significantly during the century. Male autonomy and the opportunity for privacy grew as the century progressed. Playter and Langton had few chances to meet marriageable women, and the encounters they had almost always took place in public. Wooley and Kelso, by contrast, spent much more private time with the young women they knew. The rise of a broad range of urban recreations was a special boon to Kelso, for it gave him far greater opportunity to meet young women casually and to be alone with them in the anonymity of the urban crowd.

Thirdly, the space allotted the rural bachelor for the initial phase of courtship was rather more free of adult oversight than was the case in towns and cities, particularly after 1850. Wooley acted very much like a late twentieth-century adolescent, except that he drove his girl friends in the family buggy or cutter and not the family car. Dick moved in a circle of friends who regulated their conduct quite apart from their seniors' influence. Even the comparatively free Kelso had less autonomy than Wooley and Dick.

Finally, we can see the faint outlines of differences in courtship space according to social status, at least in urban areas. There the scope of elite courtship was narrower than for other social groups. Men met possible mates in much more restricted environments than did those lower down the social hierarchy. On this point compare Freeling, Smith, and the men who courted the young Ridout women with the youthful Kelso. The former saw single young women of their own social rank only in closely supervised settings. Kelso met his female acquaintances in many locations, some supervised, some highly impersonal. The most rigid rules of propriety, so it seems, belonged to the social elite.

Woman's place was much more circumscribed. The home was her primary space and she claimed it as her own. Compared to men, women had less autonomy in their social relations. They were not free to come and go as they pleased and to meet whomever they wished. These limitations were more significant when women sought marriage than at any other time in their lives, especially at the beginnings of the search for a mate. The size of their courtship territory, so much smaller than that of men, required far different strategies of them as they pursued their ends. Unable to roam at will, they had two broad goals before them when they set about finding a husband. They had to win male attention when in public view, and they had to attract possible suitors into their own domain. These requirements had obvious implications for men as well; while a man might travel widely in search of a wife, in the end he had to meet a woman on feminine ground. Thus, since one of the ends of courtship was to meet an optimum number of possible mates from among which a spouse could be chosen, the differing territories of each gender set them quite different tasks. Men met this goal by moving about the community and meeting women in many public and domestic settings. Women met it by drawing bachelors into their own social space.

The records which women have left us from eighteenth and nineteenth-century English Canada are none too abundant, but they speak to us quite clearly about the courtship space of women. The first such history we have comes to us from the pen of Rebecca Byles, daughter of Mather Byles. Byles and his family had fled Boston during the early months of the American revolution. But they kept up a correspondence with their Yankee relatives, and from their letters we can learn something of Rebecca's courtship by the Halifax physician, William Almon, in 1784 and 1785. Almon, aged thirty, evidently pressed his suit in the usual bachelor manner. He called at the Byles home and may even have boarded there for a time. He joined the family and friends on a rural excursion in June of 1784. Through repeated encounters in the Byles family parlour an intimacy grew up between him and Rebecca, and they married in August 1785. At twenty-three, Rebecca showed herself in full control of her courting territory. On an early visit she teased the doctor about his marriage prospects. She reported to her Boston aunt, who had just written with rumours of his impending marriage,

a few hours after I received yours his [Almon's] friendly Tap at the Parlor Door presented me with an opportunity [to discuss the rumour]. after he was seated, & the customary Compliments passed, he enquired if I had any Letters from Boston. Yes Sir – any news – Yes Sir replied I with as grave a Face as I could assume I am told you are just goine to be married. I, exclaimed the Dr. with a look of surprise – I have Sir a very particular account of it, which if you wish to hear, I will read You & I drew the Letter from my Pocket, and very innocently began with, "I hear he is on the point of Marriage." he said the Dr. with a most provoking accent, pray who is meant by he and what introduced the subject? dont Miss Byles begin in the middle of a Sentence. my curiosity is on the rack. Mortified & vexed with myself for my inadvertence, I hastily returned the Letter into my Pocket, & having call'd the most expressive Frown into my Countenance I could possibly assume, I sentenced him not to be married this twenty Years, as a Punishment for raising a Laugh at my expence.[46]

Somewhat later, when she herself had begun to contemplate marriage with Almon, Rebecca described female courting strategies in an extremely revealing letter to her Boston aunt. In this instance she put her comments in a series of questions about the proper conduct of women toward men during courtship. But these were far from earnest and innocent requests for guidance. They were descriptions about the state of her relations with Almon phrased in interrogative form, most likely to preserve an element of privacy about ongoing, delicate negotiations (whose outcome still was uncertain) while still confiding important family news to a close relation. "Your returning an immediate answer to the following questions," Rebecca wrote, "will greatly oblige your constant reader."

1st what is a Lady to understand when a Gentleman tells her she looks mischievous, funny and Satirical.

2dly does a Gentleman pay a Lady a compliment, or does he not, when he desires that part of the civil things he says to her may be placed to the account of her Friend.

3 does a Lady descend from her proper dignity when she expects a Gentleman who courts her & whom she means to encourage to constantly attend her.

4th in what manner is a Lady to prevent a Gentleman who she is partial too from paying her too particular attention when he is not explicit.[47]

These questions have much to teach us about the course of courtship in general, but for the moment we need only be concerned with what Rebecca's comments may tell us about her use of courtship territory. Here questions three and four are particularly revealing, for they indicate how Rebecca sought to manipulate the attention she received from Almon. On her own home ground, where her suitor waited on her, she tried to reckon the optimum amount of desirable attention. Too little, of course, meant neglect. Too much might expose her to loss of dignity on one hand, and to inappropriate familiarity on the other – leading, perhaps, to no marriage proposal at all. This last point is pure conjecture, and it may attribute to Rebecca an unduly designing character, but is it beyond all probability? At any rate, through these queries, she illustrates the great task of the courting female in early colonial society: to attract bachelors into her territory and then to encourage or discourage their attention at her pleasure.

Mary Gapper O'Brien offers us a view of the feminine counterpart to John Langton's courtship experience. One of that remarkable group of cultivated Englishwomen who lived in frontier Upper Canada, she wrote long letters home about her backwoods experiences after her arrival in 1828. She had come with her widowed mother to visit two of her brothers, half-pay officers who had taken land north of Toronto. Still single at thirty, Mary had abandoned hopes of marriage, having promised to return to England and help her married sister raise her several children. If Mary's letters are any guide, she did not try to attract male company while at her brother's home in Thornhill. But single women of her status and accomplishments were scarce in pioneer communities, and Mary soon won the close attention of Edward O'Brien, an old friend of one of her brothers, and like them a British half-pay officer carving a farm from the hardwood forests of old Ontario. She found him attractive as well. Yet Mary's courtship posed a dilemma, for it offered her two very different prospects: the life of a maiden aunt in rural Somerset or that of a married woman in frontier Upper Canada. No doubt this predicament influenced her bearing toward O'Brien, though her correspondence does not reveal this. What we do know is that Mary met O'Brien almost exclusively in her brother's home – that is in woman's domain (though in this instance she was something of a visitor too). Apart from occasional outings to church, a very few trips to nearby Toronto, and the odd stroll through woods and fields to the nearby farm of her other brother, Mary almost never left home. She met her future husband and made her marriage arrangements on her own territory.[48]

The key to a woman's influence upon courtship during its early phases lay in controlling who entered her domain. Here men were outsiders. The social rules of introduction – which, despite Kelso's forwardness, normally required strangers to meet through a mutual acquaintance – were instruments women commonly used to receive or rebuff attention. The remarkable, and most unusual, courtship correspondence of William Douglas and Jane Hudson reveals the power of these conventions. In 1861 William was a young lawyer newly established in practice in Chatham; Jane, twenty-one at the time and daughter of a deceased army captain, lived with her mother in Toronto. In July William wrote anonymously to Jane declaring that though he did not know her name he had admired her from afar for years. He asked for an introduction in hopes of becoming her friend (though he betrayed a more serious intent by allowing that if she were already engaged he did not wish to meet her). He declared his character, prospects, and social position to be unexceptionable and a source of no difficulty. He then asked her to keep their correspondence secret for the present and requested a reply in care of a friend of his near Chatham. In conclusion he promised to send his name in return for hers.[49]

Jane was astonished by the letter but pleased by its tone. "If you are the person I think you are," she wrote, "I have no objection to be acquainted with you." Nor did her mother object. Jane told her mother about the letter despite his request for secrecy because "Mamma always has had my perfect confidence and I make this case no exception to my general rule of telling her everything, to which you cannot possibly object." With her mother's consent, Jane sent her name and address.[50] Four days later, in reply to another note from William, Jane wrote suggesting that he call on her mother when he was next in Toronto and she [Jane] would contrive to be at home.[51] A final letter, just before their first meeting, noted "we shall be most happy to see you tomorrow evening as we expect to be quite alone, which will be less embarrassing to you, and pleasanter for all."[52] William and Jane met under highly exceptional circumstances, though this proved no bar to their later marriage. Yet this exception offers much insight into the workings of territoriality in the nineteenth-century courtship. In this instance the rules of etiquette were stretched somewhat to bring the young couple together, but after this irregular introduction the crucial meeting occurred in female space and under parental supervision. Jane and her mother controlled the right of access to the domestic space which William had to enter in his quest for a bride. Few mid-Victorian English Canadians could have met their future spouse in quite this way, but the episode was entirely typical in that William and Jane made a match on her territory.

Women had great influence, too, over the processes leading to marriage. House parties were such common events that they seldom drew more than passing notice in the diaries and letters of our nineteenth-century ancestors. Older adults seem to have given most parties, though, like the informal gatherings attended by George and Honorine, these occasions commonly included adolescents as well. The past also yields many scraps of evidence that, during the second half of the century at least, youths often organized their own social lives quite apart from parental initiative. As we have seen, the diaries of Thomas Dick and J.H. Wooley offer young men's views of these events in rural Ontario during the 1860s. The evidence left to us by young women is by no means abundant, but it reveals the same processes at work. The journal of Louisa Bowlby – seventeen in 1862 when she kept notes on her experiences – makes passing reference to a party she was having for young friends. More than a decade later her sixteen-year-old sister Hattie, a diarist as well, jotted down several comments about youth parties she had sponsored or attended.[53] The Bowlby girls and their young female friends used the feminine prerogative of invitation to hold social events in their family homes and encourage the boys in whom they were interested.

Honorine Tanswell's courtship initiatives reveal still another feature of women's control of social space. Far from the passive recipient of George's attentions, she used her friendship with George's sisters to enlarge her own territory. They gave her a ready excuse to call at George's home, making her company available to him in other places than her own, at other times than those of George's choosing, and clearly on her initiative. Much more aggressive than many mid-nineteenth century women, Honorine manipulated George's domestic space in her pursuit of him. In fact, both men and women often relied on siblings and other relations to establish networks of friends among the opposite sex. Women commonly used such techniques to organize social visiting, employing them to overcome the conventional limitations that hindered their movements and thus give them more room in which to manoeuvre their social lives.

Outside the home, however, women's autonomy was limited. Respectable girls and young women required chaperons in public, at least according to convention. Samuel P. Jarvis, the Toronto Tory placeman and descendant of a leading loyalist family, remarked to his wife in 1843, "I think you were right in not allowing Ellen [their seventeen-year-old daughter] to go to the picnic under the circumstances you mention; nor do I think she should be permitted to go to such places unless under the protection of some elderly person who will look after her; as for the boys, I imagine they think too much of their own pleasure to be much protection to their sister."[54]

In 1855 the widower A.N. Buell, an ageing reformer and office-holder, cautioned his daughter Nazip (then an unhappy inmate at a Boston finishing school) "that if you do not wish to be talked about you must be particularly careful how you allow yourself to go to the theatre or any public place with Mr. Edward Rockwood unaccompanied by his sister. I know nothing about him. He may be a very nice young man, he may be very generous with his cakes and sweetmeats, he may be very good, very upright and very honorable but I dont think it would be prudent or proper for you to go with him to church or any other place unaccompanied by others."[55] Buell's daughter evidently chafed at these restraints, and her rebellious behaviour troubled her family greatly. Soon after her father's chastisement she returned to live with an older married sister in Brockville, the family home. Her sister complained to their father: "Nazip is not under the slightest restraint here. I don't know anything about where she goes, or who she goes with, where she spends her mornings or evenings. Accordingly I hear of her being at Mrs. Dana's on the islands, but she goes when and where she pleases. I have told her two or three times I thought she ought to tell Mrs. Church or me where she was going, but she does not pay any attention to me."[56] In this instance an adolescent girl's independence, her free movement without a chaperon, was a source of anxiety. When courting took a more intimate turn chaperons became still more important. Even in the advanced stages of courtship, men and women were seldom alone. And when they were, this was cause for concern. When Laura Ridout spent an evening at home alone with Vernon Wadsworth less than a month before they were engaged her mother was scandalized.[57]

Yet the evidence on this point is far from conclusive. These examples come to us from socially prominent families in urban Ontario. We do not know how deeply this custom penetrated into society. At very least we should note some indications of its limits. An eighteen-year-old Britton Bath Osler, the future famed criminal lawyer, told his brother in 1857 that "I was out riding this morning with Miss Law of Hamilton it was previously arranged that I should be one of a party of six, but accidently or on purpose Miss Law and myself had to go alone. She is 16 years of age and when in Dundas the rest of the ladies may dry up."[58] Certainly the girls who took drives with Wooley in rural Simcoe County during the early 1860s often went with him alone. Frances Tweedie, another rural diarist of the Confederation era, lived on a farm in Whitby Township, just east of Toronto. Her journal indicates that she came and went quite freely. In a cryptic report in February 1867, the eighteen-year-old Tweedie noted, "Went down for Em [a girl friend]. We dressed & went to spree in afternoon. got to tea had a gay time. We each got beaus. Ems Millar, mine Milne gay fellows had a splendid time going & coming. Said many things."[59] The holiday diary of Lois Bigelow, a student at the Horton Academy in Wolfville, Nova Scotia, describes her vacation trip to Canso in the summer of 1878. While spending six weeks with her relatives, she too moved freely about the community, alone and with male and female friends.[60]

In fact this was no contradiction at all, but a sign of changing conditions. In the conservative circles of English Canada's urban elites, chaperonage persisted until almost the end of the century. But the rules of right conduct which bound most other women gradually relaxed after 1850. No source makes this point more clearly than does the Kelso diary, which reveals the dramatically new social circumstances of young women in the late nineteenth-century Canadian city. Kelso's account indicates that city women in the 1880s and 1890s enjoyed unprecedented freedom to move about in public. New opportunities for work and leisure drew them out of the home and into the community, away from the supervisory gaze of their relations and neighbours. Here, too, we can see a sharp contrast between the situation of most women in English Canada and those in upper and middle class British society. As Davidoff and Hall note, in England "the canons of respectability prevented middle-class women from being seen except in a few narrowly specified places: the church, certain shops, select concerts, garden parties, exhibits."[61]

This new freedom had obvious implications for courtship. The anonymity of the city and the greater ease of movement for older girls and young women gave both sexes easier friendly access to one another. The urban courtship moved steadily into the public domain and women's courtship space gradually expanded to approximate that of men. By the end of the nineteenth century women could meet and be met, court and be courted, in settings well beyond the reach of direct family influence. For bachelors seeking a wife these changes had equally important implications. They no longer needed to pursue their suit into the parlour of their preferred one – space which was obviously hers. Instead they could canvass the marriage market and perhaps even make their marriage proposals in the privacy of public space, before the indifferent eyes of an anonymous urban populace. Precisely when this shift began, and whether it first occurred in the countryside or the city, we cannot know for certain. But by the dawn of the twentieth century, women in English Canada moved more freely than before in a world much larger than ever. And to the extent that they did, they yielded up that collective control over courtship which had traditionally been theirs.

Yet this new freedom soon encountered its own limits. The mobile young men and women of the later years of the century found themselves confronted with restrictions on their new liberties when they left home to live, work, or study in one of the larger institutions which enfolded the lives of increasing numbers of Canadians toward the end of the nineteenth century. Invariably these limits were defined in the name of moral respectability. The rise of co-educational normal schools and universities, for example, raised the prospect of unsupervised social relations between unmarried young men and women. Assuming the dual roles of moral guardian and community censor, these institutions carefully regulated the social lives of the students whom they taught. The Toronto Normal School forbade any communication between its male and female students either on or away from its premises; predictably, the rule was often broken and the school disciplined offenders severely.[62] Queen's University routinely drew up a list of boarding houses approved for its students.[63] By the turn of the century, when the numbers of women students had grown considerably, the university began to make special provisions for female students. It established a women's residence in 1901 and soon after required that men and women who boarded in private lodgings live in separate houses unless they were members of the same family.[64]

By the early twentieth century a new series of courtship rites governed the social lives of the men and women who lived in college and university dormitories, customs which veiled institutional supervision in the cloak of common practice. The women who lived in Annesley Hall at Victoria College in Toronto received male visitors in the Hall drawing room. A man called by previous arrangement, either at a woman's invitation or by his own request. One of the major student functions at Vic was the annual promenade, an evening when men and women gathered together to hear speeches and musical entertainments. Because Vic was a Methodist college no dancing was allowed, but each woman had a card like those used at balls which men signed for the opportunity to walk about and converse with her for part of the evening.[65] At Queen's the annual Conversazione, an evening of music, speeches, dancing, and refreshments which fell under the patronage of the chancellor and principal, was the major social event of the year.[66]

The fact that men and women in nineteenth-century English Canada moved in different social spaces had important implications for the process of seeking a spouse. Because companionate marriage – the idealized form in the English-speaking world by the end of the eighteenth century – rested upon mutual regard, and because friendship and sympathy required time to grow, those seeking a husband or wife needed special places for courtship, places where they could meet prospective mates and come to know at least one of them well. Until mid-century each sex possessed its own forms of courtship territory and each, acting collectively, rivalled the other through its control of courting space. Men were the dominant force in public hospitality, women prevailed in domestic social life. The key to their authority was the power of invitation, of admission to and exclusion from the pool of potential mates.

After 1850 men rapidly abandoned their shared influence over the marriage market. Changing patterns of mobility, the rise of urban centres, and (at least in Ontario) increasingly favourable sex ratios all improved their marriage chances. Through their control of domestic hospitality, women maintained their collective authority over matrimony much longer than did men. The demographic and social changes favouring bachelors forced spinsters to defend their marriage interests by clinging to whatever traditional means lay at their disposal. Yet the rise of the city affected the mobility of women as well as men, and as the century advanced women attained more and more freedom to come and go as they wished. New opportunities for education, work, and recreation altered woman's space, and these changes had important implications for courtship. By the later nineteenth century the sexes held much courtship territory in common. The parlour remained women's courting preserve, but men and women had greater access to one another in public spaces over time, spaces free of restrictions on entry and free of close oversight.

It might seem contradictory to suggest that women maintained a firm hold on domestic space while at the same time venturing into the terrain of men. In fact the contradiction is more apparent than real. Women's social space enlarged gradually and at different rates amongst different social groups. The process commenced in rural communities and in the middling ranks of urban society. Upper-class women, whose social position rested most firmly on prevailing codes of right conduct, felt these changes somewhat later. Moreover, the first feminine steps outside woman's traditional sphere were hesitant and tentative. Courting women were bargaining over the most important contract they would make in their lives. For this reason, especially given the heightened Victorian atmosphere of anxiety about sexual propriety, they had every incentive to move cautiously. A woman might make acquaintances with men in the wider world. When courting became serious, however, she could retreat to her home and force her admirer to negotiate on her terrain. In 1900, then, women courted in familiar as well as unfamiliar places. By moving into the domain of men they had broadened their opportunities for male friendships. But when the prospect of marriage arose women found security in their own traditional province.

CHAPTER FIVE

The Rituals of Romance

Nineteenth-century romantic rituals fulfilled important functions for courting couples and communities alike. They gave social form to the personal experience of taking a spouse. For those who wooed and wed, courtship and marriage were intensely private acts. They flowed from the intimacy between a man and woman who turn their backs to the world and gaze into each other's souls. The chosen one was cherished above all others while the secret bonds of a loving union were veiled from the onlooker's eyes. But courtship and marriage also were social processes, for society has always had a great stake in family formation. While formal rules and regulations exercised some control over these relations, informal codes and conventions enforced the greater part. These customs ruled private conduct far more effectively than laws possibly could, and they found their clearest expression in the rituals of courtship and marriage. In addition they constituted a rite of passage, a moment of teaching "when the society seeks to make the individual most fully its own, weaving group values and understandings into the private psyche so that internally provided individual motivation replaces external controls."[1] Yet, while rituals disciplined each step which men and women took along the path to married life, they were not simply a tool for the social regulation of private behaviour. Courting men and women also used them to direct the course of their relationship. Involved as they were in some of life's most delicate negotiations, they used the customs of courtship to serve their own private ends.

Each phase of the process of taking a spouse had its own distinctive rituals. Some of those typical of the courtship stage have already been discussed: calls and visits, balls and parties, held important implications for courting men and women. Their territorial significance apart, these occasions wove courtship into the fabric of everyday sociability in Canadian life. They were convivial occasions for both sexes and all ages, not just the young and unmarried.

Among all occasions for courting, outings were much the most common. They came in many forms. When William Helliwell, a Don Mills brewer, went walking with his "dear girl" in the spring and summer of 1833, the pair followed the most popular of all courtship customs.[2] In an age when walking was the chief means of getting about, a stroll around town or countryside could be a social event. It gave pleasure, cost nothing, and was accessible to all. It might have a destination or it might be an end in itself. But the Canadian courtship walk was never clearly distinguished from casual social strolls, unlike the ritual courtship promenades of contemporary English and European youths. John Gillis has noted that walking out was a seasonal, youth-regulated courtship rite among the respectable working class in Victorian England, one gradually replaced by less public forms of courtship toward the end of the ninteenth century.[3] Edward Shorter has described similar scenes in early modern French and German village life.[4] But when courting couples went strolling in Victorian English Canada the act had none of the class overtones and few of the formal characteristics of the customs which Gillis and Shorter describe. Instead they followed one of the most common of all Canadian pastimes and, far from setting themselves apart from the community when courting, they integrated themselves into conventional social life.

For those with horses, riding, driving, and sleighing offered other possibilities for courtship. We find many examples in the family papers of nineteenth-century Canadians. In 1839 the sharp-eyed Lewis Wallbridge of Belleville told his sister, "Adelaide Coleman is quite a young woman. She goes out riding with the young men."[5] Much later in the century the Ontario farm boy Charles Steen told Sarah Hillis of his own and his sister's experiences. "She has got more driving this summer than a little, more than I have anyhow, although you seem to imagine that I was a great fellow for driving the girls, but it is not so. I have given Lil a few drives in the evening and another girl where she boards would sometimes get in with us."[6] These practices grew more closely tied to social status during the second half of the century, at least in towns and cities, where only the prosperous segments of colonial society had easy access to horses, carriages, and sleighs. The several admirers of Fanny Marion Chadwick, daughter of the Toronto lawyer and United Empire Loyalist genealogist E.M. Chadwick, often took her for country drives during the early 1890s.[7] But less affluent town and city women had to court on foot.

Alicia Killaly's delightful illustrations of the adventures of Miss Muffin and Captain Busby, published in 1868, offer some vivid fictional evidence on the role of sleighing in courtship. The captain and Miss Muffin drive out from Quebec on a fine winter's day to slide on the snow cone at Montmorency Falls. After an afternoon of pleasure and mild misadventure they return rather late to be greeted at the door by her concerned parents. The fact that the term "muffin" was mid-Victorian bachelor slang for an eligible young woman makes the context quite explicit. Until mid-century at least, groups of unmarried young men occasionally organized winter sleighing parties to pursue their courting plans. The letters in the Shanley papers yield a striking example. In February 1847 Harry Allen wrote his friend Frank Shanley,

We went down to a Cal Call party at the Squire's on Monday – and really it was as pleasant as a think [sic] of the sort could be. A driving party had been announced for the next day and Dr. Going and myself drove down from London both with the determination of driving Clara – he because he is in love with her – and I – because I wanted to make myself in love with her I suppose, for I know no other reason. However, he was dancing with her and I next with Fanny Summers, and I turned to Clara and asked her to drive in my sleigh the next day which she immediately promised to do; and consequently the Doctor went back to London in disgust the same night. We had a delightful drive the next day to Rawlings – where we lunched – and Keir had to pay the bill, as he says "he always has" – and on coming home yesterday I was obliged to say to myself – "Well, I am not so much surprised at Frank having fallen in love with that girl, for I am damned near it myself.[8]

The purpose of the outing could not be more clear. Toward the end of the century the faint outlines of the modern "date" appeared in urban places. These new courtship occasions usually centred upon paid public amusements which couples attended alone, invariably at the invitation and expense of the male suitor. In one early example, the free-spirited feminist Elizabeth Smith went to see *Hamlet* with a young man in her class at the Ottawa Normal School in March 1880.[9] In another, Charles Sippi of London loaned his son the family horse and cutter "to take Miss Jones to see 'Husband and Wife' in the Opera House" in 1893. It was young Charlie's twenty-first birthday.[10] By the early twentieth century the custom had become common. When the Toronto student Main Johnson invited his future wife, Gladys Robertson, to the University Theatre night in 1907, he followed the new courting custom of socially well-placed urban youths.[11] Courtship had begun to assume its modern commercial, more private guise.

Valentines also formed part of the courtship ritual, albeit a sometimes ambiguous one. Originally a valentine was a person of the opposite sex

Captain Busby drives Miss Muffin (NAC, C-42296)

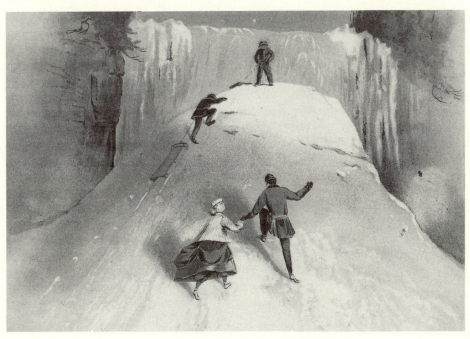

How they climb up the cone (C-42259)

Coming down is easier but more dangerous (C-42289)

On the way home, off the track, Captain Busby would very much like to know where they are (C-42273)

Assisted by some obliging inhabitants, they regain the road (C-42299)

They get home at last (C-45576)

chosen on St Valentine's Day as a friend or sweetheart for the coming year. Well into the nineteenth century in England the custom of choosing a valentine remaind playful, dedicated as much to love as to lovers.[12] But as time passed valentines became sentimental messages sent on 14 February and their exchange grew more closely tied to romance. The earliest surviving valentine from British America, sent to Amelia DesBarres (natural daughter of J.F.W. DesBarres, a major Nova Scotian land-holder and lieutenant-governor of Cape Breton) by Rebecca Byles's brother in 1784, conformed to the ancient tradition. It comes to us courtesy of Rebecca herself who, a bit of a snoop, copied it out and sent it on to her Boston aunts. A sixty-line verse in rhyming couplets with elaborate pastoral allusions, it asked Miss DesBarres:

Would you with scrutinizing eyes
Detect my follies as they rise,
With honest freedom deign to tell
The numerous faults you see too well.
Would you one Year your Power Assert.
The Virtues you possess impart.
How widely different must appear
Your Pupil in the following Year;
How should I bless the happy Hour
That plac'd my conduct in your Power.

According to the amused Rebecca, her brother was the very model of the moonstruck youth.[13] Before published greeting cards became pop- ular toward the mid-nineteenth century, valentines were rather like that of Rebecca's brother, handwritten bits of poetry or doggerel sent by men to women. Because they were original compositions or poems copied from books, the custom of sending them must have been confined to the literate. Most of the surviving examples from this era are lushly romantic, for example the unsigned valentine sent in 1842 to Laura Moorhead in Quebec City (likely by John Neilson Jr whom she later married):

How shall my faithful heart, my fair,
Declare the bliss it feels,
The balm to soften ev'ry care
Which mutual love reveals?

When prudence joins the faithful tie,
In vain will sorrow prove;
And every spark of grief will fly
Before the breath of love.[14]

A valentine for Miss McDonald (NAC Picture Division)

Yet early valentines were not inevitably romantic. Some were comic,[15] while others were written for the very young. Catherine Parr Traill spent a day writing doll valentines for her children, nieces, and nephews in 1838.[16]

The rise of the printed greeting card vastly extended the tradition of sending valentines and, in doing so, broadened its meaning. While romantic messages persisted, valentines lost some of their sentimental associations. Children received them, adolescent girls mailed them to boy friends, men sent them to various female friends at the same time. As Louisa Bowlby told her journal on 14 January 1862, "One month from today is Valentine's day. I think I shall write a few and I expect I shall get some. Belle (McCall) thinks of sending one to Abb. Wonderful."[17] The practice penetrated deeply into rural society. On Valentine's Day, 1867, the Ottawa Valley farm lad Thomas Dick told his diary, "In the woods today. In the evening went to L'Original & posted too letters the ware Valentine."[18] A generation or two previously, men of Dick's literacy would never have done such a thing. In 1879 and 1880, while in her early twenties, Elizabeth Smith received romantic and nasty valentines, the former from admirers, the latter presumably from an envious model school rival.[19]

Beyond their written message, valentines often conveyed complex meanings. The handsome, hand-tinted papercut which an unnamed admirer from Montreal sent Mary McDonald in St Andrews, Canada East, in 1855 was much more than an exquisite piece of greeting card art; it was a popular icon of love, rich in romantic imagery.[20] Two lovers stroll, arm in arm, in an idyllic pastoral setting. He gestures and leads her toward the little country church where they soon will wed. The symbols of romance surround them: love (cupid, golden doves), harmony (the harp), domesticity (flowers, lambs) and, not incidentally, fertility (nesting birds, luxuriant foliage). In broader terms, the gesture of sending a valentine might express a wide range of sentiments – budding friendship, flowering romance, or the full bloom of love. It might also use humour to convey the same message, indirectly and therefore ambiguously. It might even pervert the custom and use the form of the valentine to express converse emotions. Whatever the intent, valentines were a means of expressing interest in someone of the opposite sex and of attracting their interest in return.

Couples exchanged many other tokens of affection during courtship. Two early examples come to us from the rather precocious courting career of Henry Bliss of Fredericton, son of a loyalist émigré and leading government official. At fifteen he received presents of maple sugar from a youthful female admirer.[21] In a romantic gesture four years later, he asked Sarah Anne Anderson to name his dog. Sarah Anne, one year older and the adopted daughter of the chief justice of Nova Scotia, understood the full meaning of Henry's request. "I am very much pleased in being allowed to give him a name," she told Bliss. "If you have no objection, pray let it be *Caro*."[22] No doubt she intended the name for Bliss rather than his spaniel. Soon after, Sarah Anne sent Henry a blue ribbon for his watch and asked him to wear it for her sake.[23] We have no note of any gifts from him to her, however, for only her letters have survived.

George Jones used more tangible tokens in his suit with Honorine and she replied in kind. His first opportunity came when she gave him a Philippina and he deliberately lost the subsequent contest so he had a reason to give her a present. As they grew more familiar he pressed her with other gifts: a ring, notepaper and envelopes, mottoes, engravings, and a very expensive album in which to mount them. In return she gave him a pencil case, a seal for his watch chain and – in fine Victorian fashion – a lock of her hair. As his plight grew more desperate George also gave presents to Honorine's mother and father, hoping to ingratiate himself with them.

We see a similar pattern of gift-giving in the courtship of Fred Wightman and Lillian Williamson during the early 1880s. Fred was a New Brunswick blacksmith and carriage-maker who began to study for the ministry during his engagement to Lillian; she lived on her family's farm some distance up river from St John. Compared with Henry and Sarah Anne or George and Honorine, who moved in higher social circles, Fred and Lillian were ordinary folk in colonial society. In the early stage of their courting career Fred gave Lillian photographs of himself, an Easter card, and some sheet music. After their engagement a ring, seasonal cards, and an autograph book followed. Evidently Fred's presents were modest because of business difficulties. Lillian seems to have given him no gifts at all.[24]

The conservative proprieties of gift-giving in late Victorian times were neatly illustrated in a brief Christmas message from Mary MacGregor, a school teacher in Amherst, Nova Scotia, to her fiancé Robert Dawson, a merchant in distant Bridgewater, in 1893. "I have just been smiling all to myself as I did up my parcel for you," she wrote, "just thinking what a change from other years when you would send me a card or booklet & I never *dare* send you even that."[25]

The larger importance of these exchanges lies beneath the surface of the gifts themselves. The social meaning of giving presents is bound up in the roles of the donor and receiver, the intended and actual consequences of the donation, and the symbolic meaning of the gift. The fact that men took the initiative in giving courtship gifts is deeply significant, for it gave them a large measure of influence over the direction and pace of courting. It allowed them to express the depth of their own commitment and to encourage the degree which they sought in return. At the same time they had to reckon their timing with care in order not to bestow a present at an inopportune moment and thus give offence. A woman might, though she need not, reciprocate with a gift of her own. Whatever her acknowledgment, she responded on terms established by the suitor who had given her the gift. Women could take the initiative in other spheres of courting, but in the important matter of presents they conventionally deferred to men.

Courting gifts fulfilled some of the same ends served by valentines. They expressed interest, affection, or love, depending on circumstances. But gifts had more powerful effects, for they also created bonds of obligation between the receiver and the donor. Because the initial recipients were female, the practice of giving courtship gifts customarily indebted women to men. The offer of a gift could thus be met in one of three ways. A woman might refuse it and run the risk of affronting the donor, she might accept it and offer one in return, or she might accept it and reciprocate in another fashion. The first alternative raised the prospect of a social rupture between the parties, an outcome not often desired. The second might possibly discharge the "debt" but was much more likely to reinforce whatever bonds existed between the courting pair. The third would almost certainly strenghten those ties. Obviously, by accepting a gift from an admirer a woman greatly narrowed her options.

Gifts also had important symbolic meanings. George and Honorine exchanged mementoes and small personal articles, things with sentimental value but little utility. The modest gifts which Sarah Anne gave Henry and Fred gave Lillian were the same. An elaborate, unspoken calculus reckoned the propriety of these presents and, indeed, all gifts which passed between unrelated men and women, as Mary's affectionate note to Robert reveals. Too personal a present expressed undue familiarity and therefore might offend, but one which was too impersonal might easily suggest indifference, an equally undesirable result. The central task in giving a courtship gift was to choose an article which would please, which expressed an appropriate degree of interest and commitment, and which revealed a sympathetic appreciation of the recipient's interests, without being either too forward or too reticent.

The rituals of courtship allowed the community to monitor the courting process; in fact, this was one of their most important features. Because many courtship activities took place in open view, the public supervised them. In essence this oversight was moral. The community cared deeply about right conduct in courtship. It defined and enforced a code of conduct which denied the unmarried privacy and forbade any physical intimacy until they were virtually engaged. Gossip enforced these rules and couples guided themselves cautiously around its dangerous shoals. We see a clear example early in 1887: when another man called twice to see Jennie Miller, a thirty-three-year-old spinster who also lived in Bridgewater, she told her admirer William

Hall, "do not worry about his walking with me, he will never do that again, and do not for a moment think there will be any talk about me; there will be no shadow [*sic*] of a chance for it, about him or any one else."[26] A few months later she even discouraged Hall from paying her a visit while she stayed with a clergyman relative in Sydney Mines; she feared that this would cause talk.[27]

Women who transgressed prescribed female roles in courtship found themselves heaped with criticism. As principal of the Burlington Academy, a Methodist residential girls school in Hamilton, Jane Van Norman spoke for respectable opinion on such matters. "Poor Mary Johnson," she told a male admirer in 1848, "I half pity & more than half blame her. John did not at all like her staying there so long, he was away as much as possible. Strange indeed for a lady to get half mad after a gentleman & he care nothing about her. I am really provoked at Mary for she is making a complete fool of herself. John sent word for me to tell her candidly that he did not regard her particularly. Hopkins said if I did not he would & I suppose he will, for I do not wish to meddle in the matter."[28]

When gossip imposed behavioural codes upon courting couples it commonly reflected community norms. In this respect the social regulation of courtship in English Canada differed somewhat from common practice in much of Europe during the eighteenth and nineteenth centuries, where peer groups often controlled the courting activities of youths and young adults. Shorter describes such scenes in peasant life in pre-modern France and Germany, Gillis similar ones in urban, industrial Britain.[29] Peer group control of courting life evidently occurred in widely scattered communities across long spans of time and in strikingly different social and economic settings. But nineteenth-century English Canadian youths – much more individualistic than their European counterparts – seldom followed these traditions. Instead the entire community acted as moral policeman.

Courtship rituals also gave men and women ways of regulating the progress of their intimate affairs. Marriage was such a momentous event that few rushed headlong to the altar. What emotion drove forward, prudence usually deterred. Among the many reasons for discretion in courtship one is particularly relevant here. When a confession of love is welcomed by its recipient, a couple shares the joy of acknowledging a deep mutual commitment. But when it is unwelcome both parties suffer. The confessor loses face while the confessee receives an offence. William Wynne, a young man from the Niagara peninsula, revealed his anxieties to a friend in 1830.

I don't know how it happens – (but so it is) that I find myself when at the cottage facinated and quite at ease – and sometimes think was I prepared to commence Housekeeping that I should be more than half inclined to make an offer of my hand to some one of the inmates – (but by the by before making the offer I should take care like a prudent fellow to ascertain pretty nearly how it would be accepted – as you must be aware that a refusal on that score would be no very agreeable thing) but you know my dear John that such things with me for the present must be merely hypothetical.[30]

After becoming engaged to Agnes Rubidge in 1888, the English emigrant Reginald Drayton of Rice Lake, Ontario, confessed similar concerns about their early courtship experience in a frank letter to his fiancée: "My dear girl you were right in thinking that I would think you cold last summer, possibly we were both rather foolish for tho I have & had thought of you for a long time, I wished for some symptom of preference for me in you before I would say anything for of all things I could not bear the idea of a refusal & I am not one of the persevering kind who won't take no for a answer, in fact I had made up my mind (only some way I could not keep to it) not to get fond of you until I was sure you would have me, so that I should not feel so cut up if you said no."[31]

For such reasons couples proceeded cautiously during the early stages of courting. The rituals of courtship gave them occasions to move at their own deliberate speed, perhaps coming to know a series of possible spouses before choosing one, perhaps having a leisurely opportunity to learn much more about only one. For someone in the first stages of seeking a spouse, courting rites placed a comfortable cloak of ambiguity over the actual state of their relations with another. In this uncertain atmosphere they might pursue a single, serious romantic interest or they might meet a series of admirers with no need to take matters further. In either event they could explore the possibilities of marriage in a preliminary way without giving an affront or fearing disgrace.

When a couple's romantic interests developed to the point at which marriage became a possibility, the rituals of courtship gave way to those of betrothal. A broad range of customs distinguished this stage of a romance, a suitor's frequent visits to the home of his beloved, regular church attendance as a couple, and keeping company in public to name but three. Sitting up was another common custom leading to engagement. It was a momentous step in the courting career of Thomas Dick, who noted in his diary for 30 March 1867, "when I got my supper I went up to drill there was none. I went into John Cross's I found Ellen all alone they rest was out they come in after a while then he & they rest of them all went to bed & left Ellen & me I stoped till midnight with her. her & me had a good chat it is the firs time I ever sat up with her in that house. then I come home & went to bed I was tired."[32] At that point Ellen was mourning the death of her brother, recently killed by a kick from a horse. An oblique reference in the diary two weeks later hints that she and Dick were discussing marriage: "in the evening I went into Brokes & to the office & then into Mr. John Cross's stopt their till 12 o'clock. Ellen & me had a good chat but not *at present*. They rest of them went to bed at 9 a.m. [*sic* p.m.]"

These brief entries in the diary of a young rural bachelor describe the ritual of sitting up far more eloquently than any mere historian, far removed from the events, possibly could. The practice was simplicity itself. A suitor called for a young woman who invited him into the family home. At some point the other family members withdrew, leaving the couple alone for a few hours of private conversation. But the family would not leave unless they considered the suitor a possible marriage partner for the girl. The concession of privacy was the gift of family members and, when granted, marked their approval of a potential match. In this instance the Cross family knew Dick well. He had been a close friend of Ellen's late brother and was a familiar face in the house.

Sitting up allowed courting couples the opportunity to be alone they so often desired but so seldom obtained. It gave them time and space for the growth of mutual awareness, and it gave them a chance to taste at least some of the sensual joys of growing intimacy. We know very little about the place of caresses and kisses in nineteenth-century Canadian courtship, but likely they were most often exchanged in the family parlour. Sometimes rather more was exchanged. Pregnant and unwed, Margaret Moak of Southwold Township in Elgin County, complained to the courts in 1864 that Charles Dougherty had seduced her in her father's house under promise of marriage.[33] In fact, when taking legal action against putative fathers, many an unmarried mother claimed to have yielded to her deceiver after he had vowed to marry her. More often than not, one suspects, the sweet moment of surrender occured in the family parlour late in the evening, with mom and dad, brother and sister, fast asleep upstairs.[34]

The extent of the custom of sitting up is not at all clear. The diaries and family letters of nineteenth-century British Canadians sometimes note it in passing, and some evidence indicates that it persisted into the twentieth century.[35] It also seems to have been primarily a rural pastime, but the record is too sketchy to permit firmer conclusions.

With very few exceptions, bundling and other night courting rituals common in pre-modern continental Europe were unknown in English common in pre-modern continental Europe were unknown in English Canada. On these occasions unmarried young women entertained suitors in bed overnight. Ostensibly this allowed prospective partners to discuss their affairs in private, under the nominal supervision of family and friends.[36] Erotic contact was forbidden and both remained fully clothed though, as we might suspect, things sometimes got out of hand. Peter Russell has discovered faint traces of bundling in the Niagara peninsula early in the nineteenth century[37] but we find no other signs of the custom in English-Canadian history. In this instance the absence of evidence is particularly telling for, given the censorious outlook of so many early colonial clergymen, they almost certainly would have condemned such affronts to community moral standards.

Unfortunately, the crucial moment of the nineteenth-century betrothal – the exchange of promises to marry – is shrouded from our inquiring gaze. Our sources reveal nothing of those intensely private dramas in which a man and a woman vowed to wed one another. Perhaps it is just as well that such a luminous moment of intimacy remains veiled from the prying historian's eye. Yet betrothal had important social implications, if for no other reason than that an agreement to marry removed a couple from the pool of possible mates, a fact of general interest to the community. There was no one form in which couples advertised their intentions. The custom of giving and wearing engagement rings, now a sign of a couple's commitment, is largely a twentieth-century practice. In the nineteenth century many couples, particularly those expecting long engagements, kept their marriage plans secret from all but close family members until the wedding day drew near. Others confided their news to family and friends who, in turn, spread the glad tidings widely. In either event the process had no ritualistic associations.

Once a couple became engaged, the role of ritual in their affairs diminished. Bethrothal was a period in which the promised couple deepened their knowledge of one another, planned their wedding, and prepared for married life. The social rites which pervaded their earlier courting lives now intruded rather less for, once the community had ushered a man and woman to the threshold of marriage, the customary forms of courtship lost much of their importance. Yet while the engaged pair strove to fashion a cosy, romantic world for themselves, society maintained its claims upon them. In early modern England bethrothal had been the primary act in creating a married couple, often marked by the beginning of sexual relations. When this occurred church rites simply ratified an already existing union.[38] But by the nineteenth cenno longer bound as tightly as before, and an engaged pair's claims to privacy did not rest on the same firm prospects of a permanent relationship which they formerly had done. For this reason the community still monitored the engaged couple as it had during courtship. And couples usually behaved much as they had before they pledged themselves to one another. They walked, rode, drove, and visited, still conducting their intimate affairs in front of family, friends, and neighbours. The intensity of their relationship had changed but its social context had not.

One important betrothal ritual, the prospective groom's request to the parents of his beloved for permission to marry their daughter, is best discussed in the context of family influences on matrimony. But a striking, though far from typical, variant of this rite should be noted here. As late as the 1920s some Cape Breton Scots kept the old Hebridean custom of holding a *rèiteach* to mark a couple's formal betrothal.[39] *Rèiteach* is a Gaelic term meaning clearing, and the custom formally cleared the way for a marriage. In accordance with the tradition, a man would not propose to a woman directly but would ask an older married friend to speak on his behalf. The two would call at the home of the woman and the interceder would speak to her father for his friend.

The father would usually know why they had come, but nothing would be said outright. Instead, they would pretend they had come to buy a cow or a horse or a boat – and everything they said would have a double meaning. If it was a boat they were claiming they wanted to buy they would ask such a question as, Is she broad in the beam? Eventually they would get down to talking about the real purpose of the visit, and when the older friend had finished speaking well of the bridegroom-to-be and asking for a certain girl's hand, the father would then go through the formality of first offering his other daughters.[40]

After the father's assent had been granted, that of the girl would be sought. Once given, a celebration followed, sometimes with only the immediate participants while on other occasions friends and neighbours might attend.

Given the formal, patriarchal character of the custom, it would be easy to misconstrue the meaning of the *rèiteach*. Superficially the ritual bears the hallmarks of arranged marriages and strong paternal rule in family life. But the surviving accounts of the practice suggest that this was not the case. Whatever they once might have been, by the later nineteenth century these rites usually were predetermined events. Some time before they were held the couple had already come to a private agreement; they also knew her father's disposition in advance.

In effect, the *rèiteach* merely celebrated a couple's engagement by formally announcing it to family and friends. The rite preserved the form but not the substance of more traditional marriage customs. Like virtually everyone else in nineteenth-century British Canada, young Cape Breton Scots couples married for love and took the lead in making their own marriage arrangements.[41]

The crowning ritual was the wedding. At its heart the marriage ceremony was simplicity itself. It involved no more than a man and woman promising before witnesses to live as husband and wife from that point onward. But this was a theme with seemingly endless variations. Wedding ceremonies might be simple to the point of severity. When Stephen Chase and Nancy Bushnell married in Cornwallis Township, Nova Scotia, in 1776 they merely exchanged vows before several friends who had gathered at Chase's home. In this instance even a minister was absent.[42] At the other end of the social spectrum, Fanny Chadwick married James Grayson-Smith at an elaborate society wedding in 1898 before the Bishop of Toronto and scores of guests at St Alban's Cathedral in Toronto, following which the family invited seven hundred guests to a garden party at their home.[43] These two events mark the extremes of wedding festivities in English Canada before the twentieth century.

Unlike England, where Lord Hardwicke's Marriage Act of 1753 had fixed the times and places where lawful marriage might occur, in nineteenth-century Canada weddings were held when and where the bridal couple and their parents wished. The surviving accounts of these ceremonies reveal no clear preference for marriage in the morning, noon, or evening nor one for weddings in a church rather than a private home. An anonymous letter in the Sewell Papers sent to a Miss Quincy at the beginning of the nineteenth century amusingly describes "a most pompeous weding" among the "gentry" in the Lower Canadian countryside. It occured in a private home in the evening and was followed by a dance, after which the guests "thought best to retier and leave the bride and bridesgroom to thear privet medetation."[44] In 1816 Eliza Cottnam told her friend Mrs Boyd of a recent wedding in Windsor, Nova Scotia: "they were married at church, her Aunt, Mrs. Jades, and all his family attending. They dined at his Mother's & came home to their own house in the evening accompanied by the party, where they took cake & wine. They have rooms at the Widow Smiths which are very neatly furnished."[45]

During the late eighteenth and early nineteenth centuries most Canadian weddings were attended only by family members and a few close friends.[46] Regardless of where the wedding occurred, a party given by the family of the bride usually followed the ceremony. On some occasions there were food, drink, and dancing, on others merely a meal or even a few light refreshments. According to Miss Quincy's correspondent, these parties could be quite lively:

for my part I beged to have the gut scraper (fiddle) introduced purely for amusement, the bride an bridegroom opynd the ball with a geg (jig) and each cupple gect (jigged) it affter. As I ded not understang geging it I chose to make one in country dances, tho I must say I was sorrey I could not geg it for by that means I was at loss for a partner was obleged to take one of the chairs for a partner, cast of round a joint stool, and sat to a corner cupbard. We had trumpet mimeuet (,) butterd peas an tolle boys the new way, by which menes I had the missforten to loss the flonce tore from my skirt by a spir on one of the gentlemens boots.[47]

The tendency was for wedding ceremonies and festivities to grow more elaborate over time. When Ward Chipman married Elizabeth Hazan in St John in 1786 only the couple and three close friends attended the ceremony.[48] Even in elite circles small weddings were the norm in pioneer times. In 1808 John Powell (the eldest son of the chief justice of Upper Canada) wed Isabella Shaw (daughter of a colonel in the colony's British forces) in the bride's home with only their families present. After the ceremony the guests celebrated with a supper "and a little hop to the Col's Flute."[49] By the late 1820s we find mention of larger festivities. In 1829, while thinking ahead to her own wedding celebrations, Halli Fraser of Halifax told her fiancé Harry King about a rural double wedding she had attended in Truro.

We went to Church this morning to see the marriage ceremony performed by Bernyette it is the first country wedding I have ever seen it really presented quite a gay appearance the whole village I should think were assembled for there were a great number of persons all dressed in their 'Sunday Clothes' Two sisters married two cousins. The service was only read once. The youngest is quite pretty and very young but fifteen years of age. The bells were rung and several guns fired. I should have thought the brides would have preferred being married more privately but they did not appear to mind it in the least.[50]

Here Halli, the adopted daughter of a senior official in the Nova Scotian government, revealed the preference of her social circle for small, private wedding ceremonies. Two years later, on the eve of their own wedding, she told Harry, "I wrote to Catherine Prescott today. Told her Thursday would probably be the fatal day & requested her to officiate as Brides

Maid if perfectly convenient for her to come down. You know Susan Halliburton was also proposed but Aunt Robie thinks it better not indeed I believe our party will be somewhat diminished & I care not how few are present & I know you are of the same mind. Oh! Harry would it were all over. However I am *determined* to behave well throughout."[51] In 1832 a Brockville correspondent told her brother of a Miss Glasford's recent wedding: "They invited all the village but poor us. Passed by Maria and asked Mary Henderson. Don't you think we should be angry. They had a very splended wedding. 70 persons were there."[52] In 1839 the prominent Lower Canadian government official and businessman, Edward Hale, told his wife about an elaborate family wedding he attended in Quebec City which united a socially prominent couple. Following an evening service attended by many friends, relations, family servants, and spectators from the city, the groom's family held a reception at their home where they served a midnight supper. The affair was rather restrained, however. "The supper was a plain one – no meat – only *the* cake, jellies, blancmange etc., etc, and wine – no one sat down & it was soon over – no dancing. Fred, Buck & Jas. Sewell sang a little & everybody was quite abstemious – in fact little or no wine was drank."[53]

Later in the century, wedding arrangements among the socially prominent became more ostentatious. When Anna Dawson, daughter of McGill president J.W. Dawson, married the physician B.J. Harrington in June of 1876 her parents held the ceremony in their drawing-room, bedecked with seasonal flowers for the occasion. After exchanging their vows the bridal couple and guests sat down to an elaborate wedding breakfast laid in the dining-room and library.[54]

For urban elites, weddings became yet another article of conspicuous consumption as the nineteenth century progressed. Behind this growing display lay the social pretensions and aspirations of parents who advanced their claims to higher social status by dispensing lavish hospitality when their daughters married. Large wedding ceremonies and the ensuing festivities gave parents a chance to display their wealth and standing, to assert their place in the social hierarchy, to mark the end of their formal parental roles in an aura of material success and to locate their children in their own social milieu at the moment when a new family unit was constituted. (We may even see parallels with the west coast Indian potlatch, which celebrated an individual's accession to a new stage of life or new honours through the ritual distribution of food and goods. Here, too, the emphasis of the potlatch lay on winning community assent to claims for a particular status or honour.)

Meanwhile, with fewer reasons and resources to put on such a show, the plain people of English Canada married in much less elaborate

ways. In her journal Catherine Parr Traill described three bush weddings of the 1830s and 1840s, all of them simple affairs.[55] The wedding
of the Reverend William Gregg and his wife in Belleville in 1849 was
a family occasion. The newlyweds took supper with their relations
before leaving for his home across town.[56] Again we may turn to Thomas
Dick, that invaluable observer of Ottawa Valley social life, for a description of a country wedding in the spring of 1867. "I went to Jennie
Fairbirn wedden(.) she was married at her Fathers house(.) there was
not many their(.) I was late to see them married(.) we had tea then
she got ready and went across the river to his Fathers(.) there was no
person went across the river with them but their own friends.[57]

The symbolism of nineteenth-century wedding costume is difficult
to fathom. The surviving descriptions of bridal dress reveal that
although brides preferred white, the custom was far from universal.
When Rebecca Byles married W.J. Almon in 1785 she wore an elaborate
white gown. A century later the custom still prevailed but the rules
were far from fixed.[58] Traill described the marriage of a housemaid in
the 1840s who "was dressed very suitably in a black cotton velvet
bonnet lined with pink cambric and a gay coloured print gown and
shawl."[59] Some twenty years later Louise Bowlby, at sixteen a close
student of such matters, noted in her diary, "Martha showed us her
wedding dress but I would not of had such a dark one. It is very nearly
all black with just a very small purple stripe round it."[60] Apparently
her friend Martha had misgivings as well, for next week she got a white
dress too. But the fact that she seriously considered another colour
reveals that the white wedding was far from universal. Still another
example comes to us from the pen of Anne Richie, an Ontarian who,
in 1874, told her brother of a recent bride who "really looked so nice
in pale gray corded silk."[61]

These exceptions suggest that the twentieth-century association
between bridal white and bridal virginity was not strong before the
turn of the century. This is not to say that brides were not expected
to be chaste – we have plenty of proof that they were – but merely that
bridal costume had different symbolic meanings to those it later held.
The evidence provided by folklore offers some alternative interpreta-
tions. According to one popular saying from late-nineteenth century
Ontario, "if you marry in black, you will be in mourning before the
year is out."[62] Another old rhyme elaborated:

Married in white, you have chosen aright;
Married in gray, you will go far away;

Married in black, you will wish yourself back;
Married in red, you will wish yourself dead;
Married in green, ashamed to be seen;
Married in blue, he (or you?) will always be true;
Married in pearl, you will live in a whirl;
Married in yellow, ashamed of your fellow;
Married in brown, you will live out of town;
Married in pink, your heart will sink.[63]

Like most bits of folklore on marriage, these popular sayings concern luck and the future. Without knowing the depth of conviction beneath them, we can never know how seriously men and women regarded their truths. But they tell us that, if anything, a nineteenth-century bride's wedding dress advertised her hopes for future marital happiness rather than her virtue.

A t the heart of the marriage ritual lay an interplay between its private and public elements. On one hand, a wedding was an intensely private moment, when a man and a woman promised themselves to one another in a lifelong relationship. On the other, they spoke their vows before onlookers who attended the ceremony and later celebrated with the newly wedded pair. In fact, the creation of a new family unit was an important social act. For this reason we should scarcely be surprised to see the community play an active part throughout the wedding festivities. In fact, here we will see the vestiges of older, dying traditions of communal control over marriage.

This public role commenced during the marriage ceremony itself. Guests fulfilled an important function at every wedding, for a valid marriage required witnesses. Thus the irreducible minimum size of a wedding party was four: an official, an observer, and the couple to be wed. The wedding guests also performed another important function. By attending the ceremony they declared their approval of the union, and through them the community also expressed its assent. Those who eloped or wed in secret underscored this fact, for they often did so in order to escape disapproval. One R. Longley, an early Upper Canadian observer, made the point in a letter to her brother in 1833. "There has been a Gretna Green marriage in Brockville. Miss Mary Ann Hall and a Mr. Underwood ran away to Ogdensburg (New York) and got married last week and was back again the night before last. It is not thought a very good match as the young man is wild."[64] In 1858, when James Dunn eloped with Emily Johnson to Cape St Vincent, New York, the couple fled Emily's disapproving father, a lockmaster on the Rideau

Canal, who objected because of her youth.[65]

After the ceremony the public intruded into the private world of newlyweds in other ways. The ancient British tradition of bedding the bridal couple lingered on in parts of rural England during the nineteenth century though it had already vanished from aristrocratic circles.[66] The custom appears to have been uncommon in nineteenth-century Canada[67] but here, too, it persisted in some rural places until the later 1800s. James Gowan described an Irish Protestant bedding in a letter to the wife of his more famous cousin, Ogle, in 1836:

After my mother & Anne & Susan had come down from laying the Bride out & had retired to their own rooms the Bridegroom by his brothers *order* was proceeding with great deliberation to undress in the drawing room and performed the operation with such celerity that he was almost in a state of nudity before my father could stop him. With much solicitation however we got his brother to compromise with him for giving a ball when he went home instead of running the gantlope in his pelt four times up and down the room. This practice may have place in the north of Ireland but I must be just enough to say those of the same class in the East that [sic] are the more civilized.[68]

When J.H. Wooley's friend Kinsley Shaw married Annie Henry at her home in Simcoe County in 1865, Wooley and some other youths waited until the other guests had gone home. "We then had a grand time putting the Bride and Groom to bed and after which we all went into the room and wished them much joy and success the rest of there days and then we retired for bed which was upstairs and there we had a great deal of sport over a young man calling the pigs in his sleep."[69]

We will never know how many couples in nineteenth-century Canada were bedded in this fashion but the custom obviously represented a community intrusion into the most intimate moments of marriage. Alan Macfarlane argues that bedding was almost the only way to verify consummation short of viewing the act itself.[70] But its links with marital sexuality seem much more powerful than Macfarlane suggests. Certainly it expressed the envy, of bachelors in particular, at the privileges now open to the newlyweds. Through their pranks Wooley and his pals gave voice to their sexual jealousy. Equally important, bedding ritually expressed the recognition of friends and family members that the couple was about to commit the final act in their prolonged transition to adult status. Licit sexual relations were the exclusive preserve of married adults. Those who bedded their friends and relations marked the newlyweds' induction into the sexual world of men and women. As they did so they also expressed the lingering claims of community to a place in the most private affairs of the couple. Even the act of first intercourse had to bear some public scrutiny before the married pair forever shut the bedroom door on prying eyes.

The charivari was another social ritual through which the community oversaw marriage. A popular tradition in pre-modern Britain, France, and Germany, it took root in North America during the early years of colonial settlement and persisted well into the twentieth century.[71] Known by many other names – skimmington and rough music in England, katzenmusik in Germany, and shivaree in America – the charivari was a form of popular protest and an instrument of popular justice, a means of enforcing community standards in most societies where it was found. According to E.P. Thompson the custom had many different purposes, some public and some domestic.[72] But remarriage was probably the most common occasion for the charivari in pre-modern Europe, usually when a marriage offended local opinion. Overhasty remarriages, unions based on avarice, and May-December weddings often prompted a charivari.[73]

Bryan Palmer's catalogue of Canadian charivaris lists many which had nothing to do with marriage. Yet weddings gave rise to most shivarees in English Canada and almost always remarriage provided the occasion. Mary Gapper described a typical example soon after she arrived in Upper Canada in 1828. "After the rest of the party were gone to bed, Mama and I were startled by an unusual uproar ruffling the wings of the night. The dogs caught the alarm and added their barking to the sound of horns, guns, and shouting which came from the distance. On inquiring the cause of the uproar, we were told that it was a chivaree. That is a custom, brought from Lower Canada, of assaulting the dwelling of a newly married pair with every species of noisy uproar that can be devised, for the purpose of extorting whiskey."[74]

Susanna Moodie's well-known description fleshes out the picture:

The charivari is a custom that the Canadians got from the French, in the Lower Province, and a queer custom it is. When an old man marries a young wife, or an old woman a young husband, or two old people, who ought to be thinking of their graves, enter for the second or third time into the holy estate of wedlock, as the priest calls it, all the idle young fellows in the neighbourhood meet together to charivari them. For this purpose they disguise themselves, blackening their faces, putting their clothes on hind part before, and wearing horrible masks, with grotesque caps on their heads, adorned with cocks' feathers and bells. They then form in a regular body, and proceed to the bridegroom's house, to the sound of tin kettles, horns and drums, cracked fiddles, and all the discordant instruments they can collect together. Thus equipped, they surround the house where the wedding is held, just at the hour when the happy couple are supposed to be about to retire to rest – beating upon the door with clubs and staves, and demanding of the bridegroom admittance to drink the bride's health, or in lieu thereof to receive a certain sum of money to treat the band at the nearest tavern.[75]

William Bell, a Scottish-born Presbyterian minister in Perth, Upper Canada, recorded a charivari in his journal for March 1845.

Mr. McEachson having brought home a new wife, a charivari, of a very noisy description took place in the evening. And as the bridegroom did not immediately comply with the demands of the mob, they became very riotous, and broke in his front door, so that he was at last obliged to apply to the magistrates for protection, tho' he had, an hour before, declined their interference. I told some of the authorities next day that they ought to put down these riotous proceedings at once, or they would soon lead to serious consequences, as they had done elsewhere. They are of French origin, and are often practised in the Lower Province, only in the case of widows and widowers marrying. Horns, bells, kettles, or anything that will make noise, soon collect a mob. A coffin is carried to the door, containing one of the party, dressed so as to represent the ghost of the deceased wife or husband. The coffin is opened, the ghost walks into the house, and makes certain demands of money, which must be complied with, or mischief follows. The attendants meanwhile in all kinds of fantastic dresses and masks, or having their faces painted, are singing, dancing, making speeches, or cracking jokes.[76]

While effigies of the deceased spouse seldom cropped up in new world charivaris, their presence here underscores the close ties between the shivaree and remarriage. The victims of a charivari often resisted its threats and demands. In 1802 Ely Playter joined a "Shiverie" in York; the couple held out for three nights until the magistrates suppressed it.[77] Palmer notes another which besieged an elderly Montreal widower and his new bride for ten days to two weeks in the spring of 1823.[78] Occasionally resistance was violent. Moodie and Bell both mention incidents in which bridegrooms shot and killed one or more of their assailants.[79] But others welcomed, or at least tolerated, a charivari. In 1834, when John Dawson married his fifth wife in Kingston, he sent his wife away and, when the revellers came to call, entertained them very well.[80] Three years later some Kingston youths charivaried a recently remarried widow; she capitulated on the second night and donated £25 for the local House of Industry.[81]

During the second half of the nineteenth century the custom lost most of its traditional character. In eastern Ontario and the Maritimes, where the charivari persisted longest, it often became little more than an occasion for malicious pranks. Some two months after John McGuire of Kingston Mills remarried in 1867, a group of local men paid the couple an evening call and demanded $5 to drink the newlyweds' health.[82] When McGuire refused, they broke several windows in his house. In 1888, the day after Maurice and Dora Harlow married in Queen's County, Nova Scotia, they returned home, "put up the blinds and got a lunch of what we brought with us and thus our new home was begun. In the evening was treated to a most disgraceful Charivari by Geo. Parker, James McBain, Lem Harlow, Jamie Daily, Harry Christopher & Cleary Harlow. They crawled through the bedroom window, took possession of the sitting room and played dice for an hour. They also did foolish tricks and damage outside."[83] On a summer's eve in Kingston in 1894 local boys assailed a recently married elderly couple, breaking their windows, pelting the groom with rotten eggs and filling their well with cordwood.[84]

But not all charivaris degenerated to this level. The folklorist Helen Creighton discovered many less destructive variations of the custom still surviving in early and mid twentieth-century Nova Scotia. These events preserved elements of the tradition but little of its substance. Usually friends and neighbours serenaded the newlyweds on their wedding night or on their return from their honeymoon. In many communities the crowd paraded into the couple's yard carrying a barrel on fire, shouting, shooting guns, beating pans, ringing cow bells, and blowing horns. In some places the bride and groom were the victims of other pranks too. The couple then had to show themselves and treat the serenaders to food and drink.[85]

The broader meaning of these incidents is far from clear, in their Canadian context at least. Natalie Davis has argued that charivaris against second marriages in early modern France occurred when the young and unmarried saw remarriage as a threat to their limited marriage opportunities.[86] But marriage chances in nineteenth-century Canada were never restricted in the way that those of pre-modern Europe so often were; greater economic opportunity and high population mobility saw to that. Thus these new world charivaris cannot be seen as bachelors' attempts to control the marriage market. Nor were they the inevitable consequence when a wedding offended community opinion. For example, the Nova Scotian diarist Simeon Perkins noted two scandalous marriages in the early nineteenth century, both of which occasioned nothing more than gossip.[87]

Bryan Palmer argues that charivaris were an instrument of social regulation through which "the lower orders turned instinctively to custom, posing the discipline of the community against the perceived deficiencies of legal authority."[88] But in an age when high adult mortality made remarriage common if not almost necessary, by itself a second marriage could scarcely be considered a "domestic impropriety"[89] grave enough to warrant community censure. Nor did charivaris express class tensions, at least if Palmer's assertion that the custom was largely plebian is correct.[90] Whatever its origins in early modern European traditions of popular justice, the marriage charivari was not an instrument of social discipline in nineteenth-century English Canada.

More than anything else, the nineteenth-century charivari resembled the modern Hallowe'en: a custom entitling the young to treats and fun at the expense of others. In this case the youths were older, the treats were stronger, and the fun more violent; but the tradition of entitlement was similar. The customary right claimed in the charivari was that of hazing remarried couples and, like many forms of hazing, it marked a change in status. In doing so it punished, perhaps humiliated, and usually exacted concessions from those at whom it was directed. The participants themselves merely followed a custom which gave young men a chance to wring a donation and some discomfort from those whom tradition held hostage to their demands.

The wedding trip and the honeymoon conclude this long list of marriage rituals, one a public and ceremonial act, the other a private retreat. The custom of travelling after a wedding took root in English Canada early in the nineteenth century. Originally a luxury accessible only to the privileged, the practice diffused throughout colonial society with passing time. One early example comes to us from the Upper Canadian elite. Samuel P. Jarvis and Mary Boyles Powell, both from prominent office-holding families, took a leisurely wedding journey from York to their new home in Queenston after they married in October 1818. On their way they stopped for two or three days with his sister in Burlington, who had not been able to attend the ceremony.[91]

By the 1830s the bridal tour of the privileged classes had become more extensive. The Presbyterian minister Mark Young Stark of Ancaster described the wedding trip he and his bride Agatha Street took after they married in July of 1835: "after the ceremony and déjuné we started about 12 o'clock for Hamilton in Mr. Stevens Carriage to take the Steam boat for Toronto ... From Toronto we went next day to the Falls visiting some friends there & then crossed the Frontier to Buffalo. from thence by the Erie Canal through Lockport to Rochester where we remained 3 days and then crossed the lake to Toronto where we remained a few days & returned home on Friday last having enjoyed our excursion exceedingly but still exceedingly happy to find ourselves at home in our own little cottage."[92] In 1841 the Anglican clergyman and historian Henry Scadding and his new bride went to Hamilton,

Niagara Falls, and Buffalo after their marriage.[93] On their travels the Scaddings combined sightseeing and visits with friends. By the later nineteenth century wealthy Anglo-Canadians often took long, elaborate honeymoons. When Robert Fleming, son of the distinguished engineer and businessman Sandford Fleming, married in 1891 he and his wife travelled to Montreal, Boston, and New York, where they embarked for England, France, and Italy.[94]

Lower down the social scale, wedding trips were more modest affairs. The custom of travelling after marriage did not penetrate very deeply into Canadian society until the second half of the century, when the growth of railways made travel more easy and less expensive. Because most people had neither the time nor the money for long vacations, they usually took short wedding trips to nearby places when they took them at all. After George Jarvis and Annie McIntire of Glengarry County married in 1865 they enjoyed a brief holiday in Ottawa.[95] When James Gibson and Maggie Grant (from the Cornwall area) married in 1867 the newlyweds spent three days in Montreal.[96] (Curiously, Canadians never demonstrated the passion for a wedding trip to Niagara Falls so characteristic of the American honeymoon.[97] While some newlyweds included the Falls on their itinerary, most seem to have travelled somewhere else.) Others could not afford the time or money for a wedding trip. When W.R. Coleman, an Ontario farmer, married in 1869 he went straight home from his wedding to attend a sick colt.[98] A decade later, one of Toronto prison guard Gilbert Hartley's work mates married on a public holiday in August and was on the job at 5:30 the next morning.[99]

Like the destinations, the functions of travel after marriage changed dramatically during the nineteenth century. At first, in Canada as in Britain and the United States, couples did not remove themselves from society on their wedding journeys.[100] Like the Samuel Jarvises, the Starks, and the Scaddings, they visited friends and relations and often travelled with them too. When W.H. Merritt Jr took his new bride to England in 1853 another couple joined them on the transatlantic crossing.[101] Even late in the century, the wedding trip might be as much a convivial as a private occasion. In 1880, when the Toronto Presbyterian minister Alex Stewart and his wife Bessie spent their honeymoon in Halifax, they passed much of their time with family and friends.[102] The traditional bridal tour served an important social purpose. It re-established the links between a newly married couple, who had just severed some of their previous individual ties to family and friends, and the enlarged circle of their joint friendships and relations. Marriage created a new social unit – the couple – with a new social position – adult members of society. Couples used the bridal tour to place themselves in their social worlds as mature members of their families and their communities.

But after mid-century the wedding trip was gradually transformed into the honeymoon. Post-nuptial travel ceased to be a family affair as bridal couples increasingly set themselves apart from their friends and relations. When Anna Dawson married B.J. Harrington in 1876 the couple vacationed at a small resort near Lake Champlain where they knew no one else and could devote themselves exclusively to one another.[103] Once again the new custom of the honeymoon trickled down from its origins in privileged circles to the general populace. By the end of the nineteenth century the honeymoon had become a private idyll for all newly married couples, whatever their social status.

The older wedding tour contrasted sharply with the modern honeymoon. The former created new bonds between the couple and their kinsmen and neighbours; the latter separated the couple from their friends and relatives for an interlude of deepening emotional and erotic discovery. One underscored the powerful social basis of marriage; the other emphasized personal fulfilment as the great goal of married life.

Finally, three general points about marriage rituals in nineteenth-century English Canada. First, while public and private interests inevitably contended with one another on the occasion of marriage – the community seeking a role in regulating the marriage process, the bride and groom struggling to preserve as much privacy as possible – the couple gained the upper hand as the century progressed. Despite the rise of the large wedding among urban elites toward the end of the century, friends and relatives played a diminishing role in marriage rituals over time. The disappearance of bedding the bridal couple, the decay and transformation of the charivari, and the slow demise of the family-centred wedding trip all point to this change. So does the rise of the honeymoon, which excluded all others from the newlyweds' intimate world. Ritualistic forms of customary social sanctions had never exerted the same powerful influence in English Canada which they possessed in some parts of Britain and western Europe well into the nineteenth century. And in their weakened form they soon lost their shaping force in British North America. By the end of the century English-Canadian men and women married free from most popular forms of traditional community influence save the formal requirements needed to make a marriage valid. New rituals replaced old, the new customs based much more on the growing privacy of young love and the diminished influence of the family over the conduct of its members.

In Canada, too, we see the growing isolation of the nuclear family, and the increasing autonomy of young adults, which characterized so much of the nineteenth-century transatlantic world.

Secondly, many years ago the sociologist Arnold van Gennep observed that marriage rituals embody the processes of separation and reunification: separation in the severance of ties which bind the bride and the groom to their respective parents, reunification in the creation of a new family unit and its incorporation into the community of adults.[104] The marriage practices of nineteenth-century English Canada, while less and less distinguished by traditional customs with passing time, were ripe with the symbolism of both separation and reunification. The gift of the bride by her father during the wedding ceremony was an act of separation, the traditional wedding journey to visit family and friends was one of reunification. So, too, was the party which often followed the marriage ceremony. Still another example, the twentieth-century charivari, required the new couple to offer food and drink to the noisy band which intruded on the newlyweds' privacy. The bride and groom's hospitality symbolized their acceptance of and entry into adult roles in their community. In urban society, post-nuptial social calls and parties fulfilled the same function.

The custom of appearing in church on the Sunday following a bridal couple's wedding (or, later, their return from their honeymoon) was yet another reunification ritual common throughout the century. Around the turn of the nineteenth century, Simeon Perkins, that careful observer of social practice in colonial Nova Scotia, noted the occasions when new couples appeared at his Methodist meeting on the Sunday after their marriage.[105] Some eighty years later the Ontario farmer Johnston Paterson recorded in his diary that he and his bride received many greetings when they attended church on the Sunday after their wedding.[106] The folklore evidence from Lunenburg, Nova Scotia, suggests that the couple was not only expected to appear in church but to make a grand entrance as well.[107] In these instances, too, members of the community affirmed the new status of the recently married pair and drew the couple into their midst. Yet like the others we have noted, these old customs formed part of that vanishing world of marriage ritual in which the community laid claim to formal influence over marriage. That claim grew ever more tenuous over the years. With passing time the newly married were separated from their families and friends ever more completely, and reunified ever more informally. By the end of the nineteenth century the marriage ritual had dwindled to an irreducible minimum of customary acts: the wedding ceremony, its subsequent celebrations, and possibly a honeymoon.

Lastly, the older, often borrowed, rituals of romance persisted longest in small-town and rural English Canada, the peripheral areas of eastern Ontario, and the Maritimes. They endured longest here because these were small and relatively isolated places, where face-to-face relations governed the everyday social interaction of most community members. But these customs could not take root in places where larger populations and high rates of mobility preserved much greater anonymity. There the integration of the newlywed did not rest upon the same acceptance from members of the public. Those who married and settled in urbanizing Canada joined the community of adults through unspoken compacts which they made with their neighbours. They simply offered themselves as a newly formed couple and the community accepted them as such. They, too, had passed through a rite of passage, but it was a family and personal affair. Like so much else in the history of love, the rituals of romance in nineteenth-century Canada grew more private with passing time.

CHAPTER SIX

Families, Friends, and Property

When George courted Honorine in the mid-1840s their families took an active part in their romantic affairs. The two lovers called at each other's homes, they strolled about the city with their brothers and sisters, they attended plays and parties in the company of their relations. In fact they passed most of their moments together within a family setting. Honorine's parents closely supervised her budding romance – to the point of taking sides about George as a possible husband for their daughter. While Honorine's mother supported George, her father had another candidate for fair Honorine's hand; the senior Tanswells also consulted their older married daughter about the matter. And when they agreed that the match was not to be, their decision drove a formidable wedge between the two young lovers.

The story of George and Honorine is the stuff of Victorian fiction, all the more compelling because the tale is true. But far more important to us, this little history offers a glimpse of the power of family members in affairs of the heart. In early and mid nineteenth-century English Canada the families and friends of courting pairs played important roles in courtship and marriage. Marriage and its preliminaries altered the relationships between couples and their parents, their relatives and their acquaintances. In forming the nucleus of a new family, a man and woman discarded the role and status of unmarried persons (which implied impermanence and some measure of immaturity) and assumed the full standing of adults. Marriage also involved important considerations about property. Newlyweds required assets with which to begin married life, and families and friends often contributed to these marriage funds. Thus, because the private drama of matrimony was full of significance for the family as well as society, parents assumed a role in every scene of the tableau. Meanwhile relatives and friends hovered in the wings and the prompter's box, ready to step on stage or whisper advice whenever the moment seemed right.

When it came to encouraging a match parents could only be covert and subtle. Since the young took the lead in pairing off, their elders had little to do but set the stage for a favourable outcome, offer assistance by stealth, and hope for the best. Presumably this was what Colonel Joseph Pernette was up to when he sent a gift of ducks and squirrels to Charles Morris, the surveyor-general of Nova Scotia, late in August 1786; six weeks later Pernette's daughter Charlotte became engaged to Charles Jr.[1]

The countless house parties, at homes, dinners, and other social events organized by families of most social backgrounds could serve the same ends, especially if a marriageable daughter were in residence. The advice Marianne Howard of Milton gave to her brother Lewis Wall-bridge, twenty-one in 1838 and from a prominent Belleville family, reveals a glimpse of the process in genteel early Victorian circles. Marianne, a married woman and presumably an old hand at the game, prepared young Lewis for the social scene in Toronto where he had gone to article at law.

The city is so full of officers too, that you should not expect as much attention as at ordinary times you have been accustomed to receive, angling mammas have as much as they can do to fish for husbands for their daughters and you know you are not quite out of your time, and not quite old enough, to be an object of speculation yet amongst them it must be quite a harvest with them now that there are so many military there, but wait patiently until you are *established* and doing well for yourself in the world and you will soon see yourself invited everywhere and most graciously smiled upon, think of John Powell, how he has courted Henry Meyers for his sister Mary, and think of Benson's mean beginning, and keep your courage up.[2]

Sisterly counsel was in vain, however, for Lewis never married.

Another example of maternal encouragement comes to us from the later nineteenth century, in this case a young female correspondent of Jeanie Fleming (wife of Sandford, the civil engineer). "I met Mr. Hutch-ison last night at church," she told her friend, "and sat beside him after I was introduced to him and he walked home with me. Mamma asked him to come up often."[3] Usually, however, these parental strategies were either so artful that only the *cognoscenti* could recognize them, or so common that few bothered to note their existence. Whatever the reason, most signs of them have long since vanished from view.

Parents' attempts to frustrate courtship were quite another matter. George and Honorine, whose hopes were thwarted as we've seen, were only one of many couples whose parents opposed their courting. An early example comes to us from York, where Ely Playter pursued Sophia Beman soon after the turn of the nineteenth century. A publican and farmer in his mid-twenties, Playter began keeping company with Sophia, whose widowed father kept a shop, in the spring of 1802. Sometimes with friends, sometimes alone, he called at her home at tea time and sat up late with her in the evenings. Sophia welcomed his attentions. As he once noted rather obliquely, "I staid till late with the Lady learning more from This behaviour than I ever had before."[4]

But as spring passed into summer and his visits continued, Ely sensed that Sophia's father was growing cool toward him and this made Ely anxious. In July he told his diary, "some occurrences that had taken place in the afternoon while I was with Miss B. appeared to me again in my dreams in the night with a portended lecture that I expected from Mr. Beman." The admonition he feared came a few weeks later in a letter. Ely withdrew some distance, having "made Mr. Beman a promise not to give him further room for his jealousy." A week after the paternal rebuke, however, not having seen Sophia in the interval, he called on her again and found her low-spirited. He soon left but returned just after dark when he saw the senior Beman ride out. Ely and Sophia took tea and sang with other friends and, when later left alone, talked until her father returned. According to Ely, "I had wished an opportunity to explain to her the reason of my shiness and this was a proper one. I found her not ignorant in the case. Her father had told her what had passed between him & me. I gave her the most friendly advice I was capable upon such an occasion, found her feelings hurt and was comforting her with the prospects of more pleasing times when her father came. As he entered one door I came out the other, returned home and went to bed."[5] Three days later he was back at Sophia's as soon as her father went out, only to leave again just as Beman returned. From that point on Ely's calls grew much less frequent and he stopped sitting up with her. In the short run her father had succeeded in cooling their romance. Yet young love triumphed in the end, for the two eventually married.

Another example of parents interfering in their children's courtship, and young people's resistance to family meddling, comes to us from the mid-1860s. Jim Hall, son of a prominent Peterborough family, was seeing a local woman against his family's wishes. In the words of his sister Lily,

Jim is going on just the same only more attentive if possible. We never see him after 3 o'clock until breakfast time. He never gets home till 12 o'clock or perhaps later. We are all asleep generally. Papa is in great distress. He told Jim he did not like the girl & never could & that he (Jim) was making a fool of himself taking Clowston's castoffs. Mrs. Gilbert spent 3 hours. She said she heard we did not like it so she came to tell Mamma that it was their own doings. She had nothing at all to do with it but she would forbid Jim the house if Papa & Mamma did not give their consent. She was told that it had never been asked & that they did not think Miss G. at all suited for Jim. All they had seen of her had not been in her favour but quite the contrary but that perhaps if they knew her better they would not have such a bad opinion of her. Last night crowded all. There was no service in one church so all of us young people went to English. When lo and behold there sat Jim & the two Gilbert girls in a pew by themselves & their mother in one across the church. When it was accidentally spoken of before Papa he got in a fury & said it was just like Jim. No other girl will do. Such a thing. I even made Bingham [Higginson, her sister Martha's suitor] go into his own seat altho we were with a large party & he had been here all day.[6]

Here we find not only intergenerational conflict over courtship but also clear signs of collusion between parents to defeat their offspring's designs. Unfortunately Lily tells us no more and we do not know who prevailed in the end.

While nineteenth-century parents supervised their adolescent children, they commonly watched their daughters' courtships more closely than their sons'. In 1851 the civil engineer Walter Shanley, aged thirty-four, then boarding with a family in Prescott, Ontario, enjoyed sitting up until 2 a.m. with two of his landlord's young daughters. "Their father watches them very closely," he complained to his brother Frank, "& sometimes orders them rudely off to bed." He continued, "those Sisters in Law of Gilmans are really fine girls but so 'severely proper' you can scarcely approach them ... Mrs. Gilman, who is as fine looking a woman as I ever saw, keeps strict watch & ward over them – & it is not easy even to see them."[7]

Shanley being an older man and something of a roué, in this case parental caution was more protective than anything else. But supervision could express possessive instincts as well, as in the case of William Munro and Georgina Johnstone. William was a Scottish school teacher who emigrated to Canada in 1857. Some time before leaving home he had come to an understanding with his Irish cousin Georgina, then still in her mid-teens. They corresponded regularly until Georgina emigrated too, along with her mother, sister, and brother, and from then until they wed in 1862, Mrs Johnstone exerted a powerful influence on her daughter, to the point of reading her mail until she was twenty-one.[8] While acknowledging William as Georgina's betrothed, she also treated her grown daughter as a child, angrily calling her to bed when Georgina wished to stay up and write. In the end William and Georgina married in secret to escape her mother's tentacles. Mamma, so it seems, did not wish to see her daughter grow up.

From this brief overview we can see that parents had a small arsenal of powers at their disposal to discipline courting conduct, that of their daughters in particular. Among the most common were surveillance of social activities, the withdrawal of hospitality, and criticism or rebuke. These powers were reinforced by religious precept, by social custom and, ultimately, by the law. They were powers with clear limits, however. Like most forms of parental authority, their effectiveness depended on the willingness of the young to accept regulation. But young adults sometimes resisted their parents' authority when it weighed too heavily on them, and also when they had enough financial and social independence to allow them to push back.

Thus, as young women gained more freedoms toward the end of the nineteenth century, parental control over courtship began to weaken. Greater mobility and financial autonomy allowed them and their suitors to escape from home and elude the eyes of an older generation. In 1880 the twenty-one-year-old Elizabeth Smith, daughter of a prosperous farm family in south-western Ontario, had a well-developed sense of female propriety in these matters. The young feminist lamented to her diary, "I see around me girls making themselves cheap who act speak think things no true virtuous sensible girl should. They are all agreed on one thing – to be bold & hoydenish as concerns the opposite sex – to attract their notice – no matter at what cost – no matter that they make the first advances – No matter that they sacrifice dignity & respect so long as they gain the attention of even one milksop, they are not unhappy."[9] From the time Smith left home at the age of eighteen, however, she too moved freely in youthful social circles, well beyond the reach of her parents' supervision. When she met her future husband, Adam Shortt, in the early 1880s she did so in the less restrictive confines of a boarding house. Still, not all girls living away from home had the freedom enjoyed by the independent-minded Miss Smith. Almost thirty years later Kathleen Cowan, seventeen and staying in the women's residence at Victoria College in Toronto, wrote to her father, a Napanee doctor, for permission when a young man invited her to a concert. Father consented, but when Kathleen's admirer persisted, he told the residence dean to forbid his daughter to accompany the young man again.[10]

In most instances the young no doubt adopted the perspective of their elders, internalizing the standards and expectations of those with more experience in courtship. Lois Bigelow, a seventeen-year-old Nova Scotia schoolgirl, provided a graphic example when repulsing an ardent suitor in 1878. "I suppose you think strangely of my long silence, but reely your last letters rather startled me – in fact I am hardly yet over the shock. You should be more careful in writing. We are too young to talk about such matters. What would the Old folks say – that we were both crazy of course. Now let us be sensible and not go beyond our years. I believe in friendship. I look upon you as a sincere friend and wish you to think of me as such and nothing more. You will change your mind several times before you find your real affinity."[11]

If parents offered little but counsel and supervision in courtship, they could play a much more direct role in betrothal. The senior Tanswells refused Honorine permission to marry George and their opposition frustrated the young lovers' hopes. Normally a couple's relatives had much at stake in their betrothal. It anticipated the creation of a new household, a task which usually involved the support – including financial – of parents and other relations. For these reasons fathers and mothers, brothers and sisters, grandfathers and grandmothers, aunts and uncles, and sometimes even close friends, could become deeply enmeshed in a couple's decision to wed.

The first question a newly plighted couple likely would ask is what would their parents say? Would the old folks bless the union or would they set their backs against it? Throughout most of the nineteenth century this question had dramatically different meanings for men than women. When deciding whom and when to marry, men were far less constrained than women by the views of family members. Those whose parents lived on the other side of the Atlantic had an easy time of it. They could act as they wished and present their parents with a *fait accompli*. In 1797, when the twenty-one-year-old Quebec journalist John Neilson, a Scottish Presbyterian, took a French-Canadian Catholic wife, he sent a lengthy justification to his mother.

Since I wrote you last I married a Maria Hubert a young *Canadienne* of Three Rivers. She proves to me a tender and loving wife and I have no doubt will be a cause of my settling assiduously to Business and Shop. With the help of God I shall continue to gain in this country an honest livelihood for myself and Family. It will perhaps be a matter of astonishment to you that I should marry a person of a different nation and religion. I shall give you my reasons. Joined with the most tender esteem for the young woman I considered that I was fixed for life in Canada and where could be the harm in uniting with one of its natives by the most tender ties? I thought that it would be to reducing that monstrous prejudice between the Natives and the Europeans which is so hurtful to their respective interests and even dangerous to their safety. I found that I did not want precedent even some of the most respectable characters in the Country. It is true I consulted no one! and where could be the propriety of consulting others in such a case? Indeed a sound examination of such affairs in ones own mind at all times has proved most serviceable. However dear Mother should you find my arguments unfounded I must be subject to your censure and shall only hope that the future will justify the present.[12]

This letter is quite instructive. Neilson obviously was aware that men contemplating marriage often took counsel from others. But he had lived apart from his mother from the age of fourteen and had just assumed direction of a newspaper inherited from his brother. Obviously he considered himself his own man in most matters regardless of his youth.

Similarly, in 1835 the thirty-five-year-old Presbyterian minister Mark Young Stark of Ancaster, Upper Canada, informed his mother in Glasgow that he was about to marry, described his intended bride, and anticipated his mother's blessing.[13] Ten years later John Langton, whose long search for a wife we have already noted, announced his engagement to Lydia Dunsford in a letter to his father – though at the age of thirty-seven he could scarcely be expected to ask his father's permission![14]

Men much closer to home acted in similar fashion. Harry King, of Windsor, Nova Scotia, sought his father's approval to marry Halli Fraser in 1831. But he did so only after he and Halli had committed themselves to one another, and largely because an unpleasant family episode had suggested this as the best means of drawing his wife-to-be into the King family. As Harry told Halli soon after he had spoken to his father,

I have often said to you I wished my father and mother to be with us at the wedding and indeed I should have been very sorry if there had been the least objection – because without the sanction of my father I should almost feel, it were not an act of prudence. All that is removed by his affectionate conversation of today and his ready acquiescence in my wishes. I assure you Dear Halli My brothers marriage has turned out any thing but gratifying to my father & indeed the family. You will know more of it hereafter and my Dad has often expressed to me his hope that You would not estrange Yourself from his house and affections as Otis wife has done – to this I have always taken the liberty of freely using Your own authority for saying Your desire was to be one of the family not as my wife only, but as his daughter – and this has always been received by him from me as a healing balm to the wounds inflicted by Otis' wife's neglect.[15]

King would have married without paternal approval, but he much preferred to have it and avoid a family rupture.

Many men requested their parents' approval for their wedding plans in a much more perfunctory way. When J.C. Simpson took a wife in

Montreal in 1867 he informed his father in Penetanguishine only after the fact, leaving the senior Simpson little to do but offer congratulations.[16] This pattern of male autonomy persisted throughout the nineteenth century and on into the twentieth. In 1894 E.W. Jarvis, a member of the Maritime branch of the family, wrote from Toronto to his father in St John that he had just proposed to a young woman.[17] Like Neilson, Stark, Langton, and Simpson, he was merely passing on some important information to a loved and respected parent.

Yet not all men could marry without their parents' consent, Trevor Humphreys of Quebec, for example. This son of an English gentry family became engaged to Fanny Sewell, daughter of the Lower Canadian chief justice, in 1837. In a glowing letter to his parents he praised his love's perfection and appealed for permission to marry her.

Nothing now remains but your sanction to this most important of subjects and as it most materially concerns my future happiness in this world I hope and trust That you will not hesitate to take it into your most earnest consideration. Perhaps you may imagine that this is an attachment that I might easily overcome from my youth and that I am full young to enter the Married State. But Believe me I now feel as a man can but once feel during his existence ... I need scarcely say more than this. On this then dear Parents depends my happiness or everlasting Misery Therefore Trusting your speedy reply and hoping that you will see no objection to Miss F Sewell becoming the Wife of you[r] devoted Son.[18]

Similarly in 1846 William Kirby, then a tanner and later a celebrated author, consulted his parents about his impending marriage at the age of twenty-nine.[19]

Occasionally men also had to reckon with other authorities when making their marriage arrangements. Junior military officers might consult their superiors, or at least ask their approval, when planning to wed. "It is more than probable that ere I shall receive an answer from you...I shall be a married man," Lieutenant F. Baddely of Quebec wrote to General Sir W.H. Clinton in 1822. "I must repeat how *very gratifying* it would be to receive a letter in return, *particularly* if it should convey an *approval* of the step I have taken. The Lady in question has no fortune or at least very little (this I am afraid you will not approve) but good management in a cheap country and 300 a year (a little less than my present income) will do much."[20]

Men of the ranks required their commanding officer's consent to marry, at least if their brides were to receive the benefits given a military spouse. In 1868 Colonel F.G. Hibbert of Fort Henry near Kingston told the local Roman Catholic bishop that he could not officially sanction

Private White's marriage. "I find that there are 22 applicants for permission to marry registered before White & consequently entitled to the indulgence before it can be extended to him. At the same time, in the event of this man's marrying now his wife shall be brought on the strength of the regiment in her regular turn − when the 22 already alluded to are provided for."[21]

Student clergymen might also arouse objections if they intended to wed. "In regard to Mr. Arthurton," the Anglican Bishop Strachan told the Archdeacon of York in 1847, "I do not approve of his marrying while a student. In fact it is highly detrimental to young men who are coming forward to the Church to marry early. It brings them into difficulty in their pecuniary affairs & their exertions are clogged by the claims of Family. I shall be compelled to take some very stringent measures in this matter not only to prevent great misery to individuals but also to secure the Church against [illegible]."[22]

What divided men who sought permission to marry from men who did not was largely a matter of dependence. Those who were economically and emotionally independent made their own marriage decisions; those who were not did not. The former might consult their parents and family out of affection, loyalty, or simple courtesy, but not out of need. The latter required financial or moral support before they wed and, therefore, permission from those whom they asked for aid. The evidence suggests that most men took a wife with nothing more than their parents' blessing. They neither requested nor received permission to wed. The only clear rule was that the younger the man the more likely the possibility that he could not support a wife. Until they considered themselves established, most men probably gave marriage very little serious thought. Those few that did had to ask for the privilege.

Women, by contrast, seldom married without paternal consent, at least until the latter part of the nineteenth century. One reason was that they often felt a far greater sense of obligation to their families than men commonly did. The backwoods gentlewoman Mary Gapper offers a striking example. In 1830, when Edward O'Brien asked her to marry him, she demurred for months. What troubled her was her earlier promise to return to England and help with the education of her sister Lucy's children. In the end Mary chose marriage, but only after her mother had urged her and Lucy had released her from her promise of aid.[23]

The bonds of dependence must often have reinforced this feminine sense of duty. At a time when many women could not support themselves financially, female material ties to families usually were strong. The emotional sinews of family life were another consideration, though these are very difficult for the historian to explore. As well, religious teachings reinforced a sense of filial duty. For all of these reasons, when women wished to marry they often felt an acute sense of obligation to their relations. In turn, this sharpened the significance of parental permission to wed.

A young man's request to his loved one's parents for consent to marry their daughter was a fixed rite in the process of winning a bride. Almost invariably, by the time a suitor spoke to his intended's father or mother the couple had agreed to marry. There were exceptions, of course. When John Ross, a recently widowed thirty-two-year-old lawyer from Belleville, sought to court Eliza Baldwin, he first wrote to her father, Robert, for permission. After a few emotional misgivings the old politician handed Eliza the letter and resigned himself to her decision.[24] But this incident was highly unusual. A generation earlier, when a local doctor first approached William Bell, the Presbyterian minister in Perth, for permission to court his only daughter Isabella, Bell told him to speak to Isabella himself. The doctor did and she refused him.[25] Like most fathers, Bell expected his children to make their own marriage arrangements.

Still, until the 1880s few women would even consider marrying without their parents' approval. Sophia Sherwood, the twenty-five-year-old daughter of Justis Sherwood of Augusta Township in eastern Upper Canada, informed her insistent suitor Jonathan Jones in 1810,

At your requist dear Jonathan again I resume my pen. I did think I had relinquished it untill with a parents consent I cou'd say "Sophia will 'be Yours' till death 'takes her' from you" But alas, I know not when that time will arrive and untill it dose I very much fear I am acting wrong to encourage a hope that may never be realized. my resolution is fixed as fate. never will I change my name without the approbation of my mama. why dear Jones will you compell me to repeat this so often. was you realy in earnest when you made the requist which your last letter contains. cou'd you for a moment amagine me so inconsiderate as to consent to a proposal which must enevitably involve you in difficulties. you think you wou'd be happy ah! my frind when novelty was no more when cold reality came. in place of your expected felicity would be indifference. when struggling with an unfeeling world to gain a competancy with a partner who however willing wou'd be little able to assist, you. ah! then wou'd your eye never glance reproachfully on her, wou'd you never reflect but for her you wou'd be free and happy "Gracious" Heavens at the very Idear what horrid images rise in my amagination

Alas! my friend what a picture of happiness have I drawn and yet as little as I have seen of human life, how many examples asure me that it is a true one

You must not again asks for what it is not provided for me to grant wait my love 'till two or three more summers suns have seen there course, and then (on one condition) your patience shall be rewarded. at least if receiving a heart that never beat for any but you can be call'd a reward.[26]

Perhaps Sophia felt herself pressed harder than most women in similar circumstances, but her resolve was almost the universal opinion of her sex.

In the normal course of events the suitor himself requested the hand of his beloved. He called on or wrote to her father or, if he were dead, her mother to ask for her hand. The stilted letter Alfred Nash of Brome County in the Eastern Townships sent to Samuel Willard in 1818 is representative. "I am very sorry that your business called you from Home at the present time, as I was very anxious to see you upon business that is of the first moment to me," Nash told Willard. "As it may be some time before I can have an opportunity of seeing you I have taken the liberty of presenting my request to you by letter which is to gain your approbation of my attachment to your *Daughter Lucinda* if it should be agreeable to you. I have obtained your Daughter's leave to make this request and should it meet with your approbation I would thank you to write me the first convenient opportunity as it will relieve me from much anxiety."[27]

The examples multiply. When Vernon Smith, a civil engineer, became engaged to a woman in Woodstock, N.S. in 1853, his fiancée's father learned of their plans before Smith had spoken to him. Smith found his duty a difficult task. "After breakfast I mentioned to him about Elizabeth, it was a desperately awkward piece of business, but I was not so embarrassed as I expected to be, and he gave her to me without much hesitation."[28] Louisa Ridout's suitor faced the same ordeal in 1874. "Green came to see Mamma this afternoon & made known his intentions of marrying Louisa," her younger sister Laura recorded laconically in her diary. "Green spent the evening & clinched the bargain[.] Gussie [another sister] & myself of course retired early to bed. I hope he will not come too often as we are deprived of Drawingroom."[29]

A woman's parents normally gave a man their permission to marry their daughter when they believed that the couple loved one another, that the suitor was honourable, and that he could support a wife. "You have my consent and approbation in your intended connection with my daughter," Gideon White, a sea captain from Shelburne, Nova Scotia, told William Davis in May 1807. "Her mother most fully joins me in her assent believing as I do a mutual affection subsists."[30] The Whites and the Davises were old family friends. When a second suitor spoke to Reverend William Bell of Perth for Isabella's hand in 1835, Bell accepted his daughter's choice despite some misgivings – the young man was a lawyer. In this respect Bell treated his only daughter as he had all of his sons, respecting her choice of a mate.[31]

We see much the same process at work in the mid-century decades. In 1840, when Catherine Miller wrote to her husband Garrett, the MPP from Lunenburg, about a proposal their daughter had received he replied, "I consider your Judgement & Experience to be superier to my own and have no hesitation in approving of your decision in the matter well knowing your dicision or wish will be governed by a due consideration of the serious subject – Your wish shall be mine – from what I noticed the person when I saw him at our house appeared to me as a reputable young man and if the parties themselves appear to be well satisfied with each other which I presume to be the case from what you state I shall feel no objection."[32] In 1858 John Grist of Quebec, an open-hearted prospective father-in-law, wrote to Arthur Harvey, "I received your letter of the 18th (Thursday) last evening – and now, from this moment, consider you as one of my sons; your welfare and happiness will concern me, as much as ever theirs did or do concern me; therefore [I] shall open my mind freely and without reserve – You are now my dear son at liberty to marry my dear girl, as you have her consent, and that of her mother whenever you wish to do so."[33] A son-in-law elect could wish for little more.

Yet the parental role was often a good deal more complex than these examples reveal. While acceptable suitors made a parent's task light, and while minor reservations could easily be swallowed, fathers, mothers and other relations might also be a good deal more meddlesome. Consider, for example, a revealing note sent in 1815 by E. Odell, a female member of one of Fredericton's leading families. "I have never heard anything of Susan's attachment ... except what Mr. Ford hinted, and I confess I do not feel much flattered by it – but still I think people ought to choose for themselves unless there is some serious objection. I should be well enough pleased with Sams connection, if they were not so nearly related – and as to Graham there seems to [be] some unreasonable delay, with regard to his marriage. I wrote to Caroline sometime ago and very plainly expressed my disapprobation of such long engagements. I do not know how she will take it."[34] Clearly Mrs. Odell did not practise what she preached.

In fact, until the later nineteenth century, parents commonly refused their assent to a daughter's proposed match when they thought it unsuitable. Unsuitability, like beauty, lay in the eyes of the beholder, and therefore what parents objected to varied from one couple to the next. Among the most important concerns were a suitor's youth and inability to support a wife and family, the reasons why Honorine's father so strongly opposed George Jones. The frustrated romance of W.H. Merritt and Catherine Prendergast offers an early example.[35] Merritt met Prendergast at a St Catharines ball in 1812 when both of them were nineteen. The future canal promoter was the son of a late loyalist settler, Catherine the daughter of an American doctor who had recently moved to the area but who planned to return to New York State before long. The young couple fell in love and promised to marry each other, but her father refused to allow their union and urged them to wait two years. Merritt impetuously proposed that the two of them elope but Catherine's cooler head prevailed. She, too, urged delay, requested him not to write and moved back across the border with her family. The War of 1812 intervened and sundered the lovers more effectively than parents alone might have done, and for more than two years they had almost no contact with one another. An officer in the colonial militia, Merritt saw action several times during the war and was captured at the Battle of Lundy's Lane in July 1814. While a prisoner in Massachusetts, he found himself near her father, then in Albany, New York, and renewed his request for permission to marry Catherine. He described the scene in a letter to his beloved:

This is the first time I ever addressed you with the approbation of your Father[.] I am quite in Raptures at the Idea. in my last at Litchfield I mentioned my wish to see him. After my arrival I heard of his proceeding to New York and gave up the Thought. Yesterday we accidentally met in the Street. I took tea with him at his Quarters & the long wished for tho much dreaded subject was happily Discussed. he brought about the discourse and gave his Consent in the most affectionate and kind Manner. This approbation is enough to bind me to him forever. but I am doubly Grateful to find he does it without reluctance. he appears interested already in our future welfare.[36]

After some further tribulations they married the following year.

The parents of Aleck Lindsay and Mary Caldwell colluded to keep them apart when they sought to marry in 1814. Aleck was a young lieutenant stationed at Quebec while Mary lived with her family in Montreal. When Mary's father, a merchant, got wind of what was afoot he wrote a stern letter to Aleck's father commenting on recent developments. "If Mr Lindsay was ten years older, & in a situation to support a Family," he stated, "the connexion would be pleasing – but at his age, and in his present situation, a Wife most assuredly would entail poverty & misery upon him, her, & their offspring!...your opinion of the business coincides with mine, & I have informed my daughter that she must give up every idea of a connexion so very improper at their time of life."[37]

For those who moved in privileged social circles, status distinctions might also create an obstacle to a union, though social boundaries were much less rigid in British colonial society than they were in contemporary Britain. A case in point was the marriage of George-Paschal Desbarats and Charlotte Selby in 1841. Desbarats, who became the Queen's printer later in the year, was a thirty-three-year-old widower while Charlotte was the daughter of a leading Montreal doctor who had died some years previously. The commentator here is Edward Hale, a prominent government official in Lower Canada, who was well placed to know. "I am told that the Selby family had many scruples to overcome before they could consent, and he had to exercise great perseverance – but although he has a printing Establishment, he is really a gentlemanly fellow quite the flower of the Desbarats' and is a steady man of business, which latter quality it is supposed is the greatest charm in Madame's eyes as she requires a man of that sort in whom she has confidence to put her affairs to rights and he will probably be the means of saving the family from ruin."[38]

A wide range of additional factors might rouse parental concern. Ellen Osler tells of an engagement between two young people in Tecumseh Township, Canada West, broken off because the groom's father wished the bride's father to dower her with a marriage settlement which the latter could not afford.[39] The young military officer James B. Lundy's long pursuit of a young woman in the Niagara region during the mid and late 1840s aroused strong opposition from her family and friends, as well as from some of his. In this instance the source of their objections is not entirely clear but in part, at least, it lay in Lundy's weakness for prostitutes and old flames, which betrothal did little to cure.[40] In the end, however, the marriage took place. Elizabeth Smith's parents broke her sister Myrtle's engagement to a Mr Coon in 1886, ostensibly because the two were too nearly related but more likely because Mamma Smith considered him a farmer with no social polish.[41] This last example is a bit anachronistic, however, for by this time parental influence over a woman's wish to marry was clearly on the wane.

When faced with a parent's opposition to her marriage hopes a young woman had several alternative courses before her. She might acquiesce, as Robert Baldwin's elder daughter Maria did twice when widower Baldwin refused to part with her company. More likely she might mount a campaign to alter the decision, which was Mary Caldwell's response when her father forbade her union with Aleck Lindsay. "My Father seems not to object to our being united on condition," she wrote Aleck:

my Uncle wrote to him and said he would give [h]is consent and that you had something besides your pay, tell him to rest assured [sic] that a Lieut. pay will be sufficient for us with economy to live and that thanks to my parents I have always been brought up to that but I only wish him to write that to my Father to ease [h]is mind on that score. my Uncle ought to remember when he married that [h]is fortune was but small. it is not always money that brings happiness. another thing the prospects of the Regt being kept up is a great thing and we will be going to [a] place where every article is cheaper then here and we shall not be subject to moving for some time.[42]

In this instance, however, Mary's campaign failed for she and Aleck never wed.

The marriage of Remy Elmsley and Nina Bradshaw in 1870 offers an example of particularly determined parental opposition and equally determined youthful resistance. In this case, though, the example lies at the furthest edge of acceptable evidence: while the Elmsleys were Canadian, the Bradshaws lived in England. The only justification for considering Remy and Nina's romance here is that men like Remy from the privileged ranks of English-Canadian society often found brides in the British Isles during the nineteenth century. Remy was the son of a leading Catholic family in Toronto, Nina the daughter of a Catholic gentry family from Leamington in Warwickshire, England. When Remy first broached the subject of marrying Nina, her father refused him outright. Later, retracing his steps a pace or two, he suspended a final decision until Remy returned to Canada and satisfied the senior Bradshaw about his life's prospects. In the meantime he forbade Remy to see or correspond directly with Nina and, when Remy sent his loved one a locket, her mother returned it to him. Undeterred, Remy corresponded with Nina's mother, conveying his love for Nina through this unlikely intermediary. He also strove to meet father Bradshaw's objections which, on closer examination, rested heavily on obtaining an acceptable marriage settlement for his daughter. Lacking her correspondence, we can only assume that while Remy besieged the family fortress from without, Nina bored from within. In the end persistence and love prevailed and the couple married with her parents' blessing.[43]

Some couples defied parental opposition and married the mate of their choice. Elopements were the most extreme form of this independence and, judging from the columns of the colonial press, they were common. Few nineteenth-century Canadians lived very far from the United States and, therefore, from access to compliant pastors and the more relaxed marriage regulations of some states in the Republic. Couples on the run sometimes found it easiest to head for the international border.

More often, when the opportunity presented, they married quietly near home. Steven Conger, a justice of the peace in Picton who performed many Methodist marriages when Methodist clergymen could not legally do so, once noted in his register: "Married William McGarth and Mahitabel Simson, both of Hallowell, 5th June, 1821, regularly published by Corneleus Van Alstine, Esq. Said marriage was forbid by her Father but not for lawful reasons and no attention paid to it by me."[44] In 1850 Agnes Ann Stayner of Halifax clandestinely married Gaetano Francisco Farrugia, bandmaster of the 38th Regiment. She had corresponded with him for a year without her father's knowledge and over her mother's and sisters' objections. Eluding family vigilance she became a Roman Catholic convert and, within a day or two, married Farrugia at the local bishop's residence.[45] In another example, this one from the later part of the century, Andrew Jones told his daughter that "Andrew Wilson's daughter was married last week to a Mr. Miller from Prescott. He was a son of the merchant. Her father did not approve of the match so they were married out at ... her sisters home."[46]

But in marrying against their parents' wishes, young women risked estrangement from their families. In the early nineteenth century two of the daughters of the late Captain John Nairne, the seigneur of Murray Bay, Lower Canada, married against their family's advice, Magdalene to Peter Macnicol (son of a former soldier) whom her kin considered beneath her, Polly to a habitant named Augustin Blackburn. The family meted out harsh justice in both cases. According to Malcolm Fraser, Nairne's neighbour and friend, Magdalene and Peter "are both now here but Mrs. Nairne does not see nor will she I believe suffer Macnicol to come into her house and I think she does right."[47] Family and friends in Canada and in Scotland cut Polly off completely.[48] In these instances the Nairne daughters were excluded as well from the Anglo-Canadian seigniorial and military officer classes in Lower Canada, small islands of polite society set in a sea of their social inferiors. Thereafter their social lives were likely confined to their husbands' social milieus.

Throughout most of the nineteenth century parents occasionally used sanctions to influence their daughter's choice of a mate. But the powers at their disposal were few, perhaps more likely to invite resistance than to overwhelm it. The only instruments available to disapproving fathers and mothers were the refusal of permission to marry, and ostracization if their will was defied. The parental veto was qualified in two ways: it could only be used when families thought the best interests of their offspring were in serious jeopardy, and it could not be used more than once or twice. Suitors denied too lightly or too often invited the young to rebel. As for ostracization, it was the tactic of last resort, as painful and damaging to a parent as it was to a child. There was one other possibility – disinheritance – but it is likely that its authority was almost always held in reserve. Even then it was a limited option. Among the less affluent, children could not expect much wealth from their parents. Given the accessibility of economic opportunity during much of the century, parents who controlled small amounts of property likely had little purchase on their children in any event. Whatever influence the prospect of disinheritance might have was almost certainly confined to the well-to-do.

Toward the end of the nineteenth century, the power of parents over womens' marriage plans began to wither and by 1900 it had largely disappeared. The veto so often employed in former times literally vanished from the diaries and letters – and, more important, from the experience – of late Victorian men and women. Children still consulted their parents about their choice of a mate and prospective grooms continued to ask a bride's father or mother for permission to marry their daughter. But the consultations were advisory and the requests ceremonial. The reasons why women's autonomy in matrimony enlarged at this time are not entirely clear, but the process was linked to other changes in the status of women in English Canada during the later nineteenth century. Women's mobility, their legal rights, their educational prospects, and their vocational opportunities widened dramatically during these years. Young women, in particular, gained a newfound independence at this time. Their greater control over marriage decisions no doubt grew from the same soil which nourished these other broad changes.

Thus, when Elizabeth Smith and Adam Shortt became engaged in May 1883 they merely announced the fact to their respective parents.[49] So did Genevieve Canniff, daughter of the Toronto historian, who wrote to her father about her betrothal to Bert Gray in 1899.[50] Newton Rowell, the young Ontario lawyer, and Nellie Langford told her family of their engagement at the end of a weekend visit Rowell made in 1901.[51] According to Rowell, Nellie's father took the news calmly. By the time Elizabeth Smith Shortt's daughter was old enough to wed the new convention was firmly established. In 1916 Muriel Shortt travelled to England to meet a male admirer. Soon after her arrival she informed her mother, "just a short note. I suppose papa will get that cable today to tell you we are engaged. You see we didn't know how to word it. If he said 'May I be engaged' that was funny because we are engaged and if he said 'May I marry Muriel' we knew you'd get a fright and think he was going to do that right away and we aren't so don't worry." Her mother replied," Congratulations on your joy. He is a good sort & I am happy with you."[52] Under the circumstances she could say little else.

Before the 1850s friends sometimes played a lesser, yet significant, part in the romantic affairs of others. But here we must tread carefully to avoid a semantic confusion. Until the mid nineteenth century the term "friends" embraced both relations and close acquaintances. Before Rebecca Byles accepted W.J. Almon in 1785 she consulted her "friends."[53] In this instance she seems to have meant family members. But in 1859, when the young Quebec military officer Copner Oldfield told his mother about his long engagement, he explained that it had taken place with the knowledge of his loved one's parents and "friends."[54] Here the term was used in its more restricted, current sense. For our purpose this usage is the only relevant one; the friends discussed here were the close acquaintances, not the relatives, of the courting couples in question.

Friends played a subsidiary role in courtship and marriage as sources of advice, emotional aid and, occasionally, censure. The bantering bachelor letters which passed between Frank Shanley and his brothers and friends in the 1840s reveal a network of young courting men who exchanged reports and opinions on the progress of their romantic affairs. A group of junior military officers and young professional men from the London area, Shanley and his chums took a lively interest in each other's private lives, discussing their own affectionate liaisons in addition to those of their companions, noting relationships that had cooled or broken off and criticizing acquaintances who were pursuing unwise matches.[55]

We can see friends acting as advisers in other instances, too. In 1829 William Wynne of Queenston cautioned his protégé John Blake of York about the perils of Blake's correspondence with a young woman:

You must be perfectly aware that to form a matrimonial connexion at this time of your life considering your situation would be folly in the extreme, nay worse than that. it would be perfect madness! and if you have no such view what benefit can you expect to derive from such correspondence. admiting that the *Lady* is *handsome* and *facinating*? there are others that are her equals in these respects – and perhaps surpass them in other qualifications – and I can assure you, *John*, that there are no great difficulties for a man of good character, at any time when he finds that his situation requires it, to find a suitable companion.[56]

When James Lauder, an immigrant Scottish store clerk in Niagara-on-the-Lake, encountered difficulties while courting Jane Allerthorn of Lockport, New York, in 1838, he turned to his friend John Grant. Unfortunately only Grant's letters survive and they tell us nothing specific about the cause of the difficulty, but Grant served up generous helpings of advice and even wrote letters to Jane on Lauder's behalf (though Lauder copied them out in his own hand before sending them on).[57] Two decades later Britten Osler, yet another adviser to lovers, told his brother about a friend's predicament: "I received a letter from Dr. Orr in which he (Dr. Orr) stated that he considered it quite a match between his daughter and J. Dixon and that she was expecting him to propose every day. This as I expected put J.D. in a great stew. He wrote yesterday asking my advice on the subject and saying he did not know what on earth to do. I am now considering what I shall advise him to do."[58] Presumably Osler began his career as a legal counsellor here.

When marriage was in question, we still see friends occasionally playing an active part in the process. In 1816 the Anglican rector and educator John Strachan wrote to his former pupil John Beverley Robinson on hearing that Robinson had just become engaged to a woman in England. Strachan would have contented himself with sending congratulations were it not for the fact that "there are some particulars which require explanation." "I want to ascertain," he asked,

whether you were under any engagements directly or indirectly to Miss P[owell], whether that family had reason to entertain hopes of such a connexion, or whether [one] hopes care was taken to undeceive them. It is not from idle curiosity that I propose these queries, but from my affection for you to know how far in case of difficulty, I can be warranted in supporting you. At present things continue as usual, but perhaps I am a little more experienced in characters than you are, and am not without apprehensions of some blaming [you] if disappointment whether reasonable or not has been experienced. You know me sufficiently to be convinced, that I am not apt to shrink – but I must know the ground minutely on which I stand ... I should have saved myself and you the trouble of this letter, did I not anticipate difficulty. I may be mistaken, I wish I may, it is however good to be prepared not merely for open but covert attacks. One thing is certain, by every account the young L. was *distracted after you*, and tho such a match did not appear eligible, yet the frequency of her visits to your sister & the uncommon I might say burthensome attraction of the whole family to your sister, indicate some sort of expectation which to me requires some explanation fully to comprehend.[59]

Strachan's interrogation reveals not only the intrusive role of friends but also the importance of community opinion in accepting a match.

The opinion of friends mattered in other ways as well. Frank Shanley's correspondent Harry Allen considered it a guarantor of a promise to marry. In 1847 Allen was in love with a young woman from London, Canada West, but, unemployed and without prospects, he could not plan to marry. Despite his beloved's willingness to promise him marriage, he refused to become formally engaged. "Setting aside my own ideas of what was strictly honourable in my circumstances as they are at present," he told Shanley, "I know enough of the use to be perfectly satisfied that if a woman's inclinations change, an engagement will be very little in her way, when unknown to anyone; and therefore in the event of such a contingency, I thought it would be best to remove everything with which she could possibly reproach herself afterwards. Of course she made all of the usual protestations, which I took of course for their value with all women, and perhaps with her of all others."[60] Allen's comment on the importance of common knowledge about betrothal was perceptive; engagements were more secure when the community knew that they existed.

Some colonists revealed a great sensitivity to the opinion of friends when matrimony was at stake. William Herchmer, an Upper Canadian at Oxford preparing himself for the Anglican ministry, displayed his concerns when informing his cousin of his impending marriage. "No doubt you have heard that I intend taking unto myself a wife, before I return to Canada, unless my friends object to my proceedings."[61] He then proceeded to describe his solemn deliberations on the matter, as well as his intended wife's virtues, presumably to scotch any objections from others. Community opinion about a marriage weighed especially heavily among early colonials. When the marriage of the Anglican clergyman John Stoughton to a daughter of the Kingston Tory Christopher Hagerman approached, a rumour went round that her parents opposed the match. Hagerman denied the rumour in writing and Stoughton circulated the letter in order to contradict it.[62]

In some circumstances friends might disrupt a couple's marriage plans much more directly. A year after his own marriage William Herchmer objected to the engagement of a young woman he knew to a man of low character who was given to drink. "Rather ... than such a connexion should be formed," he declared, "I would openly confront him and strive to defeat his plans."[63] Edward Hale once took immediate action. In 1838 he heard that a son of a friend was about to make an unsuitable match. "Thinking that you would expect me to take some steps in a matter, of which you might possibly disapprove, I made it a point to see your Son who denied it, and his 2 friends Armour & Glen who confirmed it (by the by I only conversed with Armour[)]. I have reason to believe that these two gentlemen are exerting themselves to procure a delay in the affair until they can hear from you. I have every hope that they will succeed and thinking that with them the matter was in good hands I have not interfered further."[64] Here the opposition and intrusion came from friends of two generations.

After mid-century, however, friends ceased to interfere in a couple's marriage plans in such obvious ways. No doubt they continued to advise and no doubt the advice often was unsolicited. But the claims of acquaintanceship no longer authorized the degree of friendly encroachment in the intimate lives of others which Strachan, Herchmer, and Hale had taken as their right. Nor did men and women contemplating marriage formally consult their friends as they once had done. Gradually the imperatives of community opinion fell before the rise of romantic individualism and, as representatives of society in matters of the heart, friends lost most of their standing in the couple's private affairs.

In chapter 2 I argued that unmarried couples in nineteenth-century English Canada usually need not depend on their parents to give them the wealth they needed to marry and set up a household. The Eastern Townships farmer and miller George Stacey put the matter succinctly in a letter to his father in 1857. "Boys in particular in this Country long before they are twenty one years of age talk and act independently, and they can at any time if willing and able support themselves and make more in working out than remaining at home. How long Frederick and Alfred [Stacey's sons; Alfred, the younger, was twenty-one] will remain with us will entirely depend upon circumstances – they naturally look forward to a home of their own, and if either or both of them get married of course they will soon go."[65] Stacey's concern was to keep his sons at home as long as he could to help him run the farm and the mill. But the competing rewards of other jobs outweighed the benefits of any patrimony he could offer his boys.

Nor do we find clear evidence that Anglo-Canadians practised the formal traditions of bridewealth and dowry, marriage customs which transferred wealth between families and generations. No doubt property was deeply relevant to matrimony and no doubt family property sometimes played an important part in marriage arrangements. The difficulty is, once again, a lack of evidence. Few records have survived which throw any light on the role of marriage in redistributing wealth in Anglo-Canadian society. Lacking large collections of marriage contracts and similar documents we must be content with the fragmentary records which time has left us. This is a modest legacy at best and it yields only fleeting impressions.

What the minimum property requirements for marriage were in nineteenth-century Canadian society are not at all clear. No doubt they varied widely from family to family, place to place, and social group to social group. But whatever the amounts and kinds of wealth, couples required a pool of assets before they could wed, usually enough to allow them to set up a separate household at an acceptable standard of living. These marriage funds came from two primary sources: the spouses themselves, and their families. Families contributed funds according to the couple's needs and the family's resources. No clear rules seem to have governed these transactions. Contributions might come from either or both sets of parents, they might take the form of property, goods, money or less tangible forms of support, and they might come at the time of marriage or at some future date. When the Upper Canadian farm girl Mary Mullett planned her marriage in 1823 she expected to live with her new husband's family until the newlyweds headed into the bush to start their own homestead.[66] In this case Mary looked forward to the simplest form of family help. The possibilities for more generous aid were almost limitless.

In mid-century Perth County, Ontario, farm families customarily gave their daughters a feather bed and a cow when they wed.[67] W.A. Robertson, reminiscing about his Upper Canadian boyhood, remembered his sister Maggie's marriage in 1847. "Before she went away from home by getting married and at the time some effort had to be made to give her a start when she got married. a small sum of money had to be raised, to get her something for her 14 years hard work."[68] Ultimately the family raised $40 to help her on her way. (In this instance note as well the explicit association of a marriage payment as compensation for Maggie's past work on behalf of the family.) David Gagan has noted the example of a man who guaranteed his stepsister's dowry of $400, and other cases in which wills made a father's son and heir responsible for his sisters' marriage portions.[69]

In rural circles parents might give their children land to help them form the economic base of an independent household. When Thomas Moore and Margaret Steele of Rawdon Township, Canada East, signed a marriage contract in 1843, her stepfather and mother promised the couple at marriage a parcel of cultivated land and part of the oat crop then growing on it, plus some livestock, some household furnishings, and two or three bundles of hay.[70] Sons probably benefited more in this respect than daughters, if only because farm families tended to bestow real property on their male offspring. In 1854 George Bell, of Seymour Township, Canada West, settled eighty acres on his son Frank, who was about to marry, in consideration of his long service on the family farm.[71] Similarly, when twenty-two-year-old Alfred Stacey of the Sherbrooke area planned to marry in 1858, his father bought him a piece of land near the family farm.[72]

Families might contribute to a daughter's bridal fund by conveying property or money to her in trust, to her husband, or to them both (which gave effective control to him). Five examples reveal a range of possible alternatives. John Strachan gave his eldest daughter and her husband an acre lot near his own home when they married in 1833.

There the newlyweds proceeded to build "an excellent cottage which will be exceedingly elegant."[73] The Brantford area farmer William D'Aubigny's prospective father-in-law, evidently a man of some means, promised William financial help to purchase his farm after he married in 1837.[74] Agnes Poore gave her daughter Anna Maria and her son-in-law, the Cobourg industrialist Stuart Easton Mackechnie, £1,000 when they married in 1848.[75] Charles Watson married the daughter of William Sproule in Canada West in 1859 on the understanding that William would pay him a marriage portion of $1,000.[76] When Catherine Crookshank wed Stephen Heward in Toronto in 1858, the couple agreed beforehand that any real or personal property or money she received during their marriage would be set aside in a trust for her exclusive use.[77] In this case the marriage contract merely anticipated the future redistribution of wealth.

The considerations involving family property in the union of Nina Bradshaw and Remy Elmsley were more complex and well-documented than in those of any other marriage examined in this study, and are not typical of any broad patterns or trends in English-Canadian marriage arrangements. Yet the example reveals the thoughts and actions of two sets of well-to-do parents about the marriage of their children and offers us an insight into the role of property in the matrimonial strategies of privileged Anglo Canadians. Nina's parents rebuffed Remy's first marriage proposal in August 1869 and tried to frustrate any further contact between the pair. Though the Bradshaws knew the Elmsley family reasonably well, they feared losing their daughter to Canada. Also, while approving of Remy's piety, they knew nothing about his profession and were uncertain of his financial prospects. Ultimately the marriage negotiations between the two families turned on this latter point.

In order to overcome the Bradshaws' objections, Remy's widowed mother wrote to them soon after he first proposed to Nina, informing them that her son wooed with her full consent and advising them that his income would be at least £1,000 a year.[78] When pressed for further details, Mrs Elmsley assured the Bradshaws that £500 a year, plus a suitable house and grounds, would allow the couple to live as well in Toronto as they could in England on twice the income. She then offered Nina a marriage settlement of £500 pounds annually plus Barnstaple Villa, the Elmsley family home in Toronto. A brewery proprietor and land-owner in his own right, Remy would settle a further £500 a year on his bride.[79] Both settlements would come to Nina in trust. Charlotte Elmsley explained her actions to Nina's father: "I do not approve of Parents giving their daughters in marriage without securing for them some sort of independence, not altogether independent of their husbands: for that would be erring in the opposite direction but to secure to them a competency[.] Young men nowadays have an insatiable desire to acquire riches; they run all risks, which too often end in losing everything, in the meantime the family increases, and with it expenses; the end is too sad to be thought of."[80] The Elmsley offer proved enough to convince the senior Bradshaws and in December Nina sent Remy a loving note with the joyous news that her father had consented to their engagement. On their part the Bradshaws also proposed to confer an additional sum on their daughter.

But while the Elmsleys and the Bradshaws had reached an agreement in principle, they still had to work out the details. Remy soon asked J.J. Bradshaw for a large advance on Nina's marriage portion in order to help pay for renovations to the house which his mother proposed to give Nina.[81] Bradshaw objected to Remy's investment plans for the money Remy was providing to fund the trust for Nina's marriage portion. Remy intended to provide his £500 a year from rents on housing and commercial property, but the Bradshaws considered such investments much too risky and urged the greater security of mortgages and government bonds. From Remy's point of view this request posed some difficulty, for the capital investment required to produce the necessary income would be much higher if the Bradshaws' wishes prevailed over his own. When Remy later proposed to transfer to Nina his interest in lands he would inherit from his mother, J.J. Bradshaw approved, not only on his daughter's account but also for the same prudential reasons noted by Remy's mother.[82]

In the end Remy complied with the senior Bradshaws' wishes. He invested his marriage settlement funds in approved mortgages and debentures, gave Nina a life interest in further secure investments and assigned these funds to a trust. Remy and Nina jointly received the Elmsley family home with the proviso that it would not be liable for his debts in case of insolvency.[83] Remy and Nina then wed, no doubt in a state of financial as well as romantic bliss.

In spite of the unique complexity of this case the Elmsley-Bradshaw marriage had three important elements in common with many other unions in nineteenth-century British Canada. First was the role of parents in bestowing property on children when they married. In this case, while the degree of parental involvement was unusual, the practice of transferring wealth from one generation to the next at marriage was not. Though most property in Canada seems to have passed between the generations at death, matrimony was another occasion when wealth sometimes devolved from parents to children. Second, when brides received property they obtained it in the form of a trust, whether from their own families or from those of their spouses-to-be.

Third, as the example of Remy and Nina illustrates, prospective mates also brought their own property to marriage. The Elmsley-Bradshaw union provides a glimpse of these arrangements among the well-to-do, but the matrimonial property provided by each spouse was an important consideration among all but the very poor. While the forms and amounts of wealth might differ greatly from the privileged to the humble, the significance of these joint contributions varied much less. Here, too, parents might play an active part in settling the financial terms of matrimony, especially when their daughters were involved. As long as women required their parents' permission to marry, the elder generation could withhold consent until the monetary side of the bargain satisfied them. This was more likely when substantial sums were involved, but even small property-holders – and in largely rural nineteenth-century Canada this meant a majority of families – might follow this strategy if they chose. Although fathers and mothers did not have an absolute veto over their daughters' marital hopes, they could exert a great influence on the domestic bargain which she struck. The Bradshaws' pursuit of Nina's financial interest is a graphic case in point.

Family contributions apart, young men and women also gathered pools of savings in money or kind in anticipation of marriage. Girls and young women commonly spent many hours making bedding and household linen. In 1884 Lillian Williamson, a woman from rural New Brunswick with distant matrimonial hopes, told her diary that she was making a quilt and a counterpane in anticipation of a day not "at all near, only in prospect."[84] The courtship letters which Gilbert Hartley, a prison guard in Hamilton, wrote to his fiancée Mary Card during the later 1870s speak of his efforts to earn enough for them to marry and set up separate housekeeping.[85] Another courtship correspondence of the same period, between the Exeter, Ontario, farmer John Essery and his future wife Mary Harris, discussed the house which he was building for them and her plans to stock the larder.[86]

When husbands brought property to a marriage they usually kept much of it in their own names. But many well-to-do men also conveyed some of their wealth in trust to their brides, placing family assets beyond their own (and their creditors') reach. In the handful of surviving marriage contracts from Lower Canada which transferred property from husbands to wives, grooms gave their brides household furnishings. In 1837 the Montreal accountant William Clarke gave his new wife tableware, bedding and the furnishings for two rooms.[87] George Riley, a New York distiller who married Mary Reynolds of Montreal in 1847, gave her a collection of household articles worth $980.[88] A civil engineer from Brockville, Harry Abbott, gave his bride Margaret Freer furniture and effects worth $2,531.52 when the couple married in 1868.[89] In this case, though, the sum seems rather high and the groom may have been marrying for a second time (as was the bride), thus passing on the accumulation of an earlier union. In any event, these were the sorts of gifts one might expect grooms in propertied circles to give their brides.

But because these examples come to us from the comfortable classes in urban British Quebec, they reveal only part of the picture. When we shift our gaze west of the Ottawa River we find several Ontario marriage settlements which sketch in important new details. Already a wealthy man when he remarried at the age thirty-three in 1831, Allan MacNab of Hamilton placed a large quantity of lands and buildings in a trust for his new wife, Mary Stuart. The couple were to enjoy the fruits of these investments jointly during their lives.[90] Stuart Mackechnie, whose wife Anna received £1,000 from her mother when they married, also gave his bride some lands and buildings in a marriage settlement in 1848.[91] Two more examples come from further down the economic ladder. By a marriage contract signed late in 1864, John Livingston promised to pay $10,000 into a trust for Mary Applebe within a year. He did not fulfill his bargain, however, and when their marriage later failed Mary sued her husband and the trustee.[92] Four years later Blencoe Warnes, a farmer near Guelph, agreed to a marriage settlement which gave his bride Margaret Cleland $6,000 and land, buildings, and furnishings worth a further $5,000, all of it in a trust administered by her father.[93]

The task of tracing a woman's contribution to the marriage fund is more difficult still, for most women merged their assets with those of their new husbands, creating a common pool of marital property under his administration. While the records are almost mute on this point, most men likely were well aware of the benefits they might derive from taking a monied wife. The acerbic and unsentimental York bachelor Joseph Willcocks was one. As he told his brother in Dublin in 1800, "I have met a very great loss by the removal of Col. Smith from the York garrison he was uncommonly attentive to me, he had also a very pretty sister that I would have been uncommonly attentive to if she carried more metal, indeed she is a rarity for there are few Pretty Girls in the Country, but you know beauty will not make the Pot boil, which consideration alone prevents me from assuming an air of seriousness. Love & runaway matches I never was an advocate for, such proceedings may fill the bellys of women but not of men."[94] Something of a misogynist, Willcocks never married.

Some sixty years later Adam Wallbridge revealed similar sentiments when describing his intended bride to his sister: "She is one of the best Families in this County [Prince Edward], well brought up, knows how to take charge of a house, intelligent and to me good looking – almost my own size and of good constitution and well educated but does not sing, can play almost as much as you formerly did and best of all [she] is possessed of property and has no hangers on. Now there is something for you to reflect on."[95]

As we have already seen, however, not all men were this mercenary. Some bestowed substantial amounts of wealth on their wives when they wed while others allowed their spouses control of whatever assets they brought to marriage or later acquired by gift or inheritance. In 1808, when Robert Baldwin Sr proposed (unsuccessfully) to Elizabeth Russell soon after her half-brother Peter had died leaving her a vast estate, he urged her to put her fortune beyond his reach.[96] The marriage contract of the shoemaker Appleton Rice and the merchant's daughter Mary Meacham, both of Montreal, is also instructive, for it involved an exchange of wealth. When they agreed to marry in 1828 Mary gave Appleton the right to the fruits of her property for their mutual support and that of their children. In turn Appleton gave Mary the lifetime use of the profits of a piece of land with a house and shoemaker's shop.[97] Women of wealth tended to be particularly careful about protecting their economic interests through their use of marriage contracts. The affluent Louisa G. Frothingham did precisely this when she married the rich Montreal merchant John H.R. Molson in 1873. Their contract gave Louisa free administration and enjoyment of all her assets and specified that, in addition to her real and moveable property, she was to have exclusive possession of all her stocks and securities, all the furnishings and other contents of her Montreal home as well as its vehicles, livestock, implements, and other goods, and all her personal apparel, jewellery, and ornaments.[98]

Having reviewed the available evidence, we are left with some strong impressions about the importance of wealth in nineteenth-century Canadian matrimony. But we also are left with some large unanswered questions. We know nothing of the subsidiary role of friends in creating the marriage fund. They seem to have contributed little during the nineteenth-century, but with so little evidence to guide us we should treat this as mere conjecture. (During the twentieth century, by contrast, friends have come to make large contributions to the domestic assets of newlyweds through the bridal shower and the carefully orchestrated donation of wedding gifts. In this way, if in no other, the community's place in marriage seems to have broadened over the past hundred years.) We also know almost nothing about who contributed the greater share to the marriage fund, parents or children, the bride's family or the groom's, husband or wife. Presumably there was widespread variation in these matters, but the evidence is far too slender even to support guesses about broad patterns in marriage settlements. Nor can we see any clear trends over time in the redistribution of wealth at marriage except, perhaps, for the increasing tendency of friends and family members to fund a marriage. Finally, and in some ways most important of all, we cannot yet discover what relationships, if any, these patterns and trends had to the great economic, demographic, and social changes which occurred in nineteenth-century Canada. Given their magnitude, we might reasonably suspect that they influenced the distribution of property at marriage. But for the moment we must be content with vague suspicions.

CHAPTER SEVEN

The Quest for Intimacy

"On this day the most important and serious step in our lives was taken," Amelia King confided to her diary on 10 March 1852. "This evening at ½ 7 o'clock I was united to one whom I had loved long dearly and sincerely. On this evening we were made one & our whole life's happiness now solely depends on each other. Love & confidence are the chief objects to be kept in view."[1] A country girl of eighteen from Windsor, Nova Scotia, Amelia had just married Lewis Hill, twenty-four, who farmed in nearby Falmouth. In these few simple words she expressed her sense of the profound meaning of marriage and of the promises she and Lewis had just exchanged. Marriage, she believed, cast the die for the rest of one's life. Its greatest blessing was happiness. And its happiness flowed from love.

Amelia's wedding night thoughts take us to the very heart of nine-teenth-century matrimony, to its permanence, its solemnity, and its emotional intimacy. Victorian English Canadians generally agreed with her convictions when they walked the path toward marriage. They seldom thought much about the structural framework of courtship and marriage – about law and religion, family and property, territory and ritual, all those aspects of taking a mate which have concerned us until now. Instead they immersed themselves in love, the transcendent experience of courtship and marriage.

This chapter will chart the emotional course of nineteenth-century Anglo-Canadians en route to the altar. Then as now they began with ideals about the essential elements and principal ends of matrimony. While these ideals paid due regard to practical matters, they upheld mutual love as the vital ingredient in marriage and considered shared happiness to be its most precious fruit. But the experience of love differed, sometimes dramatically, from the abstract beliefs which men and women held about it. In life, love proved a jewel of many facets, some of them marred by flaws. Those who loved and loved deeply knew the joy which comes from great intimacy, but during courtship and betrothal many learned something of the darker emotions as well. Finally, whatever their personal experience (and for those in love, giving and receiving love are the quintessential personal experiences) the growth of intimacy also conformed to clear and predictable patterns of behaviour which we must explore. Set apart from all others in their own worlds of romance, even lovers shared much in common as they courted and wed.

When reflecting on the ideals of marriage, nineteenth-century English Canadians shared a broad consensus on the subject. They believed that marriage was the greatest step a man or woman took, that it shaped the course of one's life for good or for ill, and that love was the one indispensable element for marital success. The point is best made when we let them speak for themselves. Sandford Fleming pondered the meaning of matrimony when advising his sister Anna on her marriage prospects in 1856. Evidently Anna had received a marriage proposal which was not entirely welcome and she had asked her recently married brother for advice. "I consider that the choice of a husband is a choice for life and is of the very greatest consequence to your happiness," Sandford told her. "I do not wish to advise you one way or another but from your letter I can judge that you are somewhat indifferent to his proposals if so you would do well to weight [sic] the above remarks and if any doubts exist in your own mind it would [be] most consistent with prudence to take the safe side. Many take a step in the dark and find out the mistake only when it is too late."[2]

The Irish-born journalist Michael Leeson reflected similar thoughts when he considered the subject of marriage in a letter to his bride-to-be, Eleanor Donnelly, in 1880. "It is said that marriage, as we understand it in the Catholic Church, is a solemn thing – a choice for life – a most important event. My idea of it is that it should take place after the contracting parties thoroughly understand one another; then after a full religious preparation." It "is a great undertaking, and should not be concluded in a hurry; and when entered upon should be carried out as faithfully as the honourable, wealthy merchant meets his engagement to his creditors."[3]

During the early part of the nineteenth century, when men and women spoke of the need for love in marriage they sometimes tempered their appraisal with more prudential considerations. For example, William Macaulay, the Anglican rector of Picton, who married Anne Geddes in August 1829, looked to his bride for an amalgam of love, practicality, deference, and respect for his family. A week after their wedding he wrote to his mother in Kingston, "I find myself very happily married to a wife, who I trust, will unite affection & prudence in her conduct as respects myself & who will be doubly dear to me, if she answers, as I trust she will, the expectation that I have, that she will be an excellent & dutiful daughter-in-law."[4]

Another Anglican minister, Robert Cartwright (of the Kingston loyalist family) echoed Macaulay's wish for affection mingled with prudence, and added a religious desideratum when anticipating his marriage to Harriet Dobbs in 1832. "I feel that my judgment fully coincides with my affection," he told his former mentor, John Strachan, "and that I am not swayed by a blind partiality but by rational conviction when I express my belief that I shall find in Harriet a true friend, a rational companion, and a useful assistant. As in every thing human there must be drawbacks and disappointment, but as you observe where-ever there is sound Christian principle there must be on the whole comfort and satisfaction."[5]

As well as considering happiness the principle end of marriage, the young Francis Baker believed good character the preferred quality in a spouse. The son of a Prince Edward County family then evidently on the decline, Baker advised his mother on his sister's marriage proposal in 1833:

the Solemnization of Marriage is an all-important Contract as it fixes for life our weal or woe – and therefore should not be lightly or speedily entered into. the future welfare of my only sister is as dear to me as my own. & for the best fortune in the possession of any man I would not have her marry any one in the least degree unworthy of her. although the fortunes of our family have materially changed, we yett have a good & honourable name and I am too proud to bestow my sister as a wife to any man on Earth if he was not of her own Choice. I ask no favours of this World as respects getting a living in it. for I can live & spare Something. if sister cannot better her condition in life and that permanently by accepting Mr. S. she ought not to do so for I shall see that she does not want, but if Mr. S. is the person of her own choice & she thinks she could live happily with him and add to his as well as her own Happiness she ought to accept. What his circumstances are I cannot tell. his Character as a Gentleman I believe stands fair.[6]

Margaret Leoore thought kindness the most necessary attribute in a husband. We know nothing of her background, though judging from her prose she came from modest circumstances; but perhaps she spoke for many women when advising her friend Mary Hinchley on affairs of the heart in 1834. "The [reason] I wright you this is to let you know all Mr. Dickens friends is combed back from Dundass and Dawson is with [them.] he is lick a fish out of the water for want of you he is proposing to comb and see you on sabeth first he will comb if he is well his love is as strong as ever. I ask you as a perticlar favour not to be sasyie [sassy] to him when he comes he is a kind creature he will mack a good husband to you a better one than Jock."[7] Reading between the lines, Margaret valued a tempered affection above a powerful attraction.

We must be cautious at this point. We need not think that Macaulay, Cartwright, Baker, and Leoore considered love less important in marriage than we do today, or that their measured words expressed feelings any less deep or compelling than modern professions of love. The late eighteenth and early nineteenth century language of the emotions was more formal and reserved, less spontaneous and passionate than that of later times. Yet it was not necessarily any less expressive. It may well have spoken of feelings as powerful as any we know.

We find ourselves on more familiar ground in the case of the Fredericton university lecturer James Robb who, when praising his new bride in 1840, took a more romantic view of wifely virtue. "Ellen and I are one," he wrote exuberantly to his mother in Scotland.

I have gained the best and sweetest of all wives, friends and companions. She is *beautiful*, she is good, she is fond and affectionate. She is, in short, the very person whom you yourself, my own dear Mother, would have selected as the fittest for your James. If I am ever to be happy, it will be with Ellen; and since the beginning of our union, my life has been one of calm tranquillity and delight. I now have an object to live for, and one also worthy of all and more than all I can ever do for her. She is peaceful and gentle and more affectionate than a dove, in short, my Ellen is everything I could wish.[8]

Having concluded his hymn to love he continued by praising her family background, her education, her principles, and her musical accomplishments. In the first blush of marital bliss, Robb considered his wife the very embodiment of companionate love.

Sandford Fleming underscored the importance of love in his long note of brotherly advice to Anna.

Consider well the nature of the step you propose taking – remember that although a very little affection is sufficient to mary [sic] on it requires a *large stock* of it afterwards -perhaps the novelty might divert you for a short time, but remember the connection is for life, you have seen the best of him, he has of you and it is quite possible that both of you may discover faults & enow you do not now anticipate ... [I]f you really like the man if you think he possess[es] that tenderness & delicacy & then tastes & feeling [sic] which are similar to your own then you might find in the husband a lover a friend an equal companion – otherwise you may soon be tired with insipidity, shocked with indelicacy, or mortified with indifference – and if you marry a man without liking him with a fullness of heart a very short time with him will suffice to disperse any feelings you may now possess. I can well imagine a feeling akin to gratitude for a man who has made certain advances & kind promises – but do not mistake gratitude for affection or it will soon be turn[ed] to hatred and for ever embitter your married days – if under these circumstances you enter into a life long state of dependance [sic] & misery through little other than mercenary motives you will find none to compassionate or sympathize – and you will even repent relinquishing the ease & independence of a single life to become the slave of one you cannot love.[9]

For Sandford, successful marriage rested on the mutual sympathy of close companions, which could only be born of love.

Sandford shared the views of his wife Jean who, several months before they wed in 1855, revealed her feelings for him and her hopes for their married life. "Since my engagement to you my feelings have been those of perfect confidence. I have looked upon you as a *second* self – as a *friend* from whom there should be nothing secret and into whose heart I could pour mine with perfect effusion, whose joys and sorrows would be in common with my own[.] Without such feelings and such sympathies I cannot think the married state a happy one."[10] In Jean's view, candour and intimacy were the most important elements of married life.

A later observer appraised the place of love in marriage even more directly. Ellen Chapman, of Sault Ste Marie, considered it the main requirement for a successful union. "I was a little surprised to hear of Maria Robinson's marriage," she wrote to her sister in 1874. "She has certainly made a great change, still if she really loves William Kirk it may be the making of her, outward circumstances are not of so very much consequence where love & unity exist between husband & wife. drawbacks only draw them together, of course where only fancy instead of fondness exists it is a different thing."[11]

In Michael Leeson's eyes, a passionate love was necessary for marriage but it was not sufficient in itself. Like Francis Baker, he held that companionship and good character were also important if a marriage was to succeed.

A girl should never marry a man, who has *only* his love to recommend him. It is very fascinating; but it does not make the man. If he is not otherwise what he should be, there never will be happiness. The most perfect man who loved not, should never be a husband. Now though marriage without love is terrible, love, alone, will not do. If the man is dishonourable to other men, or given to any vice, the time will come when the girl he betrayed will either loathe him or sink to his level. It is hard to remember amid kisses and praises that there is anything else in the world to be done or thought of but love-making; but the days of life are many, and the husband must be a guide to be trusted – a companion, a friend as well as a lover. Many a girl has married a man whom she knew to be anything but good, "because he loved her so." The flame died out on the hearth-stone before long, – and beside her was sitting one, that she could never hope would lead her heavenward – one, who, if she followed as a wife should, would guide her to perdition.[12]

For future reference, we also should note Leeson's assumption about sex roles in marriage: good character in a husband was essential because he was a teacher and guide; a wife's role was to follow his lead.

Turning to the more practical side of matrimony, most Anglo-Canadians shared the conviction that financial security was necessary before one could marry. Among all but the very poor the assumption was that a man should not marry without stable economic prospects: an income sufficient to support a wife and the children that surely would soon follow. Nor should a woman marry a man who could not provide this support. We see this belief clearly expressed in Ward Chipman's congratulations to Jonathan Sewell Jr in 1793: "I am rejoiced most sincerely my dear Jack at your uncommon success in business – the instance is unparalleled and marks most signally your merit as well as good fortune. I consider your situation now as fixed & your income permanent & certain & therefore most highly approve your matrimonial scheme."[13] Our hero George Jones faced the problem of limited means in the mid-1840s; it was the primary obstacle to his happiness. Almost two decades later the Smith's Falls resident G.C. Shaw passed along a bit of homely bachelor wisdom on the subject to his friend James Reynolds: "it is a great mistake for a young man to get engaged before he knows how he intends keeping himself and wife."[14] The Torontonian Margaret Drayton reflected a woman's sense of the same point of view when relating a piece of family news at the end of the century. "Harry last week passed well in both his exams as barrister & solicitor ... I daresay you will also be startled to hear that he is engaged to Edith [illegible]. You may remember she is the eldest & lives over in Rosedale. Her father is comfortably off but Harry of course will have to carve out his own fortunes first before he can dream of asking for her in matrimony. So with that end in view, Harry is leaving no stone unturned to fit as junior partner in some firm."[15]

Newton MacTavish weighed the competing claims of financial security and marital happiness in a long soliloquy nine days before he married Kate Johnson in 1903. The twenty-nine-year-old MacTavish was correspondent and business representative in Montreal for the Toronto *Globe*. Methodically he had consulted two friends, a bachelor and a married man, about the wisdom of marrying. Not surprisingly, he received conflicting advice, his bachelor acquaintance cautioning him about the financial burdens of taking a wife, his other friend extolling the many blessings of married life. MacTavish had no doubts about where he stood.

Although my expenses will be high in accordance with my income, my wedding approaches only too slowly. I have no fear of the result. My love for Kate Johnson is too great to ever let the desire to amass wealth replace it. I sometimes wonder what persons of the world *wd* say if they could read my thoughts. I am so thoroughly in love that I am almost ashamed of myself. "Poor fellow," some would say, "he will soon have his eyes opened." All I can say is that I await the opening, firmly believing that it will never come. With my wedding day nine days off, I am just as impatient as the small boy waiting for the company to finish dinner. I know my impatience is outrageous; but there it is. I simply live in the future all the time. Everything I do seems to have some bearing on my life after a week from Tuesday. Even the writing of this is the result of a fancy that perhaps some day Kate would find pleasure in reading it with me, some day when the scene has changed, when our experience will have taught us much; some day when we shall know the truth or the untruth of my whole view of the future – that our love is as near perfection as it is possible to be in this world, that it will live throughout all the trials and the joys that are sure to come, & that it will ever be the chief source of our happiness & comfort.[16]

The question of religious compatibility also worried some couples as they considered marriage. For many, denominational differences were an active concern, especially when one party was Catholic and the other Protestant. For others, spirituality was the larger issue, quite apart from institutional membership. An undated letter from the earlier nineteenth century offers a telling illustration. Alicia Bowen explained her views on religious sympathy to an admirer whom we know only as Frank.

I feel that (God sustaining me) I must henceforth live to Him and this world & its follies have no more a place in my heart. The husband of my bosom must be one who feels as I do and who will be willing & desirous to follow after the things that pertain unto everlasting peace – to take up his cross daily & follow the Lamb whithersoever he goeth. I feel that without the bond of Christian fellowship there could be no confidence – no happiness – for us either here or hereafter. Answer me – pause before you do so and let the answer be in sincerity & truth – can you – or rather *do you* sincerely desire better things from joys than the unsatisfying pleasures of this world? My firm resolve is to give up gaity and whatever can draw my heart from following after righteousness & peace. Can you dear Frank assist in strengthening my resolution then indeed I were blest − if it is otherwise with you let us forget the past.[17]

The problem of religious compatibility also troubled William Dawson (Anna's Presbyterian father) during his long and difficult transatlantic courtship of Margaret Mercer, a Scottish Baptist, in the 1840s. Under these circumstances it is not too surprising that the ambitious farm lad from Nova Scotia stressed the importance of religious opinion over sectarian membership.[18] Given the importance of religion in nineteenth-century Canadian society, no doubt many couples wrestled with similar problems.

A final, and to our eyes jarring, note in these expectations of married life is the strong hint of feminine submission in some of the letters which passed between courting couples. The long, patronizing letter which the leading Montreal lawyer David McCord sent to his future bride Letitia Chambers in 1878 is a striking example. Letitia, three years McCord's senior, was a nurse, a former matron of the Montreal smallpox hospital, and a religious educator in a Toronto prison. A woman in her later thirties, she stood well beneath his high position in the Montreal Anglo-Canadian elite and some members of his family had objected to their union. Despite her mature years and wide experience, McCord addressed her with great condescension and, given the fact that she married him soon after, she must have accepted his intense paternalism. He wished Letitia to gratify his ego in a number of ways, by devoting her life to him, by pleasing him, and by accepting his guidance. Surveying her character and demeanour, McCord also urged her on to heroic acts of self-improvement. He wished her to be humble and serious, sweet and gentle, ladylike and refined. He also expected her to submit to his correction whenever it pleased him, promising that he would offer it tenderly. Commenting freely on her personal appearance, he praised her youth and beauty, then advised her on her clothing.[19]

We might think Letitia's submission an aberration were it not that other letters and diaries reveal examples of feminine subordination which, while not as extreme, display a similar pattern in male-female relations. On the day Amelia King became engaged to Lewis Hill in 1851, she noted the momentous event in her journal. "I am leaving my dear parents roof no longer under a Father's and a beloved & kind one too under his watchful eye continually. I must think and judge more for myself again. I have a fond & dear husband to whom I can go for advice and I feel that his advice will be good."[20] On New Year's Day,

1852, again anticipating her approaching marriage, she noted "I must be watchful of my conduct public & private. My husband will be a guide." Amelia thought of herself as passing from one man's guardianship to another's. In 1861 Georgina Johnstone wrote to her fiancé William Munro in a similar vein. "I have no desire William to shape my own destiny. I fear I would do it very badly. I would much rather leave it in your hands."[21] As a young woman Anna Dawson shared the same cast of mind. In 1875 she remarked of her husband-to-be, "he always knows his own mind, so in future I shall let him make up my mind for me & it will save a great deal of mental anxiety."[22] The courtship letters which Edith Carey wrote to J.B. Tyrrell, the young geologist whom she married in 1894, place him on a pedestal too.[23] Not surprisingly, men held the same point of view; recall the assumptions underlying Michael Leeson's relationship with Eleanor Donnelly. Note, too, the promise William D. Hall, a small-time Nova Scotian mine promoter, made to his fiancée Jenny Miller of Bridgewater after a lover's tiff in 1887. I am willing, he told her, "to take charge of you for life."[24] Jenny was thirty-three at the time.

What can we make of these passing observations? Perhaps not very much. After all, McCord's letter apart, all of them were casual remarks written in haste. But then these may be Freudian slips betraying a much deeper meaning. If so, they bespeak a broad acceptance of male dominance and female submission in marriage, not just in the public dimensions of male-female relations (where we have already observed the phenomenon) but also in the most intimate moments couples knew on the threshold of married life. We can only speculate what this must have meant later in the day-to-day relations of husband and wife.

From this limited evidence of nineteenth-century English Canadian views on marriage three observations can be made. One is that these brief literary fragments reveal an outlook broadly shared by both sexes. A second is that these remarks were made in anticipation of marriage and therefore tell us nothing about the interior life of the married couple. But they do reveal some of the expectations men and women had as they approached matrimony. In particular they imply that Victorian English Canadians entered marriage accepting deep-rooted patriarchal assumptions about their future roles as husbands and wives.

Finally, of the themes running through these meditations on the necessary elements of a good marriage, most important by far was the emphasis placed on the emotional bonds between spouses. Whatever ties they might have to friends and relations, husband and wife were to be sufficient unto themselves, the ultimate sources of joy and companionship for one another. Happiness was the holiest grail which matrimony offered and only those who loved one another could attain it.

Beyond this goal lay others which, though not quite so central, still were exceedingly important. Compatibility, good character, and kindness also were vital to a successful marriage. The essential point for us to note is that all thoughts revolved about the couple itself and not its social setting. By the nineteenth century the ideology of marriage in the western world had isolated the couple from the world about it.[25] Though in retrospect we can see that courtship and marriage were social processes as much as personal acts, our ancestors thought of them only in individualistic terms.

A t this point we must turn from the ideal to the real, from abstract thoughts about romantic love to its lived experience. Since the decision to marry usually rested upon love and expectations of an affectionate union, the emotional content of courtship and marriage are central to our inquiry. But here the historian enters yet another trackless forest, a dark and tangled thicket of feelings which our gaze can scarcely penetrate. The archives tell us little enough about these matters, and most of what we can learn comes from the second half of the century. Moreover, the sources are couched in language which seldom conveys the deeper emotional meanings of the words which nineteenth-century lovers exchanged. Here more than at any other place in this study we face limits to what we can understand about the intimate lives of our forbears.

The first important question is what men and women understood love to be, not as an abstract proposition but as a lived reality. When pondering the issue in the mid-1780s Rebecca Byles distinguished between friendship and love in relations between women and men. "What is your opinion of Platonism," she rhetorically asked her aunts,

and how far it may be indulge'd without being in danger of being degraded into Materialism. may not a Sensible, prudent Girl indulge a Friendship for an agreeable pleasing improved Man in the same manner & in the same degree that she would for a Lady. are their not many Characters that would please as Companions and as Friends with whom we should shudder at the idea of a nearer connexion. between the Sentimental Friend and the passionate Lover methinks their are bounds which it is in every Person's power not to overleap. a Lady in the course of her acquaintance meets with many agreeable Men. she can Love but one. perhaps none of them suit her particular taste as a partner for life. yet must she not distinguish their Merits because they are Gentleman and may not one among the rest be distinguished by her Friendship and that Friendship innocently returned. and under some little restrictions may not such an intercourse be productive of mutual and lasting advantages, and afford the most Heart felt satisfaction.[26]

At this point Rebecca was seriously considering marriage with William Almon. Perhaps uncertain of her feelings, she identified two central features of married love, its passionate intensity, and its exclusive character.

Some fifty years later Mary Gapper told her sister Lucy Sharpe about the loving feelings she had for Edward O'Brien, whom she had promised to wed. For Mary the decision to accept Edward had not come easily, as we have seen. A woman of thirty, she had grown used to her own comfortable ways. Marriage required her to yield up things which she valued. "It costs me something even in prospect to give up my independence, my power of motion, my hermitage, my philosophizing life, my general utility & alas(s) some of my more particular associations," she confessed. But in exchange she received the love of a man whom she loved deeply. As she put it,

I am more and more contented to make these sacrifices from the certainty that I should receive in return the possession of a heart capable of entering into all my views & feelings & attached to me with an affection so exactly suited to my own humour that I sometimes almost fancy that I must myself have dictated it tho' I can by no means guess how & from the pretty sanguine assurance that I should more essentially contribute to the happiness of this heart's owner than to that of any other person; besides this there is the feeling which I am almost afraid to trust to & ashamed to admit to speak of even to you, lest it should originate in presumption & be mistaken for hypocritical seeking to throw a veil of sanctity over my secret wishes – the feeling that it is perhaps the work assigned me by providence to promote his more important interests whilst I am at the same time convinced that I should in return incur no hindrance but receive assistance & encouragement on my own onward progress towards the great goal.[27]

Here Mary touched the very heart of romantic love, the transcendent feeling of oneness, the sense of common purpose and mutual support shared with a dear and intimate friend.

Jane Hudson also emphasized the intimacy, the joy, and the exclusiveness of love in a bit of poetry which she wrote, but seems not to have sent, to William Douglas after their first meeting in 1861.

Oh! tis pleasant to know there are beings about us
Who tune the most exquisite strings in our heart,
To feel that they would not be happy without us

And that we, in our loneliness sigh when we part.
Oh! there's something devine [sic] in the thoughts that we cherish
A star beam within that shines from above –
To know that if all the world gives and should perish
The greatest of fortune still dwells in our Love.[28]

In 1874 Amelia Holder, then eighteen and from a small New Brunswick village, reflected on the meaning of love in a dramatically different way when confiding to her diary about an unrequited passion. A pall of melancholy, isolation, and hopelessness hangs over the journal. "My heart is broke. I shall go stick sark staring, mad. *He's* going to Tyree. It was in our paper Friday. I had great hope that *he* was coming here and was looking for his [presence] for here all the time when the first thing strikes my eye is sailed for Tyree. I don't know exactly where that is but I think it is in the *East Indies*. I suppose I must give him up now, so farewell my dreams and hopes and let us plow on in the dreary sameness of this life."[29] And like Jeannie Douglas, though in a much different frame of mind, Amelia turned to poetry to express her sentiments:

Tired, so tired!
Heart soul and brain,
Utter the same sad plaint,
Feel the same dull, heavy pain.

Yet in her suffering, Amelia revealed the same sense of a loving relationship which Jeannie affirmed. What Amelia lacked but yearned for was the emotional bond which Jeannie so obviously had found.

When men discussed love they defined it in much the same way. In 1848, when Henry J. Boulton, a member of a prominent Toronto family, wrote to his intended Charlotte Rudyard in England, he emphasized the exclusiveness and the inward-looking emotional self-sufficiency of the loving couple.

In possessing you I shall think I possess all things and I think it not selfish to wish that all your happiness should be centred in me. This is not vanity or conceit it is but the effect which I should wish to realize of that mutual love and sincere affection wh. will make us all in all to one another. To you would I confide myself my hopes my happiness my all and it is not too much to wish for a complete return It is but my love which makes me wish dearest in these [things] and you will not misconstrue them. I tell you all I feel all I think and do it truly from that you may judge how I regard you.[30]

When the Prescott lawyer James Reynolds wrote to the woman whom he was courting in 1863, he thought of love in terms of ardour, trust, and generosity. "I am a firm believer in Curinus definition of the divine passion," he wrote to his good friend Mary. "'Love is a noble & generous passion founded only on ardent friendship or on an exalted respect or on an implicit confidence in its object' and being so won't dictate to you as to flirting correspondence or anything else in which a lady unfettered by obligations might properly indulge."[31] In this case the context of the remark is instructive. James and Mary were not engaged, but he sought a more secure relationship while acknowledging that they had made no formal commitments to each other.

The young professor Adam Shortt, writing to his fiancée Elizabeth Smith some thirty-five years later, idealized love as deep, pure, ennobling, and exalting.

Often of late have the lines occurred to me while thinking of you dearest Beth 'Oh how sweet it is to love and to be loved again!' That is, where the love is not of that insipid, warmed-over variety, which comes on like a mild attack of intermittent fever, and leaves as quickly as it comes, but where it is the genuine affection, the purest & deepest manly & womanly love, of two whole natures for each other. How elevating to the whole character is the consciousness of being able to love in such a manner & oh how precious it is to know that one is the object of such a love. Tis a stronger barrier against all base or evil inclination than a thousand good resolutions. The test of such true love is its strength during separation; when, instead of burning low & perhaps going out altogether, the lamp of true love shines brighter & brighter – instead of coldness & forgetfulness there is a constant remembrance & a continuous longing for the presence of the other one, the absent self.[32]

Like others whose experience of love we have examined, Shortt underscored its power, its intimacy, and its exclusiveness, as well as the oneness of the self and the beloved.

But some thought that women loved in ways different from those of men. Jean Hall expressed a common belief when she told Sandford Fleming, "womans love cannot be given more than once & it is I believe unchangeable."[33] This conviction placed Hall in an awkward spot for she had once encouraged another admirer. "Mine [my heart] I at one time thought I had given everlastingly away but it was not so. It was a mere *childish fancy*," she explained to Sandford, "which I very soon got over & of which I have long been very much ashamed." Sandford accepted Jean's view, though he did not apply it to himself. When proposing to her he admitted to a previous love – from whom (and this he did not admit) he had parted a scant five months before – but assured her that his affections were no longer divided.[34]

It was sometimes assumed, as well, that women might love less intensely than men. Reginald Drayton accepted this truth when he committed himself to Agnes Rubidge in 1888. Reginald, a thirty-eight-year-old Ontario bachelor from a well-to-do English landed family, told Agnes, "it is a great joy to me to have at last found in you my dear girl one who can fill that void & hunger of the heart which has been mine for many years. I know I cannot expect you to love me very strongly yet (for you have seen comparatively little of me) but I hope you will do so in time. A life without love is like a day without sun."[35] The ardent letters which William Hall sent to his fiancée Jenny Miller often refer to her tepid feelings for him. Unlike Drayton, however, Hall could not accept this situation easily. He was plagued by doubt over the depth of Jenny's commitment to him and very anxious for security in love.[36]

Occasionally courting men and women expressed their ambivalence about love. One of James Reynolds' friends, caught in the backwash of a broken engagement, believed that "men should be made of stronger & prouder stuff than to suffer the fickleness of a dainty girl to stir us from the career of our honour ... unless a fellow is weak enough to love it's hard to put one's unhoused & free condition into circumspection and confine, for the bauble of a pretty face. However, I suppose it's our common doom whether we like it or no."[37] Mary MacGregor, a school teacher from Amherst, Nova Scotia, felt this same ambivalence when, a few weeks before her engagement to Robert Dawson, she cautioned him about her forthcoming visit to his family. Apparently Robert hoped that they would become formally betrothed. Mary was more cautious: "try not to build too much on this visit Rob. Nevertheless I do hope it will end in a satisfactory way for us both. I go down with this wish & if I cannot give you all you want at the end of it, it won't be my fault. Love cannot be forced. I shall do all I can. We will enjoy the three weeks anyway."[38]

Mary's caution speaks to the fact that many couples found the growth of intimacy a troubling experience, a time of turbulent feelings, some of them far from happy. Despite the joy of blooming love, men and women frequently knew darker emotions as well; doubt and depression, jealousy and possessiveness could often be the counterpoint of romantic passion. Courtship was a time of insecurity and vulnerability, a time when men and women risked self-esteem in their quest for permanence in a loving relationship with another, a moment when the need for trust might well outweigh the possibilities that it could be achieved. Although betrothal promised to improve those possibilities, engagement was an interim position between the emotional uncertainties of courting and the seeming emotional stability of marriage. Hence the often troubled nature of these ostensibly happy times.

Doubts about love's constancy were probably a source of greater anxiety than any other cause. Soon after he became engaged to Jean Hall, Sandford Fleming became concerned about their prospects for marital happiness. Jean reassured him but also offered to release him from his promise if he doubted that their union would be happy.[39] Some of Sandford's worries came from his reaction to Jean's earlier love. According to him, he feared marrying a woman who could not love him unreservedly. "As we cannot know each other too well," he wrote to her in June 1854,

I may as well & at once point out [that] the foundation of my uneasiness is to be found in an expression in your own letter and told with that candour which I much respect. First that you "had given your heart everlastingly away" the two last words of which appear so unchangeable that they after quoting give rise to strange, uneasy feelings; as if all efforts on my part however strenuous and true would proof [sic] unavailing in gaining its possession – again you say it is "everlastingly mine" but then after it has been *everlastingly away* how can it be? To become my wife with a heart [illegible] would be a mere matter of expediency. a heart everlastingly away! and to such[.] no! it cannot be, it would be unjust, too bad – surely I am not borne [sic] to be entirely miserable. No your letter breath [sic] too much kindness for that. These are my occasional day dreams[;] it must be my fault to allow such thoughts to enter my head but they will creep in and trouble me.[40]

Obviously Sandford looked for security in love, something which still eluded him. But – and here we speculate – what may have troubled him most was jealousy that the woman he loved had loved another before him.

Fears of inconstant love particularly afflicted couples who lived far apart and those involved in long engagements. During the later 1880s William Hall, whose understanding with Jenny Miller lasted for three years before they married, felt repeated pangs of unrequited love which drove him to beg for reassurance.[41] Living some distance away from Agnes Rubidge for much of their engagement, Reginald Drayton reassured his intended, "do not as you hinted in one of your letters for a moment think that I for a moment doubt your affection for me. I do not. I know that you love me my dear and you must go on doing so."[42] Hall and Drayton had each learned painful lessons about the volatility of affection.

Nineteenth-century diaries and love letters sometimes included references to a loved one's flirtations with others, thin veils which failed to disguise anxieties about fidelity in courtship. James Reynolds bantered with his Mary about flirting in the letters he wrote her in 1863-64.[43] But usually the subject was not a laughing matter. Gingras caused George Jones no end of anguish when he sought Honorine for himself, as George so painfully recorded. William Hall was jealously possessive of Jenny Miller, and he confronted her with his feelings in 1887 when his concerns grew acute. "I have every faith in you Darling and know you will try to do what is right if possible for you to do so, but I fear that it might overcome you as it has done before. I wish now that I had not heard about the first it seems to me something *frightful*[.] I cannot account for it. I have been trying years to win your love but *how* have I succeeded while others succeed without trying[.] it is strange, and makes me verrey sad[.] God nows Darling I would do anything in the world for you, and your happiness."[44] Fear of losing his loved one troubled Hall's sleep as well. "I was dreaming of you last night Dear," he told Jean, "and somebodey else also[.] you were out driving. I thought you passed me never looked at me, laughing and talking at me[.] I felt bad even in my sleep. I woke up trembling like a leaf[.] Did not sleep again and have felt bad all day, but *I know it cannot be*[.]"[45]

Even when no alternative lover threatened a suitor's peace of mind, courting men and women often were moody and depressed. Annie Affleck, the Nova Scotia Catholic who married John Thompson (the future prime minister) in 1870, frequently felt cross, dissatisfied, and petulant during their three-year courtship. No doubt the origins of her discontent were complex, but the uncertainties of her blooming romance must surely have been among them. The peace which she found came from Thompson's company, who responded to her darker moments by coaxing her out off her unhappy humours.[46]

William Coleman, a thirty-six-year-old Ontario farmer, was melancholy in the weeks leading up to his marriage in 1869. Coleman and his bride-to-be only met infrequently prior to their wedding, and then only in the company of others. Likely they did not know one another very well before they wed. Coleman's despondency seems to have come from thoughts of his approaching nuptials and from his changed relationship with his father, whose farm he took over at marriage.[47]

The distinguished physician Sir William Osler noticed a similar problem in 1906. Osler's niece Gwendolyne Francis was soon to marry Bertram Andras and he was to give the bride in marriage. Shortly before the wedding he wrote to her, "Marjorie showed me a letter the other day from Bertram which has made me very uneasy. It was very morbid & unnatural. Have you noticed anything odd about him recently. It would never do to risk a nervous breakdown. Would it not be safer to postpone the wedding until Xmas? Send me a line in confidence. If there was anything seriously wrong you surely would have noticed it.

He seems a natural enough fellow and devoted to you. It may be only the pre-matrimonial neurasthenia in aggravated form to which many young men are, under the circumstances, subjected."[48]

For couples who lived far apart, separation itself was a source of anxiety. The nineteenth-century letters of the betrothed are filled with loneliness and longing for the company of their beloved. "I have not yet become reconciled to your absence," Halli Fraser told Harry King in 1829, "tho your likeness (for it really is one) comforts me very much still it never answers my questions and when I kiss it it is so cold and *heartless*."[49] Jane Allerthorn, the American woman courted by James Lauder, a shop clerk in Niagara-on-the-Lake, wrote even more eloquently on the subject. "I wated with all the patians that I possibly could muster for an answer to my letter," she informed Lauder in 1838.

I whent to the post Office repeatedly but no letter disappointment took possession of my mind I began to look back on past times on the many happy hours we have spent in each others Company of the many rambles we have took on the banks of that sweet river where the fresh brees forever blow where I have listened to the many fond tales and thought of futurity and of the happyness that I anticipated whould be my lot but alas I had given myself up to disappointment when yesterday Mr. Pancett handed me youre very affectionat letter but judge of my surprise to see it dated June the 13th and I have waited with all the anxiety that can possibly exist in the human brest. I am very sorry that you are so low spirited imagine the time will come when we shall not be absent from each other I wish I could see you I whould try to rouse youre sprites.[50]

At mid-century, Jane Van Norman, the Methodist girls school principal in Hamilton, empathized with her fiancé Dunham Emory when he complained of the pain of their separation. But she also advised him not to "lean too much to any arm of flesh for happiness. If you do you'll be disappointed. We should reflect how much better off we are than others."[51] Like Emory, Georgina Johnstone, the young Irish fiancée of William Munro, was beset with grief and anguish at their separation when William emigrated to Canada in 1857.[52]

A few months before she married in 1881, Mary Harris, a young farm woman from near Oshawa, spoke of her aching loneliness to her future husband John Essery, a farmer and lay Methodist preacher who lived in Huron County, Ontario.

Last Sunday was the most lonesome day I ever put in, in my life. If I had only had wings I should have flown to you. Two or three days more like that would soon send me where I should never feel lonesome anymore. I suppose what made me more lonesome was that the people at St Marys [where Essery lived] were enjoying the company of one whom I would like to see. I drempt about you but not the night you wrote, it was last Saturday. It wasnt very pleasant either. I thought the time for our union was set but that you did not come. Then in the excitement a coffin came but who it was for I do not know.[53]

When contemplating marriage some women – though seemingly no men – anticipated another source of anxiety, parting from their parents. While Amelia King felt confident that she would be happy in marriage, she also knew that leaving her family home would be "a sore trial."[54] Similarly, when at church just a few days before she married William Douglas in 1863, Jane Hudson experienced a "very strange feeling that came over me two or three times during the service. I could not help thinking when I sat down at the Lord's table with Mama that it was likely the last time I should do so (at all events before we are married) and perhaps the last time with dear Mama, Anna & Richard."[55]

Still, whatever the trials of a burgeoning romance, many couples learned the great joy which comes from a growing sense of oneness with a beloved other, for romantic love lay at the very heart of nineteenth-century courtship and marriage. This was true at all times, in all places, and in all social ranks. "Be assured every day increases my affection," a twenty-one-year-old Robert Baldwin told his future wife Eliza Sullivan in June 1825.[56] "I love you with all my affection," the lawyer Harry King wrote Halli Fraser in 1831. "God knows Dearest I seldom affect to be possessed of very refined or even enthusiastic feelings – but *all* my affections are placed upon You. I know of nothing on earth that can be preferred to or placed in competition with You – and I have the happiness to know that you are satisfied with that – and also that I possess your warmest love & confidence in return."[57] Georgina Johnstone described her sense of loving intimacy in a letter to William Munro: "I have spoken to you on subjects that I never spoke to mortal on but yourself & you could sympathize with and have patience with me – and moreover could understand me."[58]

Four further examples from the later part of the century testify further to the fact that romance knew no social rank. In 1878 the Toronto prison guard Gilbert Hartley told his beloved Mary Card, "It is a great comfort to me isolated as I am to know that there is one dearer to me than all else besides who does not forget me and in whose thoughts I am ever present conscious of this I am strengthened to meet the obstacles that daily arise and look forward to the happy coming future."[59] The engagement letters exchanged in 1881 between John Essery and Mary Harris, both from farm families, overflowed with endearment and affection.[60] Those of the aspiring scholar Adam Shortt and the feminist doctor Elizabeth Smith, written between 1883 and 1886, were highly charged with loving emotion. So too were the letters of Main Johnson and Gladys Robertson, Torontonians who married in 1912.[61]

Anne Gilpin revealed another facet of the growth of intimacy in courtship when she affectionately scolded her future husband, the Anglican clergyman Jacob J.S. Mountain, in 1846. He had travelled on a Sunday and neglected his health, and she disapproved on both accounts.[62] Although light-hearted in manner, her letter bore a serious message: it chastised Jacob for failing to act as she wished he would. Anne's example reveals that growing intimacy brought new rights to courting couples. As a relationship developed, a wider range of emotional responses between men and women became acceptable. Where once only positive and congenial feelings could be expressed, now criticism (suitably phrased) was permissible. The higher levels of trust and security found in maturing relationships broadened the limits of acceptable responses between courting couples.

Anne displayed a degree of candour open only to those very close to one another. Candour was highly prized by courting men and women, who saw it as essential to their relationship. Once more we turn to the long and difficult courtship of William Munro and Georgina Johnstone, so rich in examples of the tribulations besetting those in search of intimacy. During their slow progress to matrimony, Georgina took the lead in emphasizing the need for open communication.[63] Gilbert Hartley provides another example. When his fiancée complained of letter-writing, he warmly defended the practice: "I think that an art that yields so much pleasure and allows us to convey our dearest thoughts, wishes, and desires so easily should of all others be cultivated."[64]

Marriage brought the long process of courtship and betrothal to an emotional culmination. The pleasures and anxieties of anticipation gave way before the solemn exchange of irrevocable promises and the first taste of licit sexual joys. We know little about the emotional denouement of nineteenth-century marriage, for only a few brides and grooms recorded impressions of their new circumstances. But this history of love would be incomplete without some mention of the subject, so let us glance briefly at the first blush of married bliss. We have already discussed the measured response of William Macaulay, who spoke of his tempered affection a week after he wed, and also that of James Robb, much more passionately committed to his new bride. Amelia King also recorded the deep happiness she and her husband both felt on they day after their marriage.[65]

Georgina Johnstone Munro was much more forthcoming when she wrote to her new husband William soon after they secretly wed in 1862.

"I can think of nothing but my sweet Will and his absence is every day becoming more intolerable. He is here in my dreams, but when I come to the bitter conscious[ness] of the real state of things O! – Is it wrong to tell it now that I am his own. Surely it would no longer seem impudent. As a miser counts his [coins] one by one so I shall count the days as they pass until you are come again."[66] But Will was more taciturn about the state of his feelings. "What a niggardly creature you are about your words of love William," Georgina berated. "Even now you hardly let one slip in 3 or 4 pages of a letter." Whatever her William's sentiments, Georgina found marriage a release for long-pent-up passions.

Most revealing of all, perhaps, is the long meditation on his bride of six months which Newton MacTavish wrote in 1904, during the first lengthy separation after their marriage. He found married life a far richer experience, and his wife a far finer woman, than he had anticipated.

It is impossible to enumerate the many ways in which she excels all my best hopes. I am with her immeasurably wealthier than I was without her. As I look back, my life seems to have been very, very barren and incomplete before last September fifteenth. It would seem a calamity to have to go back to it.

We have been far happier than we ever expected to be, & we live in the most complete harmony. We have had no quarrel, not even the little tifs of which one hears so much. Our opinions are expressed freely, and if we differ, we differ agreeably. Some might say that we have not met a vital difference. That may be, but all I can say is that we are not afraid of any and are not looking for any.[67]

It would be hard to find a finer example of the Victorian marital ideal, the loving companionate union of two kindred spirits.

There is a timeless, almost universal quality about the evidence weighed in this chapter. When it came to love, things seem to have changed very little during the century, and they differed surprisingly little from one couple to the next. From the late eighteenth century onward, love has been the principle motive for marriage in English Canada. This was true among all social groups – urban and rural, wealthy and poor, high status and low. The love match was the universal goal of those who sought a spouse, and it cut across all social boundaries in the colonies. When men and women courted they sought and expected to find someone with whom they shared empathy, a sense of oneness, and (while they seldom admitted it) an erotic bond. When they married they believed that love justified the lifelong commitment they had made. When they thought about love in the abstract, they considered it the one essential element in any successful union, the only sure route to marital happiness. When they experienced it in their lives they discovered its powerful joys as well as its troubled uncertainties. And in courtship, as the paths of a man and a woman converged, they strove to fashion a permanent relationship from love's volatile emotions. For virtually all couples, marriage offered the only possible way to transform romantic love into lifelong intimacy.

Conclusion

As Sigmund Freud once observed, "civilization threatens love with substantial restrictions."[1] The long history of western marriage bears out the truth of his observation. From time out of mind the intimate relations of men and women have mattered deeply to their families, friends, and neighbours. Through ideologies, laws, customs, institutions, and informal practices the community in the western world has always shaped the course of matrimony. In places and at times when family wishes and property matters assumed more weight in marriage than private inclinations, the role of society in making a match was highly visible. It was not so evident in the era of the couple, that period after the mid-eighteenth century when, at least in northern Europe and the English-speaking world, marriage came to be founded on romantic love and personal preference.

Yet long after the young had assumed the lead in making their marriage arrangements, basing their choice of partners on sentiment more than prudence, society preserved great influence over the process of taking a spouse. As we have seen, when couples courted and wed in nineteenth-century English Canada, elaborate public constraints hedged them in while they pursued their private interests. Perhaps most important among them was the Christian context of marriage. At the heart of Christian doctrine lay a common body of belief and tradition: the sacred character of matrimony, free consent of both partners, lifelong monogamy, and the restriction of sexual intimacy to married couples. The legacy of centuries of Christian history, these teachings established the framework within which most men and women approached and lived their married lives. They accepted religious precepts on marriage almost without question, and those who did not could only dissent on the sly. Each church used its own means to defend its views, to punish transgressors, and to reconcile them with the religious fellowship when they repented their misdeeds. And each offence, each punishment, each reconciliation marked the line between right and wrong conduct, reinforcing acceptance of the church's views on matrimony.

Law formed another set of constraints upon courting and marrying. Its understanding of gender relations rested heavily on Christian tradition but its influence moved well beyond the concerns of religion and into the secular world. The laws which touched on courtship in Canada defended the integrity of a promise to wed and reinforced the rule of chastity outside the bounds of marriage. As for matrimony, the law performed two vital functions. It established the condition of lawful wedlock and, by making divorce extremely difficult, it upheld the permanence of the marriage bond. In these ways the law powerfully reinforced the stability of family life. Beyond these functions lay the laws of marital property, rules with powerful implications for the control and distribution of wealth between husbands and wives, parents and children, but which men and women often overlooked when they wed.

The act of choosing a spouse was also governed by more impersonal factors, among them some leading characteristics of the Canadian population. For any bachelor or spinster the range of possible mates was restricted to the number of unmarried women or men they would meet who themselves were seeking a spouse. Age was an important limiting influence on the size of this group, for men and women tended to marry someone close to themselves in age, wives usually being slightly younger than their husbands. In effect this meant that men usually found potential spouses from among the unmarried women they knew who were a bit younger than themselves and who ranged in age from their late teens to their late twenties. Most women found potential husbands from the bachelors in their acquaintance who, a few years their senior, were in their twenties and early thirties. Within this age range men found that the available selection of possible mates tended to increase as they grew older, while women saw their range of choice diminish as they matured. In addition to age, geography, ethnicity, and religion also shaped the marriage market. Most often, people married someone from their own community. They also tended to marry within their faith and their ethnic group. When nineteenth-century Canadians searched for a consort, these various forms of preference limited their choice of acceptable partners.

Laws, institutions, and demographic patterns apart, communities had many less formal ways of guiding private conduct during courtship and marriage. One involved the control and supervision of social spaces for courting activities. The nineteenth-century Canadian practice of separating men from women in the course of everyday life created a special problem in courtship: society had to find occasions and places for the young to mingle and develop romantic ties. These special times and locations gave community members a chance to oversee the process of pairing off. They also gave the young of each sex a great deal of control over whom they might admit into courtship's charmed circle.

Complex rituals also framed the private experience of taking a lifelong partner. These customs varied considerably across the century and throughout the colonies, but seen in aggregate they served three complementary ends. Most important of all, rituals gave community members ample opportunity to intrude into the private world of couples as they courted, made commitments, and wed. Throughout the century society preserved the right to scrutinize and comment at every stage of the process, though the forms of this oversight changed dramatically over time. The rituals of courtship and marriage also initiated couples into the community of adults, instructing them in its values on marital ties and family life. Meanwhile men and women took advantage of these customs, using them as a chart to guide their steps over unfamiliar ground. Following the paths which ritual marked for courting couples took some uncertainty out of the quest for a mate. It allowed men and women to reveal their general intent while preserving control over the degree of their commitment.

Family members had the most immediate influence of all external factors which impinged on the couple. Courtship often unfolded within the confines of the family, particularly during the early and mid-nineteenth century and, while parents and siblings played little more than a passive role in courting life, they still formed part of the supporting cast in these intimate social dramas. As participants they could encourage or frustrate a courtship as they wished. These efforts usually centred on the courting activities of daughters who, more likely to be living at home than their brothers, were more subject to family influences than were sons.

When it came to betrothal, however, fathers and mothers moved much closer to centre stage. While men often asked their parents to approve their marriage plans, and did so earnestly hoping that approval would be granted, they seldom needed permission to wed in the same sense that women did. A man of independent means might marry whom he wished whatever his parents thought. Women lacked the same freedom. Until the later years of the century young women almost never married without their parents' formal permission. Most often it was given when requested but, when a father and mother strongly objected to their daughter's marriage hopes, their objection normally prevailed unless she could overcome it. Like most forms of parental power, this one was far from absolute. It could not be used often or capriciously without inviting defiance. Ultimately, as women gained more autonomy toward the end of the century, it fell into decay.

Within the confines of these laws, these institutions, these rituals,and these relationships the young pursued their quest for intimacy. In many ways oblivious to the limits which confronted them at every turn, they sought a spouse whom they loved and who would love them in return. Throughout the nineteenth century young English Canadians regarded romantic love as the ideal form of intimate relations between men and women. They believed love to be a powerful form of empathy, a sense of deep mutual understanding, a unique and exclusive bond with another, a feeling of enduring oneness shared by two individuals. Men and women expected to marry for love, while single they searched for someone to love, they committed themselves to marriage when they fell in love, they married feeling that they were in love, and they believed that love would last for all their wedded years. Yet reality often was far removed from this ideal. In the course of their romantic lives young lovers frequently learned that love was a complex emotion, with a dark and troubling side to its powerful joys. Doubt and anxiety, jealousy and possessiveness,were often as much a part of romance as was the contentment borne of love.

Social restrictions on the intimate world of romance gradually eroded from the mid nineteenth century onward. Everywhere we look in English Canada during these years we see the increasing freedom of the young in affairs of the heart. Although Christian precepts defined the essence of marriage, throughout the century churches lost much of their influence over courtship. At the same time, older patterns of sexual territory gradually broke down, giving the young more ease of movement, more opportunity to meet beyond the range of the family's vision. The emerging cities of the colonies offered a new anonymity to couples who moved courtship into the streets, an impersonal public setting which gave them far more privacy than could be had in their homes. The decline of traditional courtship and marriage rituals was another sign of faltering public influence over matrimony, as was the rise of new marriage customs such as the honeymoon which preserved a couple's privacy. The most telling sign of growing autonomy could be seen in the very heart of the family where, by the later nineteenth century, women gained formal control over their own marriage decisions. In early twentieth-century Canada, courtship and marriage still took place in settings bounded by complex rules and customs, as well as by powerful influences from families and social institutions. But when making their marriage arrangements, the young of the pre-war decade had far more control over their actions and decisions than earlier generations of Canadians had ever known.

What caused these far-reaching changes in English Canadians' intimate relationships? The question is much easier to ask than to answer. They occurred at a time of massive economic, demographic, and social change in Canada. High rates of migration and population increase, shifting patterns of fertility and mortality, the growth of towns and cities, the development of agriculture and resource extraction, and the beginnings of industrial manufacturing progressively altered the face of British America during the nineteenth century. In particular, the 1840s were a watershed dividing the simpler, fragmented societies and economies of the colonies, based on local or regional patterns of commerce, farming and resource production, from the more urbanized, integrated, and economically advanced community of the second half of the century.

The links between some of these broad changes and the new climate of family formation are clear. The rise of towns and cities in nineteenth-century Canada left its mark upon courtship. By removing many youths from family surveillance and introducing them into the less demanding company of comparative strangers, urban places freed them from close supervision when they set about finding a mate. High rates of immigration and internal migration had much the same effect. In a community consisting principally of first and second generation immigrants, newcomers quickly abandoned traditional courtship and marriage customs and adopted those of English Canada instead. As the cultural boundaries between immigrant groups grew fainter, the importance of ethnic background in the choice of a spouse also declined.

But in other instances the ties between sweeping change and contemporary marriage practices are far less obvious. According to some historians of the European family, industrialization had a great impact on the process of taking a spouse. Because it gave urban youths and young adults financial independence from their parents much earlier than their counterparts in rural societies, it freed them from family restrictions on marriage. The results included higher rates of illegitimacy, lower ages at marriage, and decisions to marry based upon sentiment rather than calculation.[2] In Canada industrialization had no similar impact. Illegitimacy rates were very low both before and after the rise of industry, and marriage age differed little from rural to urban places. It also appears that economic opportunity was generally greater in nineteenth-century Canada than it was in contemporary Europe, freeing Canadian young men and women from the old folks' clutches rather sooner than their European counterparts. Then, too, Canadians fell heir to an important cultural legacy, the romantic revolution of the eighteenth century. By the time settler societies took root in the lands which later became Canada, British and western European youths had taken the lead in making their own marriage decisions, basing their choice of mates on romantic love. In colonial society this was the case from the early years of settlement, long before the rise of industry.

Concerning demographic change, fertility rates in Canada began a gradual decline in the second half of the nineteenth century, as married couples deliberately began to limit the size of their families. This process had important implications for conjugal life, for it involved a new responsibility shared between husband and wife. Its significance for those contemplating marriage, however, is anything but obvious. We know very very little about how unmarried nineteenth-century Canadians anticipated marital sexuality, about their knowledge of contraception, and about their sense of an ideal family size.[3] Did men and women approach marriage with a strategy for reproduction and the knowledge and means to pursue it? Or did they simply do their conjugal duty and accept the results? We do not, and probably cannot, know.

Finally, the history of courtship and marriage holds broad implications for three further issues in the social history of nineteenth-century Canada: the problem of working-class culture, the question of women's status, and the forming of a national popular culture. In recent years some historians have argued that a working class took form in Canada during the nineteenth century. They claim that, apart from its dependent position in the capitalist social order, the most important feature of this new labouring class was its distinctive culture: a rich mixture of beliefs, traditions, institutions, rituals, behaviours, and aspirations which set working people apart from, and in opposition to, the dominant class in Canada.[4] This argument draws its inspiration from Europe, where the first industrial revolution created large urban proletariats, communities within communities deeply divided by culture, status, wealth, and power from the bourgeoisies and aristocracies above them. Among the distinctive features of these plebian cultures were their courtship and marriage practices, rituals which set working people apart from their social superiors and which reinforced the bonds of community among them.[5] But even admitting the scantiness of our sources on industrial workers, in nineteenth-century Canada we look in vain for evidence of proletarian marriage customs such as those found in Great Britain. The rituals of Canadian romance had little to do with class (though they often had much to do with status and wealth – quite another matter). When a labouring man sought a wife, he followed much the same course as a professional or farmer or businessman. When a working woman (or a working man's daughter) entertained a suitor, she acted like most other women would in similar circumstances. The courtship and marriage rites of English Canadians cut across most social boundaries. They offer no support for the claim that nineteenth-century Canadian working men had a culture of their own.

Nor, should we cling too tightly to simplistic notions about the low status of women in nineteenth-century English Canada, for feminine autonomy grew substantially from at least the 1850s onward. Married women obtained new property rights, single women won control over their marriage decisions, and all women gained greater freedom of movement. These developments formed part of a broader pattern of change which reached deep into women's lives. Among the most important were wider opportunities for education and paid employment, possibilities which increased a young woman's independence. Gradually, reluctantly, Canadian universities began to admit women students, inadvertently forming a female elite with access to some of the learned professions. The growth of compulsory public schooling spread its benefits to girls and boys alike, in the process creating job opportunities for generations of young female teachers. Lower down the scale of privilege, the rise of urban manufacturing created a swelling demand for unskilled female labour while, in city, town, and country, the need for domestic servants never seemed satisfied.

Education and employment apart, womens' lives changed in other respects as well. As the nineteenth century progressed, more and more of them remained single rather than taking a spouse. Among the married, the fertility rate declined gradually from the mid nineteenth century onward. Over time women had fewer children to care for, another new circumstance with great significance for family life and women's experiences. These far-reaching changes fundamentally altered the opportunities open to women. They did not create an egalitarian paradise: even nineteenth-century feminists could not envision such a thing. But they increased the autonomy, improved the life chances, and raised the civil status of women throughout English Canada.

Finally, the absence of strong ethnic influences on courtship and marriage customs might come as a surprise to those convinced that cultural boundaries were sharply defined in nineteenth-century English Canada. Yet while significant, common ethnic origin was not a dominant factor in selecting a mate, and the courtship rituals of the British Isles were largely absent from the colonies. In the inevitable cultural pruning which accompanied migration, most of the matrimonial customs of England, Ireland, and Scotland were shorn away. The few that survived lingered in the remoter corners of colonial society, usually in much altered form. To see this circumstance as a failure of ethnic persistence is to miss a larger point: that the courtship and marriage rituals explored in this book formed part of an emerging Anglo-Canadian popular culture. In many areas of their experience English

Canadians slowly fashioned national cultural habits during the nineteenth century. Inevitably these practices revealed a good deal of diversity from place to place and group to group, but as time passed they increasingly assumed a common core. Nineteenth-century Anglo-Canadian marriage customs were deeply embedded in this emerging popular culture. When we compare the process of seeking and winning a spouse in Victorian English Canada with that in contemporary Britain, the contrast is obvious: social differences – specifically class and ethnicity – had comparatively little influence on courtship and marriage in the colonies. That fact alone reveals the distinctive character of Canadian marriage traditions and the important place these customs had in an emerging national culture.

The history of love in nineteenth-century English Canada, then, is a story without events. It is a tale of gradual, often barely perceptible, change in the social relations of our forbears. No great occasion, no basic cause, no leading actor was fundamental to this account. We look in vain for a central moment or turning point along its course. We see instead a slow evolution in the history of private lives: the growing independence of the young, the increasing autonomy of the couple, the broadening opportunities of women, the declining inequality of the sexes – changes of attitude and behaviour which touched most social groups and which trickled into the remotest parts of Canada during the nineteenth century. Intimacy thus has a history of its own and, while no dramatic events or heroic figures mark its progress, it was equally significant for their lack. These developments were as important as any social changes in nineteenth-century Canada. By degrees they altered the character of intimate relations between the sexes, between parents and children, and between the community and its young. In doing so they transformed the very basis of marriage and family life. What could have been more fundamental than that?

Epilogue

Like all good love stories, George and Honorine's tale has a happy ending. The young couple married at the Chapelle de la Congrégation on 10 February 1847.[1] We will never know how they overcame her parents' opposition, nor how they endured the tribulations of the ten months between George's last lament and their wedding, for no sequel to the diary exists. Indeed, from this point onward the newlyweds recede into the shadows of time. By 1851 they had moved to Toronto, but after that we hear from them no more.[2] In 1873 George's journal reappeared in Oshkosh, Wisconsin, with the name A.W. Jones inscribed on the cover page. How it arrived there is a mystery. Did the Joneses migrate to the United States? Was A.W. a child of George and Honorine? We will never know. All we can hope is that our young lovers lived happily together for many years, if not ever after.

Appendix

A-1
Mean Age at Marriage by Birthplace, Ontario, 1858–1900

	Groom's Birthplace				Bride's Birthplace			
Year	Canada	England	Scotland	Ireland	Canada	England	Scotland	Ireland
1858–60	24.4	26.7	27.1	25.3	20.6	22.0	22.3	22.3
1861–65	24.9	25.9	26.9	26.2	21.2	22.1	23.4	23.0
1866–70	25.3	26.2	26.8	26.3	21.4	23.1	21.6	23.3
1871–75	25.0	25.3	27.6	26.9	21.4	22.4	22.8	23.9
1876–80	24.9	26.0	28.4	30.1	21.9	23.4	22.2	25.6
1881–85	25.8	25.7	27.5	25.1	22.5	21.7	22.6	22.7
1886–90	25.9	25.3	26.8	26.5	23.0	22.3	24.6	24.0
1891–95	25.6	25.5	26.3	26.2	22.9	22.6	22.2	23.8
1896–1900	26.5	27.6	26.1	27.7	23.6	25.5	22.0	25.3
MEAN	25.4	26.0	27.0	26.2	22.0	22.6	22.6	23.2
N	4053	825	381	645	4564	498	234	569

A-2
Mean Age at Marriage by Religion, Ontario, 1858–1900

	Groom's Denomination				Bride's Denomination			
Year	R. Cath.	Meth.	Presby.	Anglic.	R. Cath.	Meth.	Presby.	Anglic.
1858-60	24.8	25.1	25.8	26.2	21.7	20.9	21.1	22.4
1861-65	26.2	25.1	26.2	25.7	22.4	21.2	22.0	22.3
1866-70	26.3	25.3	26.2	26.0	22.6	21.3	21.6	23.3
1871-75	26.1	25.2	25.7	28.3	22.7	21.5	21.7	22.1
1876-80	25.3	24.9	25.7	28.3	22.9	21.6	22.1	24.3
1881-85	26.8	24.9	26.5	25.4	23.2	21.8	22.6	23.7
1886-90	26.8	25.5	26.2	25.2	24.0	22.2	23.4	23.0
1891-95	27.0	26.1	26.1	25.0	23.9	22.8	23.1	22.4
1896-1900	26.9	26.4	26.4	27.3	24.3	23.4	23.7	24.3
MEAN	26.3	25.3	26.1	25.7	23.0	21.7	22.2	22.8
N =	1008	2740	1591	927	941	2711	1556	906

A-3
Mean Age at Marriage by Religion, Canadian and Irish Born (N = ( ))

	Grooms		Brides	
	Canadian	Irish	Canadian	Irish
Protestant	25.2 (3377)	26.3 (372)	21.8 (3867)	23.1 (373)
Roman Catholic	26.3 (665)	26.2 (273)	23.0 (932)	23.2 (196)

A-4
Mean Age at Marriage, Urban Places

	Grooms	Brides	N
Toronto	25.4	22.8	1944
Kingston	25.4	23.3	737
Other Towns	25.4	22.0	939
	1705	1915	3620

Note: In Toronto, the only community whose sample was sufficiently large to support analysis of age differences between those born in the city and those who migrated to it, the native-born married slightly younger than the migrants (25.3 years as opposed to 25.5 for grooms, 22.2 years as opposed to 23.0 for brides.)

A-5
Marriage Age Means and Sex Ratios of the Single at Prime Marriage Age

Location	(Single Men per 100 Single Women)				Marriage Age Means	
	1861 (Ages 15–39)	1871 (16–40)	1881 (16–40)	1991 (15–44)	Grooms	Brides
Ontario	130.4	123.6	114.8	113.7	(N=2872)	(N=3345)
Toronto	90.8	96.6	96.5	89.8	25.4	22.8
Kingston	92.6	86.0	86.8	84.8	26.5	23.3
Barrie/Simcoe North	142.9	146.5			24.9	21.4
Colgan/Simcoe South	203.6	141.2	130.0	125.3	26.2	22.9
Chatham/Kent	101.6	138.7	137.1	120.9	25.5	21.8
Perth/Lanark South	121.2	111.5	101.8	92.7	25.5	23.4
Caledonia/Haldimand	110.4	141.3	123.9	123.5	24.9	22.4
Dunbarton/Ontario South	104.0	111.6	111.2	111.8	25.2	21.7
Verulam/Victoria South	232.0	136.6	119.3	117.9	25.3	21.4
Markham/York East	119.5	110.4	118.0	104.6	25.4	21.8
Scarborough/York East	137.0	110.4	118.0	104.6	26.3	22.5
Eramosa/Wellington Centre	123.8	138.6	117.1	124.8	24.3	21.9
Stanley/Huron South	156.2	130.8	118.3	108.6	25.7	21.4
Brantford/Brant South/West	109.1	114.1	105.7	101.1	25.2	22.4
Caledon/Cardwell	144.1	133.5	129.0	131.2	26.9	22.4
Chinguacousy/Peel	137.1	154.5	117.3	111.9		
Hullett	143.6					
Morris Huron North	206.9	148.7	120.9		26.8	22.2
Wawanosh	187.2					

Sources: Canada, Census, 1861–1891, and the parish records sample.
Except for Toronto and Kingston, the data for 1861 are for the township level; for 1871, 1881, and 1891 they are for the county level.

A-6
Relationship of Spousal Ages at Marriage (in percentages)

	1817–29	1858–60	1861–65	1866–70	1871–75	1876–80
Same Age	6.9	5.4	7.0	7.4	8.3	8.7
Groom Older	87.0	82.4	81.9	82.9	80.9	79.1
Bride Older	6.1	12.2	11.1	9.7	10.8	12.2
N	135	501	1085	958	687	575

	1881–85	1886–90	1891–95	1896–1900	1817–1900	
Same age	10.0	13.3	12.0	12.0	9.0	
Groom older	78.1	71.6	74.1	69.2	78.7	
Bride older	12.0	15.2	13.8	18.8	12.3	
N	743	566	557	425	6097	

A-7
Mean Age Differences (Years) at First Marriage, by Age Quartiles

	Groom's Older (N = 4806)		Bride's Older (N = 750)	
Quartile	Groom Age	Difference	Groom Age	Difference
Grooms				
1	−22	2.5	−21	−2.9
2	23–25	3.6	22–23	−2.7
3	26–28	5.1	24–25	−2.8
4	29+	7.9	26+	−2.7
Brides	Bride Age	Difference	Bride Age	Difference
1	−19	6.2	−23	−1.4
2	20–21	4.9	24–25	−2.0
3	22–24	4.4	26–28	−2.7
4	25+	3.4	29+	−4.8

A-8
Per Cent of Marriages within National Groups

Years	Canada	USA	England	Scotland	Ireland	N
1858–60	72.4	21.1	38.5	40.4	54.5	505
1861–65	75.3	24.0	22.5	32.8	45.6	1064
1866–70	80.8	12.5	20.9	26.6	38.1	965
1871–75	87.9	18.8	23.2	36.4	25.0	689
1876–80	90.0	6.3	16.1	14.3	34.8	570
1881–85	91.2	6.1	18.0	19.0	28.9	741
1886–90	89.5	9.1	24.3	23.1	36.7	563
1891–95	87.4	8.0	28.9	13.3	26.3	562
1896–1900	91.2	14.3	32.1	−	14.3	430
N	4005	259	813	377	645	6099

Notes

ABBREVIATIONS

ANQM	Archives nationales du Québec à Montréal, Montreal, Quebec
AO	Archives of Ontario, Toronto
MTRL	Metropolitan Toronto Reference Library
NAC	National Archives of Canada, Ottawa, Ontario
PANB	Public Archives of New Brunswick, Fredericton, New Brunswick
PANS	Public Archives of Nova Scotia, Halifax, Nova Scotia
PMNB	Provincial Museum of New Brunswick, St John, New Brunswick
QUA	Queen's University Archives, Kingston, Ontario
RCAAK	Roman Catholic Archdiocesan Archives, Kingston, Ontario
UCA	United Church Archives, Victoria University, Toronto, Ontario

INTRODUCTION

1 Edward Shorter, *The Making of the Modern Family* (New York: Basic Books 1975).
2 Lawrence Stone, *The Family, Sex and Marriage in England, 1500–1800* (New York: Knopf 1977), 390–5.
3 Peter Gay, *The Bourgeois Experience Victoria to Freud*, vol. 1, *Education of the Senses* (New York: Oxford University Press 1984); Peter Gay, *The Bourgeois Experience Victoria to Freud*, vol. 2, *The Tender Passion* (New York: Oxford University Press 1986).

4 Ellen K. Rothman, *Hands and Hearts: A History of Courtship in America* (New York: Basic Books 1984).

5 Michael Anderson, *Approaches to the History of the Western Family, 1500–1914* (London: Macmillan 1980).

6 Jennifer S.H. Brown, *Strangers in Blood: Fur Trade Company Families in Indian Country* (Vancouver: University of British Columbia Press 1980); Sylvia Van Kirk, *"Many Tender Ties": Women in Fur Trade Society in Western Canada* (Winnipeg: Watson and Dwyer 1980).

7 For a useful introduction, see Bryan D. Palmer, *Working-Class Experience: The Rise and Reconstitution of Canadian Labour, 1800–1980* (Toronto: Butterworth 1983).

8 E.J. Chambers and G.W. Bertram state that over two-thirds of secondary manufacturing value added in Ontario and Quebec were produced in greater Montreal and Toronto by 1890. "Urbanization and Manufacturing in Central Canada, 1870–1890" in Sylvia Ostry and T.K. Rymes, eds., *Canadian Political Science Association, Conference on Statistics, 1964: Papers on Regional Statistical Studies* (Toronto: University of Toronto Press 1964), 239.

9 Gregory S. Kealey, *Toronto Workers Respond to Industrial Capitalism, 1867–1892* (Toronto: University of Toronto Press 1980), 25.

10 F.H. Leacy, ed., *Historical Statistics of Canada*, 2nd ed. (Ottawa: Statistics Canada 1983), series R12–36.

PROLOGUE

1 Her Christian name was Catherine-Eléonore-Honorine.

2 George Stephen Jones, Diary, 2 November 1845, MG24 I155, NAC.

3 Ibid., 6 November 1845.

4 Ibid., 9 November 1845.

5 Ibid., 29 November 1845.

6 Ibid., 12 December 1845.

7 Ibid., 28 December 1845.

8 Ibid., 22 December 1845.

9 Ibid., 9 January 1846.

10 Ibid., 13 February 1846.

11 Ibid., 11 March 1846.

CHAPTER ONE

1 Georges Duby, *The Knight, the Lady, and the Priest: The Making of Modern Marriage in Medieval France*, Barbara Bray, trans. (New York: Pantheon 1983), 26–8.

2 1 Cor. 7: 7, 32–4.

3 Michael M. Sheehan, "Choice of Marriage Partner in the Middle Ages: Development and Mode of Application of a Theory of Marriage," *Studies in Medieval and Renaissance History* 1 (1978): 6–7.

4 Duby, *The Knight, the Lady, and the Priest*, 33–4.

5 Ibid., 283.

6 George H. Joyce, *Christian Marriage: An Historical and Doctrinal Study* (London: Sheed and Ward 1948), 147–8.

7 Ibid., 185.

8 Jack Goody, *The Development of the Family and Marriage in Europe* (Cambridge: Cambridge University Press 1983), 139; Jean-Louis Flandrin, *Families in Former Times: Kinship, Household and Sexuality* (Cambridge: Cambridge University Press 1979), 24.

9 In 1917 the Catholic church reduced the prohibited degrees to the third. Joyce, *Christian Marriage*, 530.

10 Ibid., vii.

11 Sheehan, "Choice of Marriage Partner," 3–33.

12 Goody, *Development of the Family*, 123, 151–3.

13 Ibid., 214–6.

14 Emmanuel LeRoy Ladurie, *Montaillou: The Promised Land of Error* (New York: Vintage 1979), 179–204.

15 Goody, *Development of the Family*, 102.

16 Flandrin, *Families in Former Times*, 131–2.

17 Goody, *Development of the Family*, ch. 8.

18 Quoted in Joyce, *Christian Marriage*, 112–13.

19 Ibid., 177–84; Gerhard E. Lenski, *Marriage in the Lutheran Church: An Historical Investigation* (Columbus, Ohio: Lutheran Book Concern 1936), 334–5.

20 Joyce, *Christian Marriage*, 116–23.

21 Ibid., 531–3; Goody, *Development of the Family*, 176–7.

22 T.A. Lacey, *Marriage in Church and State*, 2nd. ed. (London: Society for the Promotion of Christian Knowledge 1947), 149–51.

23 Joyce, *Christian Marriage*, 147.

24 Ibid., 128, 194–5.

25 Ibid., 530.

26 In terms of adherents, the largest denominations in British North America during the second half of the nineteenth century were: Roman Catholics (40–45 per cent of the colonial population), Methodists (12–17 per cent), Presbyterians (15 per cent), Anglicans (13–14 per cent), and Baptists (5–6 per cent). No reliable statistics are available for most colonies during the first half of the century. In English Canada the proportion of Catholics was considerably lower and the proportion of Protestants correspondingly higher. See: Canada, *Census of Canada*,

1851–1901; and M.C. Urquhart and K.A.H. Buckley, *Historical Statistics of Canada* (Toronto: Macmillan of Canada 1965), 18.

27 Alexander, Bishop of Kingston, to the Catholic Clergy of Upper Canada, [1829], Father Ewen Macdonald Collection, AO; [Pastoral Letter on Marriage], 25 November 1840, B12•CL•1/3 RCAAK; Pastoral Letter of His Lordship the Bishop of Toronto on Matrimony, 23 January 1869, ibid., DI10 CL 9/3

28 *The Most Reverend Doctor James Butler's Catechism* (Montreal: D. & J. Sadlier 1871), 79–80.

29 J.B. de la Salle, *A New Treatise of the Duties of a Christian Towards God* (Montreal: Plinguet & Laplante 1869), 298–300.

30 C.P.T. Chiniquy, *The Priest, the Woman, and the Confessional* (London, n.d.). First published in 1875, this sensationalist tract went through scores of editions in at least eight languages during the next half-century.

31 Audrey S. Miller, et., *The Journals of Mary O'Brien, 1828–1838* (Toronto: Macmillan 1968), 78, 140.

32 Gordon to Gaulin, 24 and 29 May 1838, Catholic Archdiocesan Archives Collection, AO.

33 J.F. Leonard to Bishop Horan, 19 December 1870, DI5 C24/1, RCAAK.

34 Ibid., letter re: William Murphy and Elizabeth O'Brien, Patrick Phelan, Bishop, 11 January 1850.

35 Farling to Macdonell, 23 July 1833, Catholic Archdiocesan Archives Collection, AO.

36 Ibid., Morin to Gaulin, 23 December 1834.

37 Ibid., O'Flynn to Gaulin, 31 December 1840.

38 Macdonell to Cassidy, 28 August 1832, Macdonell Letterbook 3, RCAAK.

39 Power to Morin, 19 March 1844, Power Letterbook, 133, Roman Catholic Archdiocese of Toronto Archives.

40 Ibid., Power to McIntosh, 25 June 1844, 162-3.

41 Horan to Rossiter, [March 1860], DI8 C19/1, RCAAK.

42 Power to McDonell, 14 December 1842, Power Letterbook, 35.

43 Ibid., Power to O'Dwyer, 17 November 1842, 25.

44 Caution re: Sally Wright, 12 November 1836, AI5 ED4/12, RCAAK.

45 Power to O'Dwyer, 30 September 1843, Power Letterbook, 94–5.

46 Lee to Gaulin, 31 January 1842, Catholic Archdiocesan Archives Collection, AO.

47 O'Connor to Horan, 31 October 1865, DI7 C24/32, RCAAK.

48 Strachan to Atkinson, 18 December 1843, Strachan Letterbooks, AO.

49 Kenneth M. Boyd, *Scottish Church Attitudes to Sex, Marriage and the Family, 1850–1914* (Edinburgh: John Donald 1980), 4–9; Norah Smith, "Sexual Mores and Attitudes in Enlightenment Scotland" in Paul-Gabriel Bouc, ed., *Sexuality in Eighteenth-Century Britain* (Manchester: Manchester University Press 1982), 50–7.

50 Boyd, *Scottish Church Attitudes*, 11–14.
51 A strong tradition of kirk session discipline also persisted amongst Presbyterians in the American south. W.D. Blanks, "Corrective Church Discipline in the Presbyterian Churches of the Nineteenth Century South," *Journal of Presbyterian History* 44, no. 2 (1966): 89–105.
52 Duff Willis Crerar, "Church and Community: The Presbyterian Kirk-Session in the District of Bathurst, Upper Canada" (M.A. thesis: University of Western Ontario 1979).
53 Franktown Presbyterian Church, *Session Minutes*, 1834–1889, UCA.
54 Ibid., 21 January 1839.
55 John M. Beattie, *Attitudes Towards Crime and Punishment in Upper Canada, 1830–1850* (Toronto: Centre of Criminology, University of Toronto 1977).
56 Bryan D. Palmer, "Discordant Music: Charivaris and Whitecapping in Nineteenth Century North America," *Labour/Le Travailleur* 3 (1978): 5–62.
57 *A Form of Discipline for the Ministers, Preachers, and Members comprehending the Principles and Doctrines of the Methodist Episcopal Church in America*, 7th ed. (Philadelphia 1791), 27–8. This was the Methodist discipline used in Upper Canada before the first Canadian edition was published in 1829.
58 *The Doctrines and Disciplines of the Methodist Episcopal Church in Canada* (York: Ryerson and Metcalf 1829), 79–80. The regulations remained unchanged until at least the 1860s.
59 Ryerson to Mother, 31 May 1825, Ryerson Papers, UCA.
60 Sylvia Wright to Thomas Bennett, 26 September 1793. George A. Rawlyk, ed., *The New Light Letters and Spiritual Songs, 1778–1793* (Wolfville, N.S.: Acadia Divinity College 1983), 177–8.
61 Rawlyk, *New Light Letters*, 345, n.256; George A. Rawlyk, "From New Light to Baptist: Harris Harding and the Second Great Awakening in Nova Scotia" in Barry W. Moody, ed. *Repent and Believe: The Baptist Experience in Maritime Canada* (Hantsport, N.S.: Lancelot Press 1980), 17–18.
62 Rawlyk, *New Light Letters*, 62–3; George A. Rawlyk, *Ravished by the Spirit: Religious Revivals, Baptists, and Henry Alline* (Montreal and Kingston: McGill-Queen's University Press 1984), 82–5, 130–1.
63 Joseph F. Kett, *Rites of Passage: Adolescence in America 1790 to the Present* (New York: Basic Books 1977), 78–9.
64 *Doctrines and Discipline of the Wesleyan Methodist Church in Canada* (Toronto 1850), 37.
65 For examples, see Methodist Episcopal Church Conference Correspondence, boxes 1 and 3–6, UCA; file M/5/19, United Church of Canada, Montreal-Ottawa Conference, McGill University Archives, acc. 2201.
66 W.R. Riddell, "The Law of Marriage in Upper Canada," *Canadian His-*

torical Review 2, no. 3 (September 1921): 226–48.
67 Sigmund Freud, *Civilization and Its Discontents*, James Strachey, ed. (New York: Norton 1961), 51–2.

CHAPTER TWO

1 Earl of Halsbury, *The Laws of England*, 1st ed. (London 1890), XVI: 274–7.
2 *British Whig* (Kingston), 24 October 1874.
3 W. Peter Ward, "Unwed Motherhood in Nineteenth Century English Canada," Canadian Historical Association, *Historical Papers* (1981), 38–9, n.9.
4 Ibid., 36–8.
5 Halsbury, *Laws of England*, XX: 270–5.
6 Constance B. Backhouse, "The Tort of Seduction: Fathers and Daughters in Nineteenth Century Canada," *Dalhousie Law Journal* 10, no. 1 (June 1986): 49–50. Backhouse notes (73, n.82) that there were virtually no reported actions for seduction outside Ontario during the nineteenth century, a fact which she attributes to the absence of legislation similar to the Upper Canadian law of 1837. But it may have been the case, in Nova Scotia and New Brunswick at least, that few seduction actions were pursued in the courts because poor law provisions there gave unwed mothers recourse to financial support, whereas no such possibility existed in Ontario. Thus the Ontario penchant for seduction lawsuits may have resulted, in part, from the fact that this was the only legal avenue open for an unmarried mother and her family who sought financial redress.
7 Backhouse, "The Tort of Seduction," 80.
8 Ibid.," 79.
9 *British Whig*, 13 September 1888.
10 Ward, "Unwed Motherhood," 39–40.
11 Canada East, *Civil Code*, 1866, art. 240, s.768.
12 Ward, "Unwed Motherhood," 40–1.
13 Ibid., 42–5. See also, Angus McLaren, "Birth Control and Abortion in Canada, 1870–1920," *Canadian Historical Review* 59, no. 3 (September 1978): 319–40: Angus McLaren and Arlene Tigar McLaren, *The Bedroom and the State: The Changing Practices and Politics of Contraception and Abortion in Canada, 1880–1980* (Toronto: McClelland and Stewart 1986); and Constance B. Backhouse, "Nineteenth-Century Canadian Rape Law 1800–1892" in David H. Flaherty, ed., *Essays in the History of Canadian Law*, vol. 2 (Toronto: Osgoode Society 1983), 200–47.
14 Great Britain, *Statutes*, 32 Hen. VIII, c.38.

15 Lawrence Stone, *The Family, Sex and Marriage in England, 1500–1800* (New York: Harper and Row 1977), 35–7.

16 Whether the Hardwicke Act obtained in Nova Scotia is uncertain. English law as it existed in 1758 formed the basis of colonial law, but one early commentator on the laws of the colony states that the Hardwicke Act, passed in 1753, was not in force. Beamish Murdoch, *Epitome of the Laws of Nova Scotia*, vol. 2 (Halifax 1832), 15.

17 Richard Cartwright Jr to [Lieutenant Governor of Upper Canada], 12 October 1792 in Canada, *Report on the Canadian Archives*, 1891, 85–6; 33 Geo. III, c.5, Upper Canada, *Statutes of the Province of Upper Canada*, 1792–1831.

18 In most colonies the major denominations received authorization to perform marriages, but in Upper Canada the Church of England fought a stiff battle to keep this privilege from falling into the hands of the Methodists. For the details, see W.R. Riddell, "The Law of Marriage in Upper Canada," *Canadian Historical Review* 2, no. 3 (September 1921): 226–48. In Nova Scotia, from the eighteenth century onward, justices of the peace often performed marriages as well, even when ordained ministers lived in their communities. For an example of a jurisdictional dispute between a clergyman and a justice of the peace, see Brian C. Cuthbertson, ed., *The Journal of John Payzant* (Hantsport, NS: Lancelot Press 1981), 59–64.

19 Ryerson to Punshon, 19 June 1867, Wesleyan Methodist Portrait Album, UCA.

20 For a sample, see *Review of a Pamphlet from the Churchman's Magazine, Entitled Marriage with a Deceased Wife's Sister: A Bible Argument Long Obscured* (Toronto 1871); Hibbert Binney, *Reasons for Rejecting the Proposed Alterations in the Marriage Law of the Dominion* (Halifax 1880); William Gregg, *Marriage with a Deceased Wife's Sister Prohibited by the Word of God* (Toronto 1868); Jacob M. Hirschfelder, *A Wife to her Sister* (Toronto 1878); John Laing, *Marriage with the Sister of a Deceased Wife, considered in connection with the Standards and Practice of the Canadian Presbyterian Church* (Toronto 1868); D.V. Lucas, *Deceased Wife's Sister. Letters by the Rev. D.V. Lucas, M.A. in Reply to the Rev. H. Roe, D.D.* (Montreal 1882); [Susie A. Wiggins], *The Gunhilda Letters, Marriage with a Deceased Wife's Sister: Letters of a Lady to the Right Rev. the Lord Bishop of Ontario* (Ottawa 1881).

21 Canada, *Statutes of Canada*, 45 Vict., c.42.

22 George Elliott Howard, *A History of Matrimonial Institutions*, 3 vols., 2nd ed. (New York: Humanities Press 1964), 2: 85–117, especially 107.

23 Edgar F. Raney, *Marriage and Divorce Laws of Canada* (Toronto: Social Service Council of Canada 1915); Emily L. Purves, "Divorce in Canada"

(MA thesis: Colorado College 1931), 1; Constance B. Backhouse, "'Pure Patriarchy': Nineteenth Century Canadian Marriage," *McGill Law Journal* 31 (March 1986): 264–312; and James G. Snell, "'The White Life for Two': The Defence of Marriage and Sexual Morality in Canada, 1890–1914," *Histoire sociale/Social History* 16, no. 31 (Mai 1983): 111–29.

24 *Crim. Con.: A Trial* (Halifax 1820).

25 Quoted in Lee Holcombe, *Wives and Property: Reform of the Married Women's Property Law in Nineteenth-Century England* (Toronto: University of Toronto Press 1983), 18.

26 Ibid., 20.

27 Ibid., 21–3.

28 Ibid., 23.

29 Ibid., 37.

30 Ibid., 39–40.

31 *The Upper Canadian Law Journal* 2 (1856): 217.

32 Formal equity courts were established in Nova Scotia, New Brunswick, and Prince Edward Island in 1825, 1838, and 1848 respectively. Constance B. Backhouse, "Married Women's Property Law in Nineteenth Century Canada," *Law and History Review* 6, no. 2 (Fall 1988): 211–57.

33 Ibid.

34 Canada, *Statutes of Canada*, 1859, 22 Vict., c.34.

35 Richard H. Chused, "Married Woman's Property Law: 1800–1850," *Georgetown Law Journal* 71, no. 5 (June 1983): 1359–1425; Norma Basch, *In the Eyes of the Law: Women, Marriage, and Property in Nineteenth-Century New York* (Ithaca and London: Cornell University Press 1982); Marylyn Salmon, *Women and the Law of Property in Early America* (Chapel Hill and London: University of North Carolina Press 1986), 81–140.

36 The petitions to the Legislative Council can be found in NAC, RG14 C1, vols. 26, 42, 45, 54, 55, 57, 59, 60, 61, and 64. Those presented to the Legislative Assembly are noted in the *Journals of the Legislative Assembly of the Province of Canada*: 1855, 807; 1856, 101, 153; 1857, 100, 219, 226, 266, 273, 306, 318, and 377.

37 Backhouse, "Married Women's Property Law," *passim*.

38 James Armstrong, *A Treatise on the Law Relating to Marriages in Lower Canada* (Montreal: John Lovell 1857); Yves F. Zoltvany, "Equisse de la Coutume de Paris," *Revue d'histoire de l'Amérique française* 25, no. 3 (décembre 1971): 368.

39 Zoltvany, "Coutume de Paris," 370.

40 Armstrong, *Law Relating to Marriages*, 36–7.

41 Micheline D.-Johnson, "History of the Status of Women in the Province of Quebec," *Cultural Tradition and Political History of Women in*

Canada, Studies of the Royal Commission on the Status of Women in Canada, vol. 8 (Ottawa: Information Canada 1971), 14–16, 45.

42 E. Spring, "The Settlement of Land in Nineteenth-Century England," *American Journal of Legal History,* 8 (1964): 214–15, n.13.

43 Jack Goody, "Inheritance, Property and Women: Some Comparative Considerations," in Goody et al., eds. *Family and Inheritance: Rural Society in Western Europe, 1200–1800* (Cambridge: Cambridge University Press 1976), 10–36.

44 David Gagan, *Hopeful Travellers: Families, Land, and Social Change in Mid-Victorian Peel County, Canada West* (Toronto: University of Toronto Press 1981), 50–60.

45 For example, see Lutz K. Berkner, "Peasant Household Organization and Demographic Change in Lower Saxony (1689–1766), in R.D. Lee, et al., eds., *Population Patterns in the Past* (New York: Academic Press 1977), 53–69; and Lutz K. Berkner, "The Stem Family and the Developmental Cycle of the Peasant Household: an Eighteenth Century Austrian Example," *American Historical Review* 77, no. 2 (April 1972): 398–418. On New England, see John Demos, *A Little Commonwealth: Family Life in Plymouth Colony* (London: Oxford 1970), 164–70.

46 Goody, "Inheritance, Property and Women," 10; Hans Medick, however, notes that the decline of inheritance as a determinant in household formation in peasant societies was associated with the rise of rural industry and the proto-industrial economy. This was so because the proto-industrial family was founded on the basis of its labour potential rather than its possession of resources. Hans Medick, "The Proto-industrial Family Economy: The Structural Function of Household and Family during the Transition from Peasant Society to Industrial Capitalism," *Social History* 1, no.3 (October 1976): 303.

47 David Gagan has made much of the crisis of rural society in Canada West during the later 1850s. He argues that the closing of the Upper Canadian frontier reduced the economic options of rural dwellers in Peel County and forced them to alter a wide range of their behaviours, their strategies of marriage, fertility, and inheritance in particular. There is no need here to dispute these claims point by point, but if the economic horizons of Peel County narrowed at this time, opportunity certainly beckoned just over them. Gagan, *Hopeful Travellers, passim.*

48 Simeon and Eunice White to Simeon White [Jr], 14 July 1823, courtesy of Pat Greenwell, Ponoka, Alberta. The entire letter has been printed in W. Peter Ward, "Family Papers and the New Social History," *Archivaria* 14 no.(Summer 1982), 64–5.

49 Michael Katz, *The People of Hamilton, Canada West: Family and Class in a Mid-Nineteenth Century City* (Cambridge, Mass.: Harvard Univer-

sity Press 1975), ch. 3; Gagan, *Hopeful Travellers*, ch. 5; Stephan Thernstrom, *The Other Bostonians: Poverty and Progress in the American Metropolis, 1880–1970* (Cambridge, Mass.: Harvard University Press 1973).

50 This sample was constituted in the following manner. The marriage contracts found in the notarial archives housed in the Archives nationales du Québec in Montreal have been indexed for the period from 1800 to 1850. All sixty-seven contracts in this index between two parties with British surnames were included in the sample. A further nine contracts of the same nature drawn up by a single notary between the later 1860s and the early 1880s were also included. The sample is small and not randomly composed. But despite its statistical deficiencies, it provides a useful indication of some general trends. A more detailed analysis will have to await the comprehensive and systematic examination of this source. Montreal, Contrats de mariage, 1800–1850, and greffes de W. A. Phillips, notaire, Archives nationales du Québec, Montreal.

51 Armstrong, *Law Relating to Marriages*, 14. Armstrong noted, however, that this authority did not extend to the disposition of property, for a woman who administered her own goods still could not sell them without her husband's authorization. As he explained, this "being opposed to the dependence in which the wife is placed by nature and law with respect to her husband, would be regarded as against public policy." A woman who was a public merchant in a business separate from her husband was an exception to this general rule. She was deemed to have his implied authorization to conduct any matters related to that business. In addition, it should be noted that women who opted out of a community of goods when negotiating a marriage contract did not automatically obtain power of administration over their property. They did so only when the marriage contract expressly provided for that eventuality, or when a married woman received property on the proviso that her husband not have access to it (Armstrong, 18).

52 L.H.L., "Des contrats de mariage des commerçants dans le Bas-Canada," *Revue de législation et de jurisprudence* 1 (1845): 24–6.

53 John J. Maclaren to Alfred Ward, 28 February 1887, courtesy of A.B. Ward, Toronto.

54 Bond between John S. Cartwright and Sarah Hayter Macaulay, 16 December 1830, Cartwright Papers, AO.

55 Indenture between W.C. Gwynne and M.A. Powell, 4 May 1835, Jarvis-Powell Papers, AO.

56 Marriage settlement, William Dummer Powell Jarvis and Diana Irving, 1 October 1850, ibid.

57 Draft marriage settlement, Remigius Elmsley and Nina Bradshaw, July

1870, Elmsley Papers, box 10, Thomas Fisher Room, University of Toronto Library.

58 *Simpson* v. *Leitch*, Chancery Case Files, 115–202–69, RG22, AO.

59 *Heward* v. *McLean*, ibid., 375–70.

60 *Mackechnie* v. *Cockburn*, ibid., 122–237–69; *Chatten* v. *Bell*, 292–261–71; and *Watson* v. *Sproule*, 80–71.

61 *Beaty* v. *Stuart*, ibid., 340–90–72; *Hanscome* v. *Boylan*, 104–138–69; *Mackechnie* v. *Cockburn*, 122–237–69; *Bank of Montreal* v. *Bettes*, 324–15–72; *Livingston* v. *Blain*, 98–106–69; *Warnes* v. *Warnes*, 88–46–69.

62 Accounts of the incident can be found in *The Leader* (Toronto), 24 and 25 September 1856, and in an exchange of letters between Thomas Benson and his son Thomas Moore Benson dated 24 and 26 September and 6 and 8 October 1856, Benson Family Papers, box 1, AO.

63 *Leader* , 25 September 1856.

64 Sally Falk Moore, *Law as Process: An Anthropological Approach* (London: Routledge & Kegan Paul 1978), 2.

65 Michael Mitterauer and Reinhard Sieder, *The European Family: Patriarchy to Partnership from the Middle Ages to the Present* (Chicago: University of Chicago Press 1982), 69.

66 Ibid., 87.

CHAPTER THREE

1 Michael Katz noted an average age of 23.2 for brides and of 27.7 for grooms in Wentworth County between 1842 and 1869. David Gagan discovered a rise in mean marriage ages for nearby Peel County during these same years, from 23.8 to 26.8 for men and 21.1 to 22.9 for women. Lorne Tepperman calculated means for women throughout Canada in 1871 from aggregate census data; on average he found Canadian women married first at 23.9 years, though Nova Scotians (who wed latest) did so almost one and a half years later than Ontarians, the most precocious group. By far the most ambitious of these scholars, Ellen Gee, calculated mean marriage ages for all census years from 1851 to 1971, nationally and by province. Her estimates are somewhat above those already noted, though the only exact point of comparison is with Tepperman's means for women in 1871, Gee's being about one and a half years higher. Rather more important than this discrepancy is the trend which she described. At mid-century, Gee concluded, men married on average at just over 26, women at 23. Over the next forty years the mean age at first marriage rose steadily. By 1891 it had increased three years for both men and women; grooms were then just over 29,

their brides 26. Male marriage age remained high until the First World War, when a trend toward earlier marriage set in which lasted until the recent past. Female age at first marriage began to decline rather sooner, and it, too, fell more or less continuously throughout the twentieth century. Michael Katz, *The People of Hamilton, Canada West: Family and Class in a Mid-Nineteenth Century City* (Cambridge, Mass.: Harvard University Press 1975); David Gagan, *Hopeful Travellers: Land, Population and Social Change in Mid-Victorian Peel County, Canada West* (Toronto: University of Toronto Press 1981), 76–7; Lorne Tepperman, "Ethnic Variations in Marriage and Fertility; Canada, 1871," *Canadian Review of Sociology and Anthropology* 11, no.4 (November 1974): 329; Ellen M.T. Gee, "Fertility and Marriage Patterns in Canada, 1851–1971," (Ph.D. thesis: University of British Columbia 1978).

2 John Hajnal, "European Marriage Patterns in Perpective" in D.V. Glass and D.E.C. Eversley, eds., *Population in History: Essays in Historical Demography* (London: Edward Arnold 1965), 101–43.

3 Gee, "Fertility," 168, 314–15.

4 Martha Vicinus, *Independent Women: Work and Community for Single Women, 1850–1920* (Chicago: University of Chicago Press 1985).

5 The following parish registers were used: Trinity Anglican, Cornwall (NAC); Church of the Holy Trinity, Toronto (Anglican Diocesan Archives, Toronto); Wesleyan Methodist Church, Chatham (UCA); Chalmers Church, Kingston (Presbyterian) (UCA); Alice Street Primitive Methodist,Toronto (UCA); Caledonia Presbyterian Church, Haldimand County (UCA); Collier Street Methodist, Barrie (UCA); Dunbarton and Canton Presbyterian, Pickering Township (UCA); St Basil's Roman Catholic, Toronto (St Basil's Archive); St James Roman Catholic, Colgan (Roman Catholic Archdiocesan Archives, Toronto); St James Anglican, Kingston (Anglican Diocesan Archives, Kingston); St Andrews Presbyterian, Markham (UCA); St John the Baptist Roman Catholic, Perth (NAC); Bobcaygeon Methodist Church (UCA); Markham Circuit Primitive Methodist Church (UCA); Knox Presbyterian, Scarborough (UCA); Rockwood Circuit Primitive Methodist, Guelph district (UCA); Bayfield and Berne Presbyterian, Huron County (UCA); Playfair Circuit (Methodist), Lanark County (UCA); Chatham Station Primitive Methodist (UCA); Wellington Street Methodist, Brantford (UCA); First and Second Presbyterian Churches, Chinguacousy (UCA); Blyth Presbyterian, Huron County (UCA). These registers were selected because of their completeness and their broadly representative character. They encompass the four largest Christian denominations in nineteenth-century Ontario, in proportions roughly equal to their distribution in the population. They also reflect conditions in the most populous parts of the province, rural as well as

urban. They should not be assumed to represent other provinces in Canada for, as Gee and Tepperman suggest, mean age at first marriage was somewhat lower in Ontario than elsewhere.

6 The discrepancies between these means and those estimated by Gee are considerable. Using Hajnal's technique for calculating singulate mean ages at marriage from census data, she reported the following average bridal ages for nineteenth-century Ontario:

Year	Grooms	Brides
1851	26.7	22.4
1861	27.2	23.9
1871	28.4	25.0
1881	28.0	25.3
1891	29.3	26.6

Ellen M.T. Gee, "Marriage in Nineteenth-century Canada," *Canadian Review of Sociology and Anthropology*, 3 (1982): 320.

7 The mean for urban grooms was 25.8 and for rural grooms 25.6; the mean for urban brides was 22.3 while that for rural brides was 21.9.

8 Gee, "Marriage," 318–19.

9 E.J. Chambers and G.W. Bertram, "Urbanization and Manufacturing in Central Canada, 1870–1890" in Sylvia Ostry and T.K. Rymes, eds., *Canadian Political Science Association Conference on Statistics, 1964: Papers on Regional Statistical Studies* (Toronto: University of Toronto Press 1966), 225–58.

10 Gee, "Marriage," 318–19. But she also claims that the effects of sex ratio changes and migration patterns on nuptiality trends in general were minor between 1851 and 1971. Gee, "Fertility," 187–92, 198–9.

11 Gagan, *Hopeful Travellers*, 61–94.

12 E.A. Wrigley, *Population and History* (New York: McGraw Hill 1969), 141–2.

13 In England between 1861 and 1901 marriage age rose from 26.4 years to 27.3 for men, and 25.4 to 26.3 for women; in Scotland it increased from 26.9 to 27.5 and from 25.4 to 26.4 for the two sexes. See: E.A. Wrigley and R.S. Schofield, *The Population History of England, 1534–1871: A Reconstruction* (Cambridge, Mass.: Harvard University Press 1981), 437; Michael Flinn, et al., *Scottish Population History from the 17th century to the 1930s* (Cambridge: Cambridge University Press 1977), 331.

14 In Ireland the marriage age in 1840 was 27.5 for men and 24.4 for women. By 1861 the mean age for men was just over 30, and for women about 26. See: Cormac O'Grada, "The Population of Ireland, 1700–1900: A Survey," *Annales de demographie historique* (1979): 281–99;

Joel Mokyr, *Why Ireland Starved: A Quantitative and Analytical History of the Irish Economy, 1800–1850* (London: Allen and Unwin 1983), 72.

15 Thomas P. Monahan, "One Hundred Years of Marriage in Massachusetts," *American Journal of Sociology* 56 (1950–51): 534–45; Thomas P. Monahan, *The Pattern of Age at Marriage in the United States* (Philadelphia: Stephenson Brothers 1951), vol. 1: 157–207; John Modell, et al., "The Timing of Marriage in the Transition to Adulthood: Continuity and Change, 1860–1975" in John Demos and Sarane Spence Boocock, eds., *Turning Points: Historical and Sociological Essays on the Family* (Chicago: University of Chicago Press 1978), s120–50.

16 For example, see David Levine, *Family Formation in an Age of Nascent Capitalism* (New York: Academic Press 1977), 58–87.

17 Michael Katz, et al., *The Social Organization of Early Industrial Capitalism* (Cambridge, Mass.: Harvard University Press 1982), 279–81.

18 Modell, "Timing of Marriage," s125.

19 Gagan notes that early travellers in Upper Canada remarked on the propensity toward early female marriage and suggests that later observers thought it to be rising. Gagan, *Hopeful Travellers*, 75.

20 Etienne van de Walle, *The Female Population of France in the Nineteenth Century: A Reconstruction of 82 Departments* (Princeton, NJ : Princeton University Press 1974), 127; Martine Segalen, *Love and Power in the Peasant Family: Rural France in the Nineteenth Century* (Oxford: Blackwell 1983), 12; John Knodel, *The Decline of Fertility in Germany, 1871–1939* (Princeton, NJ: Princeton University Press 1974), 70; Ron J. Lesthaeghe, *The Decline of Belgian Fertility, 1800–1970* (Princeton NJ: Princeton University Press 1977), 54–5.

21 The prime marrying years were defined on the basis of several parish registers, parts of which listed the previous marital status of all brides and grooms.

22 Peter Laslett, *Family Life and Illicit Love in Earlier Generations: Essays in Historical Sociology* (Cambridge: Cambridge University Press 1977), 13, 42.

23 More mature grooms were 4.9 years older than their brides; more mature brides were 2.8 years older than their grooms.

24 Laslett, *Family Life*, 13; Edward Shorter, *The Making of the Modern Family* (New York: Basic Books 1975), 154–5.

25 At the age of thirty, 90.0 per cent of all first married grooms in the sample were wed, leaving 10.0 per cent to find a mate; for women the comparable figures were 98.1 per cent and 1.9 per cent.

26 The figures are 2,485 out of 3,787, or 65.6 per cent.

27 Katz, *The People of Hamilton*, 240–1.

28 Only two registers noted religious affiliation. Of 571 marriages, 66 per

cent were between members of the same denomination, 28 per cent united Protestants of two different faiths, 5 per cent were Protestant-Catholic unions, and 1 per cent were others.

CHAPTER FOUR

1 Lucienne Roubin, "Male Space and Female Space within the Provencal Community" in Robert Forster and Orest Ranum, eds., *Rural Society in France: Selections from the Annales: Economies, Societies, Civilizations* (Baltimore: Johns Hopkins University Press 1977), 152–80.

2 Erving Goffman, *Behaviour in Public Places: Notes on the Social Organization of Gatherings* (New York: Free Press 1963), 105–6.

3 Byles to Almon, 12 January 1786, Byles Family Papers, MG1, no. 163, PANS.

4 J. Ross Robertson, ed. *The Diary of Mrs. John Graves Simcoe* (Toronto: William Briggs 1911), 143.

5 Hannah Jarvis to Peters, 17 June 1793, W.B. Jarvis Papers, 254–7, MG24, I47, NAC.

6 Ely Playter Diary, 14–18 November 1802, AO.

7 Joseph Willcocks to Lucy Willcocks, 10 September 1801, Willcocks Letterbook, AO.

8 Harriette Peters to Samuel D. Peters, 1 May 1815, Jarvis Papers, 339–42, NAC.

9 Maria C. Head to Anna Maria Boyd, 28 December 1815, Jarvis Papers, PMNB.

10 W.H.E. Napier to Francis Shanley, 28 March 1856, Francis Shanley Papers, box 89, env. 26, AO.

11 Caroline Wallbridge to Marianne Howard, 6 May 1838, Wallbridge Family Papers, AO.

12 James Reynolds to Mary, 25 November 1863, James Reynolds Papers, AO.

13 Louisa Bowlby Journal, 1862, 8, AO.

14 Samuel Jarvis Jr to Mary Jarvis, 23 January 1868, Jarvis-Powell Papers, AO.

15 Robb to Elizabeth Robb, 4 January 1839, in Alfred G. Bailey, ed., *The Letters of James and Ellen Robb: Portrait of a Fredericton Family in Early Victorian Times* (Fredericton: Acadiensis Press 1983), 21.

16 Ibid., Robb to Jane Robb, 26 February 1839, 25–6.

17 W.H. Merritt, manuscript autobiography, W.H. Merritt Papers, folio 80, AO.

18 Invitation to Miss Prendergast, 18 February 1811, W.H.Merritt Papers, 42, MG24, E1, NAC: Invitation, Belleville, 4 February 1825, W.H. Merritt Papers, pkg. 59, AO; Invitation to Bachelors' Ball, Port Colborne, 13 January 1840, ibid., pkg. 60, item 61; Invitation, O'Brian Family Papers,

file 1, AO; Invitation to Miss Margaret Thompson, 1902, Thompson
Family Papers, MC 79, PANB.

19 Playter Diary, 18 November 1802.

20 John Langton to Thomas Langton, 28 February 1834, Langton Family
Collection, AO.

21 Ibid., Langton to Langton, 18 February 1835.

22 Leonore Davidoff, *The Best Circles: Society, Etiquette, and the Season*
(London: Croom Helm 1973).

23 Audrey S. Miller, ed., *The Journals of Mary O'Brien, 1828–1838*
(Toronto: Macmillan 1968), 153.

24 Wallbridge to M. Howard, 20 November 1837, Wallbridge Papers.

25 Fanny Chadwick Diary, 27 October 1892, F.M. Chadwick Papers, AO.

26 Nutting to Jarvis, 1 August 1806, John G. Harkness Papers, box 3, series
II–1, AO.

27 Ibid., Nutting to Jarvis, 4 March 1808.

28 Ibid., Nutting to Jarvis, 10 February 1810[?].

29 Playter Diary, *passim*.

30 John Langton to Langton Sr, 12 August 1835, Langton Collection.

31 Ibid., 22 September 1836.

32 W.A. Langton, ed. *Early Days in Upper Canada: The Letters of John
Langton* (Toronto: Macmillan 1926), 177n.

33 J.H. Wooley, Diary, 1861–1898, AO.

34 Ibid., 27 May 1862.

35 Maurice A. Harlow Diary, 1877–1935, PANS.

36 Edward Shorter, *The Making of the Modern Family* (New York: Basic
Books 1975), 121–4.

37 Thomas Dick Diary, 1867–1905, Mss, Diaries, I-D-4, AO.

38 Charles Askin to Alexander Hamilton, 2 September 1810, Hamilton
Papers, vol. 7, NAC.

39 Freeling Diary, 1839–1844, *passim*, NAC.

40 Mary Larratt Smith, ed., *Young Mr. Smith in Upper Canada* (Toronto:
University of Toronto Press 1980), 26.

41 Laura Ridout Wadsworth Diary, Wadsworth Family Papers, AO.

42 Andrew Jones and Leonard Rutman, *In the Children's Aid: J.J. Kelso and
Child Welfare in Ontario* (Toronto: University of Toronto Press 1981), 3–
16.

43 J.J Kelso Diary, 18 April 1888, J.J. Kelso Papers, MG 30 C97, vol. I, NAC.

44 Davidoff, *Best Circles*, 17.

45 Ibid., 41.

46 Rebecca Byles to her aunts, 17 May 1784, Byles Family Papers.

47 Ibid., Byles to Aunt, 17 January 1785.

48 Miller, ed., *Journals of Mary O'Brien*, 45–110.

49 [Douglas] to [Hudson], 17 July 1861, William Douglas Papers, AO.
50 Ibid., Hudson to Douglas, 22 July 1861.
51 Ibid., Hudson to Douglas, 26 July 1861.
52 Ibid., Hudson to Douglas, n.d.
53 Bowlby Journal, 15 January 1862, 4; Hattie Bowlby Journal, 29, 30 April, 8 September 1874, Mss, Margaret Bowlby Collection, AO.
54 Jarvis to Mary Jarvis, 27 February 1843, Jarvis-Powell Papers.
55 Buell to S.N. Buell, 11 March 1855, Buell Papers, AO. This draft of the letter was not sent, but shortly afterward Buell mentions sending such a letter to his daughter. Buell to Rockwood, 24 March 1855.
56 Ibid., Medora Cameron to Buell, 5 September 1855.
57 Wadsworth Diary, 3 October 1874.
58 Osler to Featherstone Osler, 6 August 1857, Osler Family Papers, I–2, AO.
59 Frances Tweedie Milne Diary, 20 February 1867, AO.
60 Bigelow Diary, 1878, Lois E. Bigelow Papers, Dalhousie University Library, Halifax.
61 Leonore Davidoff and Catherine Hall, "The Architecture of Public and Private Life: English Middle-Class Society in a Provincial Town, 1780–1850" in Derek Fraser and Anthony Sutcliffe, eds., *The Pursuit of Urban History* (London: Edward Arnold 1983), 343.
62 Alison Prentice, "'Friendly Atoms in Chemistry': Women and Men at Normal School in Mid-Nineteenth Century Toronto" in *Old Ontario: Essays in Honour of J.M.S. Careless*, David Keane and Colin Read, eds. (Toronto: Dundurn Press forthcoming).
63 Queen's University, *Calendar, 1871–72*, 7.
64 "The Opening of the First Residence," *The Alumnae News* 10 (November 1925): 11–13; Queen's University, *Calendar, 1912–13*, 27.
65 Kathleen Cowan, *It's Late, and All the Girls Have Gone: An Annesley Diary, 1907–1910*, Aida Farrag Graff and David Knight, eds. (Toronto: Childe Thursday 1984), *passim*.
66 Hilda Neatby, *Queen's University*: I, *1841–1917: And Not to Yield*, edited by Frederick W. Gibson and Roger Graham (Montreal: McGill-Queen's University Press 1978), 205–6.

CHAPTER FIVE

1 Barbara Mayerhoff, "Rites of Passage: Process and Paradox," in Victor Turner, ed., *Celebration: Studies in Festivity and Ritual* (Washington, DC: Smithsonian Institution 1982), 112.
2 William Helliwell Diary, Baldwin Room, MTRL. His "dear girl" was Elizabeth Bright of nearby York.

3 John R. Gillis, *Youth and History: Tradition and Change in European Age Relations, 1770–Present* (New York: Academic Press 1974), 62, 64, 129.

4 Edward Shorter, *The Making of the Modern Family* (New York: Basic Books 1975), 121–3.

5 Lewis Wallbridge to Marianne Howard, 17 July 1839, Wallbridge Papers, AO.

6 Charles Steen to Sarah Jane Hillis, 22 June 1877, Moulton Family Collection, courtesy of Carolyn Moulton, Toronto.

7 Fanny Marion Chadwick Diary, 1892–1895. AO.

8 Harry Allen to Francis Shanley, 24 February 1847, Shanley Papers, box 89, env. 3, AO.

9 Veronica Strong-Boag, ed., *A Woman with a Purpose: The Diaries of Elizabeth Smith 1872–1884* (Toronto: University of Toronto Press 1980), 161.

10 Charles Sippi, Diary, 23 January 1893, Baldwin Room, MTRL.

11 Main Johnson to Gladys Robertson, 10 January 1907, Johnson Papers, Baldwin Room, MTRL.

12 John R. Gillis, *For Better, For Worse: British Marriages, 1600 to the Present* (New York: Oxford 1985), 23–5.

13 Rebecca Byles to her aunts, 20 February 1784. Byles Family Papers, PANS.

14 To Laura, Neilson Papers, vol. 43, p. 2596, MG24 B1, NAC. For other examples, see "Cupid's Address," Alonzo Belvedira to Laura Moorhead, 14 February 1840, Neilsen Papers, vol. 43, p. 2437, and L.L. to Miss C.O. Bakker, 14 February 1835. Miscellaneous Collection, 1835/1, AO.

15 See the following undated, unaddressed and anonymous example:
     If ever I marry a wife
     I'll marry a publican's daughter
     I'll sit all day long in the bar
     And drink nothing but brandy and water.
    McCormack Family Papers, 20–148–B–1, Hiram Walker Collection, AO.

16 Catherine Parr Traill, *Journal, 1831–1895*, Traill Family Collection, vol. 2, p. 3429, MG29 D81, NAC.

17 Bowlby Journal, Mss. Margaret Bowlby Collection, AO.

18 Thomas Dick Diary, 1867–1905, Ms, Diaries, I–D–4, AO.

19 Strong-Boag, ed., *A Woman with a Purpose*, 74, 152.

20 To Miss Mary McDonald, O'Hanley Papers, vol. 1, file 7, MG29 B11, (transferred to the picture collection), NAC.

21 William Blowers Bliss to Henry Bliss, 14 June 1812, Bliss Family Papers, MG1 vol. 1598, no. 16, PANS. Whether he received the gift in response to one he had given is not clear.

22 Ibid., Sarah Anne Anderson to Henry Bliss, 27 May 1816, vol. 1604, no. 4.

23 Ibid., Anderson to Bliss, 1 July 1816. Anderson's guardian, S.S. Blowers, later accused Bliss of an improper attachment to Sarah Anne and forced them to break off their relationship. She married Henry's older brother, William Blowers Bliss, in 1823.

24 Lillian Williamson Diary, 1878–1885, PMNB.

25 MacGregor to Dawson, December 1893, Robert Dawson Papers, MS2 77, Dalhousie University Archives.

26 Jennie Miller to William D. Hall, 23 January 1887, McGrigor-Miller Collection, MG1 vol. 656, file 8, PANS.

27 Ibid., Hall to Miller, 6 August 1887, file 5.

28 Jane Van Norman to A. Dunham Emory, 1 January 1848, Van Norman Papers, UCA.

29 Gillis, *Youth and History*, 62; Shorter, *Making of the Modern Family*, 121–3.

30 William Wynne Queenston to John Blake, York, 14 January 1830, courtesy of Peter Moogk, Vancouver.

31 Drayton to Rubidge, 12 December 1888, file 2, Drayton Papers, AO.

32 Thomas Dick Diary.

33 Affidavit of Margaret S. Moak, 5 August 1864, Affidavits of Affiliation, University of Western Ontario Library.

34 For a graphic example, see Constance B. Backhouse, "The Tort of Seduction: Fathers and Daughters in Nineteenth Century Canada," *Dalhousie Law Journal* 10, no. 1 (June 1986): 57–60.

35 Lizzie Keys Carmichael to Sarah Jane Moulton, 26 January 1910, Moulton Family Collection.

36 Pierre Caspard, "Conceptions prénuptiales et développement du capitalisme dans la Principauté de Neauchâtel (1678–1820)," *Annales: Economies, Sociétés, Civilisations* 29, no. 4 (juillet–août 1974): 994–5; Martine Segalen, *Love and Power in the Peasant Family: Rural France in the Nineteenth Century* (Oxford: Basil Blackwell 1983), 23–4. See also, Shorter, *Making of the Modern Family*, 102–5, 124; Gillis, *For Better, For Worse*, 30–1; and T.C. Smout, *A Century of the Scottish People, 1830–1950* (London: Collins 1986), 170–1, 173–5.

37 P.A. Russell, "Attitudes to Social Structure and Social Mobility in Upper Canada (1815–1840)" (Ph.D. thesis: Carleton University 1982), 225–6.

38 Gillis, *For Better, For Worse*, 11–54.

39 On the Scottish origins of *rèiteach*, see Morag Macleod, "Rèiteach" in *Tocher: Tales, Songs, Traditions Selected from the Archives of the School of Scottish Studies* 30 (1979): 375–99; M. Ireland, "Will Ye

Gang Wi' Me Lassie: Scottish wedding customs and lore" in Billy Kaye ed., *Odyssey* (Edinburgh: Polygon 1980), 89–97.

40 "Reiteach, A Scottish Engagement Rite," *Cape Breton Magazine* 5 (1973): 20–3.

41 Hughie MacKenzie's reminiscences suggest that a few men did not court and sought a bride only through a *rèiteach*. But this seems to have been highly exceptional. Hughie MacKenzie, "Reiteach," taped reminiscences recorded in 1963, Beaton Institute, College of Cape Breton, Sydney, Nova Scotia, tape 3, side b; see also, P.J. MacKenzie Campbell, *Highland Community on the Bras d'Or* (n.p., Casket Printing and Publishing 1978), 42–3; and Mary L. Fraser, *Folklore of Nova Scotia* (Antigonish: Formac 1975), 112–14.

42 Declaration of Marriage of Stephen Chase and Nancy Bushnell, 28 January 1776, Cornwallis Township Records, Township Books, vol. 2, p. 21, PANS. The legality of this marriage is questionable, though it is clear that the couple considered themselves wedded in community eyes.

43 F.M. Chadwick Diary, 30 June 1898.

44 H. to Miss Quincy, n.d., Jonathan Sewell Papers, 1–2, MG23 GII10, NAC.

45 G. Eliza Cottnam to Mrs Boyd, 2 September 1816, Jarvis Papers, PMNB.

46 Simeon Perkins noted an exception in early nineteenth-century Nova Scotia, a wedding with ninety guests in attendance, most of the relations of the couple being married. C.B. Fergusson, ed., *The Diary of Simeon Perkins, 1804–1812* (Toronto: Champlain Society 1978), 210–11.

47 H. to Miss Quincy, n.d., Sewell Papers. "Trumpet mimeuet, butterd peas an tolle boys" seem to have been country dances.

48 Ibid., Jonathan Sewell, Jr to Jonathan Sewell Sr, 30 December 1786.

49 Anne Powell to George W. Murray, 9 August 1808, William Dummer Powell Papers, L16, Baldwin Room, MTRL.

50 Fraser to King, 11 September 1829, King-Stewart Papers, vol. 1, 51–4, MG24 I182, NAC.

51 Ibid., Fraser to King, 28 October 1831, vol. 2, 1039–42.

52 S. Malloch to W.B. Wells, 14 February 1832, Wells Family Papers, box 1, 1832, QUA.

53 Edward Hale to Eliza Hale, 6 November 1839, Hale Papers, McCord Museum, Montreal.

54 Sophie Browne to George Dawson, 8 June 1876, J.W. Dawson Papers, acc. 1584, ref. 3, McGill University Archives.

55 Catherine Parr Traill, *Journal, 1831-1895*, Traill Family Collection, vol. 2, pp. 3498–505, MG29 D81, NAC.

56 Mrs William Gregg, Diary, 10 and 11 May 1849, Gregg Papers, QUA.

57 Thomas Dick Diary, 28 May 1867.

58 Sarah Byles to the Misses Byles, 17 August 1785, Byles Family Papers, III, p. 86; Ellen Primrose Bell to her Aunt, 30 July 1868, Dawson and Herrington Papers, acc. 1421, bundle 6/10, McGill University; Jane M. Bell to her Aunt, n.d. [1869]: Dawson and Herrington Papers, acc. 1421, bundle 6/11; Chadwick Diary, 30 June 1898.

59 Traill, *Journal*, 3503.

60 Louisa Bowlby Journal, 27 January 1862.

61 Anne Richie to Charles Sibbald, 7 February 1874. Sibbald Family Papers, file 27, MG29 C69, NAC.

62 W.J. Wintemberg, "Folklore Collected in the Counties of Oxford and Waterloo," *Journal of American Folklore* 31 (1918): 137.

63 F.W. Waugh, "Canadian Folklore from Ontario," *Journal of American Folklore* 31 (1918): 27. According to Waugh these ideas were current in central and southern Ontario among people of British descent. For a similar rhyme from a Scotch-Irish population, see W.J. Wintemberg and Katherine Wintemberg, "Folklore from Grey County, Ontario" in ibid., 97.

64 R. Longley to William B. Wells, 10 March 1833, Wells Family Papers.

65 She was in her mid-teens at the time. Her father had Dunn charged with seduction and abduction but the judge dismissed the case on account of the couple's marriage. Clipping dated 9 April 1859, Mackenzie-Lindsey Papers, file 6008, AO.

66 Randolph Trumbach, *The Rise of the Egalitarian Family: Aristrocratic Kinship and Domestic Relations in Eighteenth Century England* (New York: Academic Press 1978), 113–17; MacFarlane, *Marriage and Love in England*, 315.

67 Miss Quincy's correspondent noticed the absence of the custom following the wedding she described. H. to Miss Quincy, n.d., Sewell Papers.

68 James R. Gowan to Mrs. Gowan, 21 May 1836 [draft], James and Ogle Gowan Papers, AO.

69 J.H. Wooley Diary, 15 February 1865. For another example from a Scottish immigrant family, see W.A. Robertson, Reminiscences, 23–5, MG29 C18, NAC.

70 Macfarlane, *Marriage and Love in England*, 315.

71 The literature on the charivari is extensive. For an introduction to the European charivari, see: E.P. Thompson, "'Rough Music': le Charivari anglaise," *Annales: Économies, Sociétés, Civilisations* 27, no. 2 (mars-avril 1972): 285–312; Natalie Z. Davis, "The Reasons of Misrule," *Society and Culture in Early Modern France* (Stanford: Stanford University Press 1975), 97–123; R. Bonnain Moerdyk and D. Moerdyk,

Sociétés, Civilisations 32, no. 2 (1977): 381–98. On the charivari in Canada, see Bryan D. Palmer, "Discordant Music: Charivaris and White-capping in Nineteenth-Century North America," *Labour/Le travailleur* 3 (1978): 5–62; E.-Z. Massicotte, "Le charivari au Canada," *Bulletin des Recherches Historiques* 32 (1926): 712–25; W.R. Riddell, "The 'Shivaree' and the Original," Ontario Historical Society, *Papers and Records* 27 (1931): 522–4; P.-G. Roy, "Un charivari Montréal en 1818," *Bulletin des Recherches Historiques* 47 (1941): 250; Anne M. Speight, "The Chivaree," *Alberta History* 26, no. 3 (Summer 1978): 34–5; Lorraine Léger, "Le charivari en Acadie," La Société historique acadienne, *Les cahiers* 10, no. 4 (décembre 1979): 164–9.

72 Thompson, "'Rough Music'," 308.

73 Ibid., 294.

74 Audrey S. Miller, ed., *The Journals of Mary O'Brien, 1828–1838* (Toronto: Macmillan 1968), 26.

75 Susanna Moodie, *Roughing it in the Bush* (Toronto: McClelland and Stewart 1962), 145.

76 William Bell Journal, vol. 9, 118–20, Robert Bell Papers, vol. 48, MG29 B15, NAC.

77 Playter Diary, 12, 13 and 14 October 1802, AO.

78 Palmer, "Discordant Music," 28.

79 Moodie, *Roughing it in the Bush*, 147; Bell Journal, vol. 9, 120.

80 *British Whig*, 18 March 1834.

81 Ibid., 19 January 1837.

82 *Daily News* (Kingston) 4 April 1867.

83 Maurice Harlowe Diary, 26 April 1888, MG1, vols. 1300-2, PANS.

84 *Whig* (Kingston), 14 July 1894.

85 Canadian Centre for Folk Culture Studies, Ottawa, Creighton Manuscript Collection: CR–C 8.1: 47, 49, 156; CR–C 8.2 (part 1): 39, 45, 48, 52; CR–C 8.2 (part 2): 203. These field notes were gathered in 1947 and 1948.

86 Davis, "The Reasons of Misrule."

87 Fergusson, ed., *The Diary of Simeon Perkins*, 63, 67.

88 Palmer, "Discordant Music," 60.

89 Ibid., 29.

90 Ibid., 49–54.

91 Anne Powell to George Murray, 2 October 1818, Powell Papers, vol. A94, Baldwin Room, MTRL.

92 Stark to Miss Young and Mrs Stark, 7 July 1835, Mark Young Stark Papers, UCA.

93 Scadding Diary, 14–17 August 1841, Baldwin Room, MTRL.

94 Gertrude Fleming Diary, MG29 C96, NAC.

95 Isabella McGillivray to George McGillivray, 22 September 1865.

McGillivray Papers, MG24 I3, NAC.

96 Thomas Dick Diary, 5 July 1867.

97 Elizabeth McKinsey, *Niagara Falls: Icon of the American Sublime* (London: Cambridge University Press 1985), 177–88; Ellen K. Rothman, *Hands and Hearts: A History of Courtship in America* (New York: Basic Books 1984), 82, 175.

98 W.R. Coleman Diary, 10 May 1869, Baldwin Room, MTRL.

99 Gilbert Hartley to Mary Card, 24 August 1879, Hartley Collection, City of Toronto Archives.

100 Rothman, *Hands and Hearts*, 81–3, 175–6, 280–2. Gillis notes that the unaccompanied wedding trip was growing fashionable in British middle-class circles early in the nineteenth century, though it did not become common until the Victorian era. Gillis, *For Better, For Worse*, 138.

101 W.H. Merritt Jr to W.H. Merritt Sr, 11 December 1853. W.H. Merrit Papers, pkg. 54, AO.

102 Bessie Gregg Stewart Diary, 12 – 22 August 1880, Gregg Papers, QUA.

103 Anna Dawson to her Mother [9 June 1876]. J.W. Dawson Papers, acc. 1584, ref.3a.

104 Arnold van Gennep, *The Rites of Passage* (London: Routledge and Paul 1960).

105 C.B. Fergusson, ed., *The Diary of Simeon Perkins, 1797–1803* (Toronto: Champlain Society 1967), 244, 434.

106 Johnston Paterson Diary, 28 December 1879, MG55/30, #167, NAC.

107 Creighton Collection, CR–C-8.1: 47.

CHAPTER SIX

1 Charles Morris Jr to Joseph Pernette, 29 August 1786, Morris Papers, MG1, vol. 1206, no. 5, PANS.

2 Marianne Howard to Lewis Wallbridge, 9 June 1838, Wallbridge Papers, AO.

3 Sarah to Mrs Fleming, 16 April n.d., Sir Sandford Fleming Papers, AO.

4 Ely Playter Diary, 27 May 1802, Ms 87, AO.

5 Ibid., 20 July, 23, 28, and 30 August 1802.

6 Lily Hall to Jeanie Fleming, 29 February 1864, Fleming Papers.

7 Walter Shanley to Francis Shanley, 16 June, 1851, Shanley Papers, box 93, env. 12, AO.

8 G.F. Johnstone to W.F. Munro, 2 October 1861, William F. Munro Papers, AO.

9 Veronica Strong-Boag, ed., *A Woman with a Purpose: The Diaries of Elizabeth Smith 1872–1884* (Toronto: University of Toronto Press 1980), 154.

10 Kathleen Cowan, *It's Late, and All the Girls have Gone: An Annesley Diary, 1907–1910*, Aida Farrag Graff and David Knight, eds. (Toronto: Childe Thursday 1984), 9, 11 December 1907 and 10 February 1908, 62–3 and 91–2. Cowan defied the dean and her father, however, by spending the night of her date out of college at the home of a friend.

11 Lois E. Bigelow to Byron Morse, 16 February, 1878 [copy], Bigelow Papers, Dalhousie University Archives, MS2 88.

12 John Neilson to Isabel Neilson, 9 August 1797, Neilson Papers, vol. 35, 7–9, MG24 B1, NAC.

13 Mark Young Stark to Mrs Stark, 14 May 1835, Mark Young Stark Papers, UCA.

14 Langton to William Langton, 17 February 1845, Langton Family Collection, AO.

15 Harry King to Halli Fraser, 11 October 1831, King-Stewart Family Papers, vol. 3, 1252–55, MG 24 I182, NAC.

16 William Simpson to Mr and Mrs J.C. Simpson, 20 October 1867, William Simpson Papers, AO.

17 E.W. Jarvis to W. M. Jarvis, 29 January 1894, Jarvis Papers, PMNB.

18 Trevor Humphreys to Father and Mother, 4 April 1837, Sewell Papers, MG23 GII10, 3715–18, NAC.

19 John Kirby to William Kirby, 18 October 1846, William Kirby Collection, AO.

20 Baddely to Clinton, 22 January 1822, Sir William Henry Clinton Papers, MG24 F53, NAC.

21 Hibbert to Bishop Horan, 2 June 1868, DI4C22/2, RCAAK.

22 Strachan to the Archdeacon of York, 8 November 1847, Strachan Letterbooks, John Strachan Papers, AO.

23 Audrey S. Miller, ed. *The Journals of Mary O'Brien, 1828–1838* (Toronto: Macmillan 1968), 84–98.

24 Robert Baldwin to John Ross, 18 November 1850. Robert Baldwin Papers, L14, Baldwin Room, MTRL.

25 William Bell Journal, 12 June 1827, vol. 4: 153–6, Robert Bell Papers, vol. 48, MG29 B15, NAC.

26 Sherwood to Jones, 9 October 1810, Jones Family Papers, QUA.

27 Nash to Willard, 6 July 1818, Samuel Willard Papers, Brome County Historical Society Collections, MG8 F13, 959, NAC.

28 T.T. Vernon Smith Diary, 7 July 1853, MG1 vols. 999–1001, PANS.

29 Laura Ridout Wadsworth Diary, 12 March 1874, Wadsworth Family Papers, AO.

30 White to Davis, 16 May 1807, White Family Papers, no. 859, PANS.

31 William Bell Journal, vol. 7, 75–6.

32 Garrett Miller to Mrs Miller, 23 March 1840, McGrigor-Miller Collection, MG1 vol. 501, folder 4, PANS.

33 John Grist to Arthur Harvey, 21 November 1858, Arthur Harvey Papers, Thomas Fisher Room, University of Toronto.

34 Odell to David Ford, 12 September 1815, Ford Family Papers, AO.

35 For the courtship correspondence of Merritt and Prendergast, see William Hamilton Merritt Papers, pkgs. 43, 43a, AO; W.H. Merritt Papers, MG24 E1, 50–2, 60–3, NAC.

36 Merritt to Prendergast, 9 August 1814, Merritt Papers, pkg. 43, AO.

37 Caldwell to William Lindsay, 17 February 1814, John Ashworth Papers, vol. 1, 28–30, MG24 B164, NAC.

38 Hale to Eliza Hale, 21 January 1841, Hale Papers, McCord Museum, McGill University.

39 Osler to Featherstone Lake Osler, 27 June 1843, Osler Family Papers, Bound Correspondence, vol. 4, AO.

40 See the letters from Lundy to Frank Shanley in the Shanley Papers, box 89, and also A.W. Gordon to Walter and Frank Shanley, 23 December 1849.

41 Elizabeth Smith to Adam Shortt, 7 December 1886, Elizabeth Smith Shortt Papers, file 849, Library, University of Waterloo, Waterloo, Ontario.

42 Caldwell to Lindsay, 5 August 1814, Ashworth Papers.

43 For the complicated correspondence on the Elmsley-Bradshaw courtship, see boxes 3, 4, 5, and 7 in the Elmsley Papers.

44 Steven Conger, Marriage Register, 1803–1823, UCA.

45 William Stairs to T.A. Stayner, 26 June 1850, William Stairs Papers, no. 129, MG1 vol. 880, PANS.

46 Jones to Lucia Jones, n.d. [c. 1880s], Jones Family Papers, additions, box 1, file 1, QUA.

47 Fraser to James Ker, 29 August 1803, John and Thomas Nairne Papers, MG23 GIII 23, 324–27, NAC.

48 Miss Beck to Christina Nairne, 16 March 1814 and 17 March 1815, Nairne Papers, 744–49 and 795–802.

49 Smith to Shortt, 6 May 1883, Elizabeth Smith Shortt Papers, file 809.

50 Canniff to William Canniff, 22 December [1899], William Canniff Papers, AO.

51 Margaret Prang, *Newton Rowell: Ontario Nationalist* (Toronto: University of Toronto Press 1975), 45–6.

52 Muriel Shortt to Elizabeth Shortt, 30 November 1916, Shortt Papers, file 506; Elizabeth Shortt to Muriel Shortt, 10 December 1916, file 507.

53 Byles to her aunts, 2 July 1785, Byles Family Papers, part III, MG1 no. 163, PANS.

54 Copner F. Oldfield to Mother, 21 June and 28 July 1859, Copner Francis Oldfield Papers, MG24 F91, NAC.

55 For example, see the letters of James B. Lundy, J.G. Williams, Harry

G.A. Allen, Walter Shanley and Coote Shanley to Frank Shanley in the Shanley Papers, box 89.

56 William Wynne to John Blake, 29 July 1829, courtesy of Peter Moogk, Vancouver.

57 John Grant to James Lauder, 25 April, 10 May and 14 June 1838, Lauder Papers, AO.

58 Britten B. Osler to Featherstone Osler, 26 May 1857, Osler Papers, I–2, loose correspondence.

59 Strachan to Robinson, 30 September 1816, Sir John Beverley Robinson Papers, AO.

60 Allen to Shanley, 23 July 1847, Shanley Papers, box 89, env. 3.

61 Herchmer to John Macaulay, 27 July 1835, Macaulay Papers, AO.

62 Ibid., Stoughton to John Macaulay, 12 June 1821.

63 Ibid., Herchmer to Macaulay, 13 November 1835.

64 Hale to A. Peterson, 29 January 1838, Hale Papers.

65 George Stacey Jr to George Stacey Sr, 9 January 1857, George Stacey Papers, MG24 I177, NAC.

66 Mullett to Hannah Clothier, 6 April 1823, Hannah Clothier Papers, MG24 I132, NAC.

67 Thomas and Lucy Baldwin to Steven and Francis Filmer, 17 November 1852, courtesy of Mrs Ann Logan, Toronto.

68 W.A. Robertson, "Reminiscences," 15, MG29 C18, NAC.

69 David Gagan, *Hopeful Travellers: Families, Land, and Social Change in Mid-Victorian Peel County, Canada West* (Toronto: University of Toronto Press 1981), 50–60; David Gagan, "The Security of Land: Mortgaging in Toronto Gore Township, 1835–85" in F.H. Armstrong, et al., eds., *Aspects of Nineteenth Century Ontario* (Toronto: University of Toronto Press 1974), 143.

70 Marriage contract of Thomas Moore and Margaret Steele, 5 July 1843; Joseph Dufresne, notary public, no. 2760, ANQM.

71 *Chatten v. Bell*, Chancery Case Files, 292–261–71, AO.

72 George Stacey Jr to George Stacey Sr, 21 June 1858, George Stacey Papers, 241–4.

73 Strachan to James Brown, 28 September 1833, Strachan Papers.

74 D'Aubigny to Samuel Street, 5 September 1837, Samuel Street Papers, AO.

75 *Mackechnie v. Cockburn*, Chancery Case Files, 122–237–69; see also, Peter Ennals, "Stuart Easton Mackechnie," *Dictionary of Canadian Biography* VIII, 1851–1860 (Toronto: University of Toronto Press 1985), 555.

76 *Watson v. Sproule*, Chancery Case Files, 80–71.

77 *Heward v. McLean*, Chancery Case Files, 375–70.

78 Charlotte Elmsley to Mary Bradshaw, 8 September 1869, Elmsley Papers.

79 Ibid., Charlotte Elmsley to J.J. Bradshaw, 14 October and 18 November 1869.

80 Ibid., 28 December 1869.

81 Remy Elmsley to J.J. Bradshaw, 18 February 1870.

82 J.J. Bradshaw to Remy Elmsley, 16, 30 March, 6 May 1870.

83 Remy Elmsley to J.J. Bradshaw, 10 June 1870.

84 Lillian Williamson, Diary, PMNB.

85 Hartley Collection, Toronto City Archives.

86 Essery-Harris Correspondence, 1881, courtesy of Mrs Dorothy Hall, Toronto.

87 Marriage contract of William R. Clark and Margaret Miller, 6 April 1837; J. Blackwood, notary public, no. 773, ANQM.

88 Marriage contract of George Riley and Mary Reynolds, 21 August 1847; J. Blackwood, notary public, no. 1102, ANQM.

89 Marriage contract of Harry Abbott and Margaret Amelia Sicotte Freer, 18 February 1868; W.A. Phillips, notary public, no. 2101, ANQM.

90 *Beaty* v. *Stuart*, Chancery Case Files, 340–90–72.

91 *Mackechnie* v. *Cockburn*, Chancery Case Files.

92 *Livingston* v. *Blain*, Chancery Case Files, 98–106–69.

93 *Warnes* v. *Warnes*, Chancery Case Files, 88–46–69. Soon after the couple married Margaret returned to her father's home and Blencoe sued for the return of his property, charging that father and daughter had colluded to deprive him of his wealth.

94 Willcocks to Richard Willcocks, 3 November 1800, Joseph Willcocks Letterbook, AO.

95 Wallbridge to Marianne Howard, 19 April 1862, Wallbridge Family Papers.

96 Baldwin to Russell, 3 November 1808, Baldwin Papers, AO.

97 Marriage contract of Appleton Rice and Mary Meacham, 13 July 1828; A. Jobin, notary public, no. 4583, ANQM.

98 Marriage contract of Louisa G. Frothingham and John H.R. Molson, 29 April 1873; W.A. Phillips, notary public, no. 5640, ANQM.

CHAPTER SEVEN

1 Amelia Hill Diary, 10 March 1852, PANS.

2 Sandford Fleming to Anna Fleming, 2 November 1856, Fleming Papers, AO.

3 M.A. Leeson to Eleanor Donnelly, [1880], Leeson Papers, University of Western Ontario Library.

4 William Macaulay to Ann Macaulay, 1 September 1829, Macaulay Papers, AO.

5 Cartwright to Archdeacon of York, 22 May 1832, Cartwright Papers, AO.

6 Francis B. Baker to Mother, 6 March 1833, McDonald-Stone Papers, 2282–4, MG23 HII1, NAC.

7 Margaret [Leoore] to Mary Hinchley, 27 August [1834], Lauder Papers, AO.

8 James Robb to Elizabeth Robb, 29 December 1840. Alfred G. Bailey, ed., *The Letters of James and Ellen Rob: Portrait of a Fredericton Familly in Early Victorian Times* (Fredericton: Acadiensis Press 1983), 52–3.

9 Fleming to Fleming, 2 November 1856, Fleming Papers.

10 Jean Hall to Sandford Fleming, 22 May 1854, Fleming Papers.

11 Ellen Chapman to Hannah Walton, 12 August 1874, Thomas Walton Papers, AO.

12 Leeson to Donnelly, [1880], Leeson Papers.

13 Ward Chipman to Jonathan Sewell, Jr, 23 February 1793, Sewell Papers, MG23 GII10, 831–34, NAC.

14 G.C. Shaw to James Reynolds, 17 June 1862, Reynolds Papers, AO

15 Margaret Drayton to Agnes Drayton, n.d., Drayton Papers, file 1, AO.

16 Newton MacTavish Diary, 6 September 1903, Newton MacTavish Papers, MG30 D278, NAC.

17 Alicia Bowen to Frank, n.d. Hale Papers, misc. 51, McCord Museum.

18 J.W. Dawson to M.A.Y. Mercer, 30 November 1844, acc. 1377, 15–B–35, Dawson Papers, Dalhousie University Archives. S.B. Frost, "A Transatlantic Wooing," *Dalhousie Review* 58, no. 3 (Autumn 1978): 458–70.

19 David R. McCord to Letitia Chambers, 8 June 1878, McCord Papers, McCord Museum.

20 Hill Diary, 1 December 1851.

21 Georgina Johnstone to William Munro, 13 September 1861, Munro Papers, AO.

22 Anna Dawson to George Mercer Dawson, 20 September 1875, Dawson Papers, acc. 1421.

23 Edith Carey to J.B. Tyrrell, 1892 to February 1895, box 14, J.B. Tyrrell Papers, Thomas Fisher Room, University of Toronto Library.

24 W.D. Hall to Jenny Miller, 4 September 1887, McGrigor-Miller Collection, vol. 656, file 4, PANS.

25 Edward Shorter, *The Making of the Modern Family* (New York: Basic Books 1975), 148–61.

26 Byles to Aunt, 17 January 1785, Byles Family Papers, PANS.

27 Mary Gapper to Lucy Sharpe, 26 March 1830, Mary Sophia O'Brien, Diary, 1828–1838, Ms 199, AO.

28 Jane Douglas to William Douglas, 13 September 1861, draft, William Douglas Papers, AO.

29 Amelia Holder Diary, MC 665, PANB.
30 Henry Boulton to Charlotte Rudyard, 23 March 1848, Henry John Boulton Papers, Baldwin Room, MTRL.
31 James Reynolds to Mary, 18 June 1863, Reynolds Papers, AO.
32 Adam Shortt to Elizabeth Smith, 30 June 1883, Elizabeth Smith Shortt Papers, file 809, Library, University of Waterloo, Waterloo.
33 Jean Hall to Sandford Fleming, 26 March 1854, Fleming Papers, AO.
34 Ibid., Fleming to Hill, 21 March 1854. On his previous flirtation, see the references to his occasional meetings with B. in 1853. Sandford Fleming Diary, 1853, *passim.*, especially 4 November 1853.
35 Reginald Drayton to Agnes Rubidge, 29 November 1888, file 2, Drayton Papers, AO.
36 Hall to Miller, 19 August, 25 August and 11 September 1887, McGrigor-Miller Collection, vol. 656.
37 James Reynolds to Mary, 16 September 1863, Reynolds Papers, AO.
38 Mary MacGregor to Robert Dawson, 13 July 1893, Dawson Papers.
39 Hall to Fleming, 22 May 1854.
40 Fleming to Hall, 20 June 1854, draft.
41 Hall to Miller, especially the letters for early 1887, McGrigor-Miller Collection, vol. 656.
42 Drayton to Rubidge, 2 February 1889, Drayton Papers.
43 Reynolds Papers, 1863–64.
44 Hall to Miller, 20 January 1887, McGrigor-Miller Collection, vol. 656, file 5.
45 Ibid., Hall to Miller, 30 January 1887.
46 P.B. Waite, *The Man from Halifax: Sir John Thompson, Prime Minister* (Toronto: University of Toronto Press 1985), 24–8.
47 William R. Coleman Diary, 1 January to 10 May 1869, S88, Baldwin Room, MTRL.
48 William Osler to Gwendolyne Francis, 29 June 1906, Osler Papers, Thomas Fisher Room, University of Toronto Library.
49 Halli Fraser to Harry King, 11 November 1829, King-Stewart Papers, vol. 1, 77–80.
50 Allerthorn to Lauder, 8 July, 1838, Lauder Papers, I.B., AO.
51 Van Norman to Emory, n.d. [c.1847–48], Van Norman Papers, UCA.
52 Johnstone to Munro, 17 March 1858, Munro Papers.
53 Harris to Essery, 31 August 1881, Essery-Harris correspondence, courtesy of Mrs Dorothy Hall, Islington, Ontario.
54 Amelia Hill Diary, 1 January 1852.
55 Hudson to Douglas, n.d. [c. April 1863], Douglas Papers, AO.
56 Baldwin to Sullivan, 27 June 1825, Baldwin Papers, MG24 B11, vol. 4, NAC.
57 King to Fraser, 2 October 1831, King-Stewart Papers, vol. 3: 1237–40.

58 Johnstone to Munro, 1 October 1861, Munro Papers.

59 Hartley to Card, 19 December 1878, Hartley Collection, City of Toronto Archives.

60 Essery-Harris Correspondence, February to November 1881.

61 Elizabeth Smith Shortt Papers, files 809 to 849; Main Johnson Papers, boxes 1 and 2.

62 Anne Gilpin to J.J.S. Mountain, 30 April 1846, Mountain-Roe-Jarvis Papers, box 1, 1–B–b #12, Anglican Church of Canada, General Synod Archives, Toronto.

63 Johnstone to Munro, 17 March 1858 and 12 August 1862, Munro Papers.

64 Hartley to Card, 8 June 1879.

65 Hill Diary, 11 March 1852.

66 Johnstone to Munro, 27 July 1862, Munro Papers.

67 MacTavish Diary, 2 April 1904.

CONCLUSION

1 Sigmund Freud, *Civilization and its Discontents* (New York: W.W. Norton 1961), 50.

2 The classic statement is found in Edward Shorter, *The Making of the Modern Family* (New York: Basic Books 1975), 79–167. See also, John R. Gillis, *For Better, For Worse: British Marriages, 1600 to the Present* (New York: Oxford University Press 1985), 119, 165–9; David Levine, "Industrialization and the Proletarian Family in England," *Past & Present* 107 (May 1985): 180. The contrast with circumstances in continental Europe is striking. In Vienna, for example, industrialization frustrated working class marital aspirations, with the result that illegitimacy rates were extremely high by British standards. Michael Mitterauer and Reinhard Sieder, *The European Family: Patriarchy to Partnership from the Middle Ages to the Present* (Chicago: University of Chicago Press 1982), 132–3.

3 Angus McLaren and Arlene Tigar McLaren, *The Bedroom and the State: The Changing Practices and Politics of Contraception and Abortion in Canada, 1880–1980* (Toronto: McClelland and Stewart 1986), 15–31.

4 Gregory S. Kealey, *Toronto Workers Respond to Industrial Capitalism, 1867–1892* (Toronto: University of Toronto Press 1980); Bryan D. Palmer, *A Culture in Conflict: Skilled Workers and Industrial Capitalism in Hamilton, Ontario, 1860–1914* (Montreal: McGill-Queen's University Press 1979); Bryan D. Palmer, *Working-Class Experience: The Rise and Reconstitution of Canadian Labour, 1800–1980* (Toronto: Butterworth & Co. 1983).

5 Gillis, *For Better, For Worse*, 152–60.

EPILOGUE

1 *Journal de Québec*, 13 février 1847.
2 Manuscript Census of Canada, 1851. Ville de Québec, Palace and St Louis Wards, folio 47, reel C–1155.

Index